CEREMONIES OF POSSESSION IN EUROPE'S CONQUEST
OF THE NEW WORLD, 1492–1640

This work of comparative history explores the array of ceremonies that Europeans performed to enact their taking possession of the New World. Frenchmen reproduced the grandeur of royal processions wherever possible, always ending in dialogue with the indigenous peoples. Spaniards made solemn speeches before launching military attacks. Dutchmen drew intensely detailed maps, scrutinizing harbors and coastlines as they disembarked. The Portuguese superimposed the grid of latitudes upon lands they were later to take by the sword. The English calmly laid out fences and hedges in the manner of their native shires. Through such activities each power considered itself to be creating imperial authority over the Americas; yet each failed to acknowledge the same significance in the ceremonies of other powers. This book develops the historic cultural contexts of these ceremonies and tackles the implications of these histories for contemporary nation-states of the postcolonial era.

CEREMONIES OF POSSESSION IN EUROPE'S CONQUEST OF THE NEW WORLD, 1492–1640

PATRICIA SEED
Rice University

CAMBRIDGE
UNIVERSITY PRESS

PUBLISHED BY THE PRESS SYNDICATE OF THE UNIVERSITY OF CAMBRIDGE
The Pitt Building, Trumpington Street, Cambridge CB2 1RP, United Kingdom

CAMBRIDGE UNIVERSITY PRESS
The Edinburgh Building, Cambridge CB2 2RU, UK   http: //www.cup.cam.ac.uk
40 West 20th Street, New York, NY 10011-4211, USA   http: //www.cup.org
10 Stamford Road, Oakleigh, Melbourne 3166, Australia

© Cambridge University Press 1995

First published 1995
Reprinted 1997, 1998

Printed in the United States of America

Typeset in Baskerville

A catalogue record for this book is available from the British Library

Library of Congress Cataloguing-in-Publication Data is available

ISBN 0-521-49748-5 hardback
ISBN 0-521-49757-4 paperback

CONTENTS

ACKNOWLEDGMENTS

A book of this scope could not have been written without the gracious cooperation of colleagues in a number of fields who have steered me in useful and highly productive directions. I would particularly like to thank seven of my colleagues at Rice University who allowed themselves to be subjected to multiple versions of the same arguments – George E. Marcus, who encouraged its anthropological ambitions; Katherine Drew, who has been an enormous help to me in terms of clarifying the technical dimensions of medieval law; Ira Gruber, who steered me away from many a pitfall in early American history; and Mehti Abedi, Michael M. J. Fischer, Paula Sanders, and David Nirenberg, who restrained some of my enthusiasms about the Islamic world while inspiring others. I was particularly fortunate in having extremely helpful reviews of the entire manuscript from James Axtell, Karen Ordhal Kupperman, Peter Hulme, and George Winius. In addition, individual thanks are due to many who have helped with separate sections of the book.

For the Portuguese sections I would like to thank Linda Lewin, George Winius, Alcida Ramos, Wilson Trajino Filho, and Ellen and Klaus Woortman; for the history of science, Bernard Goldstein, Albert Van Helden, and John Polking; the History and Anthropology departments of the Universidade de Brasilia, the History Department at the Universidade de Campinas, especially Leila Mazan Algranti and Michael Hall, as well as members of the Latin American Program at Yale University.

For the English sections of the book, Tamsyn Donaldson, members of the Center for Aboriginal Studies, Canberra (Australia), Getty Center for the History of Art and the Humanities, Michael McGiffert, Ira Gruber, Ranajit Guha, Warren H. Billings, Peter Hulme, and James Axtell; for the Dutch sections, George Winius, Pieter Emmer, Leonard Blussé, and Albert Van Helden; for the Spanish sections, Mehti Abedi, Michael M. J. Fischer, Paula Sanders, David Nirenberg, Ira Gruber, Geoffrey Parker, Hamid Naficy, Robert Lindsay, and George E. Marcus, as well as audiences at Indiana University, New York University, and the Fine Arts Department of the University of

British Columbia; for the French sections, Hugh Elton, Sam Kinser, and Pierre Boulle.

Libraries whose staff and leadership I have greatly appreciated are (in chronological order) the National Library of Australia, Library of Australian National University, John Carter Brown Library, James Ford Bell Library (University of Minnesota), William Clark Library (UCLA), UCLA Research Collections, Bancroft Library (Berkeley), Library of the John Paul Getty Center for the History of Art and the Humanities, Huntington Library, Rare Book Collection of the University of Chicago, Beineke Rare Books Collection at Yale University, the Sergio Buarque de Holanda Library of the Universidade de Campinas (Brazil), the Library of the Faculdade de Direito da Universidade de São Paulo, the Algemeen Rijksarchief (The Hague), and the Library of the Royal Anthropological and Linguistic Society (Leiden). I also owe an enormous debt of gratitude to Jennifer Geran and the Interlibrary Loan Division of Rice University.

INTRODUCTION

CEREMONIES OF POSSESSION IN EUROPE'S CONQUEST OF THE NEW WORLD, 1492–1640

Landing on the soil of the Bahamas on October 12, 1492, Christopher Columbus planted the royal banners of the king and queen (Ferdinand and Isabel) and called upon members of his expedition to witness his solemn declarations instituting Spanish authority over the New World.

Four months after reaching the isle of São Luis Maranhão at the mouth of the Amazon in 1612, the French company under Lord de la Ravadière marched in elaborately conceived procession, after which "the Indians *themselves* placed this standard of France, placing their land in the possession of the king."[1] By contrast, during the first English act of possession at St. John's Harbor (Newfoundland) in 1583, Sir Humphrey Gilbert "had delivered unto him (after the custom of England) a rod [small twig] and a turf of the same soil."[2] Humphrey Gilbert had a solid clump of dirt dug up and formally presented to him, along with a stick. No particular words were uttered by Gilbert as he took the sod.

Eight years after Columbus's arrival, a Portuguese fleet reached the coast of what is now Brazil. Stepping off the ship Nicolau Coelho began by trading, establishing the first commercial contacts with the Tupi. After several days of sailing and trading along the coast, the expedition's astronomer and chief pilot, Master John, disembarked and measured the height of the midday sun and described the position of the stars. Portuguese possession was initiated not by the dirt or earth below, but by the stars above.[3]

On August 16, 1616, Cornelius Henricxson declared to the States General that he "had discovered a new land between the 38 and 40 degrees [latitude]."[4] When informing the States General of his finding,

---

1 Claude d'Abbeville, *Histoire de la Mission des Pères capuchins en l'isle de Maragnan et terres circonvoisins* (Graz, Austria, 1963; orig. pub. 1614), 161–161v (emphasis added).
2 Richard Hakluyt, *Voyages to the Virginia Colonies*, ed. A. L. Rowse (London, 1986), 32–33.
3 Abel Fontoura da Costa, "O Descobrimento do Brasil," in António Baião, Hernan Cidade, and Manuel Múrias, eds., *História da expansão portuguesa no mundo*, 3 vols. (Lisbon, 1937–1940), 2: 359–370.
4 *Resolutionen der Staten Generaal*, ed. A. Th. van Duersen, vol. 2 (The Hague, 1984),

he enclosed a latitude-scaled map to "more fully" describe the region.[5] In later years Dutch commanders were explicitly ordered to make "perfect maps and descriptions" of their findings.[6]

Colonial rule over the New World was initiated through largely ceremonial practices – planting crosses, standards, banners, and coats of arms – marching in processions, picking up dirt, measuring the stars, drawing maps, speaking certain words, or remaining silent. While military might effectively secured their power over the New World, sixteenth- and seventeenth-century Europeans also believed in their *right* to rule. And they created these rights for themselves by deploying symbolically significant words and gestures made sometimes preceding, sometimes following, sometimes simultaneously with military conquest. But these symbolically significant gestures were not always the same.

At times they used speeches, and at other times they did not. Columbus made a solemn speech, his statement recorded by official notaries. But no notaries appeared to authenticate speeches accompanying Henricxson's completion of the map for the States General, Humphrey Gilbert's reception of the turf and twig, Master John's astronomical observation, or the Tupi planting of the French standard.

Even the physical gestures establishing authority differed. Gilbert grasped the ground, but no one else touched it. La Ravadière, Gilbert, and Columbus planted an object in the ground or on a tree, but Master John and Henricxson did not. A totally different set of distinctions emerges by looking at the person performing the action. Gilbert, Columbus, Henricxson, and Master John all created authority for their respective European powers by themselves. But in La Ravadière's expedition, it was the Tupi natives who actually instituted French authority.

Some practices were dictated by European political authorities; the Spanish crown, for example, gave strict instructions to Columbus about how and what he was to do. The Dutch Estates General gave Henricxson similar instructions. So, too, had the crown of Portugal. But in other cases – La Ravadière in the Amazon or Gilbert in Newfoundland – expeditionary leaders simply performed those actions they believed most clearly established their own country's right to rule over the New World. The ceremonial gestures, speeches, objects, even the persons used to initiate political possession, all clearly differed.

680. A slightly different version dated Aug. 18, 1616, appears in *Documents Relative to the Colonial History of the State of New York*, 15 vols. (Albany, 1853–1887) 1: 12.

5 "Resolution of the States General on a Report of Further Discoveries in New Netherland," Aug. 18, 1616, in *Documents*, 1: 12.

6 "Instructie voor den schipper commandeur Abel Jansen Tasman, Aug. 13, 1642," in R. Posthumus Meyjes, *De reizen van Abel Janszoon Tasman en Franchoys Jacobszoon Visscher ter nadere ontdekking van het zuidland in 1642/3 en 1644* (The Hague, 1919), 147.

While all Europeans aimed to establish their right to rule the New World, their means differed substantially.

Yet histories often homogenize the five major powers colonizing the Americas into a single identity: "Europe." French, Spanish, Portuguese, Dutch, and English ceremonies and symbolic means for initiating colonial authority are frequently lumped together, as if there were a single common European political picture of colonial rule. What Europeans shared was a common technological and ecological platform – trans-Atlantic ships bearing crossbows, cannon, harquebuses, horses, siege warfare, and disease. But they did not share a common understanding of even the political objectives of military action.[7] Differentiating rather than homogenizing Europe enables us to examine differences as well as similarities in the means of creating colonial authority over the New World.

This book compares how Europeans created political authority over New World peoples, lands, or their goods between 1492 and 1640. It is not, therefore, a history of first contacts, nor is it an account of the many expeditions of trading and fishing between New World and Old.[8] Rather it examines the initial attempts to own the New World, to claim it for England, Spain, Portugal, France, or the Dutch Republic.[9] Yet achieving this understanding presents several obstacles.

Rarely did colonists and their leaders explain why they did what they did to establish their political rights. To each group of Europeans, the legitimacy of their or their countrymen's actions could be readily understood. Their rituals, ceremonies, and symbolic acts of possession overseas were based upon familiar actions, gestures, movements, or speeches, and as such, were readily understood by themselves and their fellow countrymen without elaboration, and often without debate as well.

Yet while each group of Europeans understood the significance of their or their compatriots' actions, these meanings are not always so clear to us, nor were they obvious to other Europeans at the time. To understand why, this book will render explicit the often unstated yet distinct

7 See Patricia Seed, "The Conquest of the Americas, 1492–1650," in Geoffrey Parker, ed., *Cambridge Illustrated History of Warfare* (Cambridge, 1995).
8 "Elle [la pêche] n'est guère 'peuplement.' " Jean Meyer, Jean Tarrade, Annie-Rey-Godzeiguer, and Jacques Thobie, *Histoire de la France coloniale: Des origines à 1914* (Paris, 1990), 22.
9 Pierre Chaunu, *European Expansion in the Later Middle Ages,* trans. Katherine Bertram (Amsterdam, 1979); Charles Verlinden, *The Beginnings of Modern Colonization* (Ithaca, N.Y., 1970); Robert Bartlett, *The Making of Europe: Conquest, Colonization and Cultural Change, 950–1350* (Princeton, N.J., 1993); Claudio Sánchez-Albornoz, *España, un enigma histórico,* 2 vols. (Buenos Aires, 1956), 2: 500–513. All argue for continuity of political and economic institutions with medieval ones. Yet all pick very different objects, utilize different explanations, and invoke different medieval origins. None treats the problem of political legitimacy.

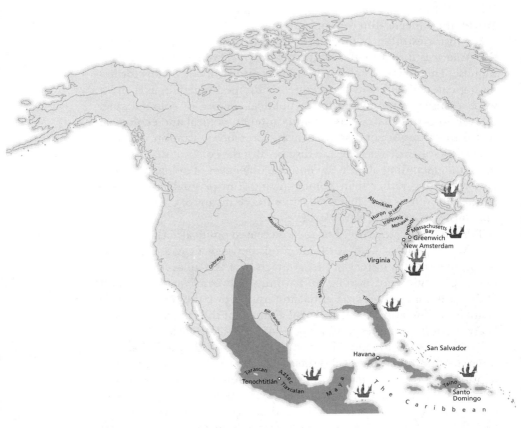

Major European arrivals in the Americas, 1492–1640.

embedded histories and locally significant systems of meaning behind the symbolic actions and statements creating overseas authority.

 These historic cultural assumptions stemmed from three fundamental sources: "everyday life," a common colloquial language, and a shared legal code. They originated in the first place in what Ernest Gellner called "cultural shreds and patches" of everyday life, seemingly arbitrary, but not accidental.[10] The "turf and twig" ceremony of

---

10 "Cultural shreds and patches used by nationalism are often arbitrary historical inventions . . . but . . . [not] contingent and accidental." Ernest Gellner, *Nation and Nationalism* (Oxford, 1983), 56. Williams writes of "a whole body of practices and expectations over the whole of living . . . a lived set of meanings and values – constitutive and constituting – which as they are experienced as practices appear as reciprocally confirming. It thus constitutes a sense of reality for most people in the society, a sense of absolute . . . reality beyond which it is very difficult for most members of the society to move." Raymond Williams, *Marxism and Literature* (New York, 1977), 110.

the English in the New World, for example, stemmed from gardening rhetoric, land ownership practices, and agricultural fertility rituals. Its origins were visible to sixteenth-century Englishmen in everyday objects such as landscapes and buildings, heard in popular biblical interpretation, and seen performed in ordinary folk rituals. By contrast La Ravadière's procession was modeled on royal coronation and city entrance ceremonies witnessed by thousands of Frenchmen. Ferdinand and Isabel ordered Columbus to make a solemn speech, but the content of that speech soon became fixed, reflecting a newly elaborated practice created from traditional Iberian Islamic traditions of declaring war. Master John's ceremony on the coast of Brazil originated in a totally different domain, an elite tradition of Islamic and Hebrew astronomy and mathematics. Although borrowing heavily from Portuguese ideas of nautical discovery, Dutchmen registered their claims primarily in maps and highly detailed descriptions rather than numbers. A different set of cultural histories, even different domains of history – science, religion, warfare, agriculture, theater, navigation – guided the actions of subjects and citizens of each European state in creating rights to rule the New World. Yet within each European society, its members easily understood these actions as establishing legitimate possession because of their links to conventional experiences and customs.

A second factor rendering overseas colonial authority seemingly comprehensible and legitimate to its contemporaries was ordinary language. Colloquial languages were the languages of everyday life. They were seen as "natural" because even small children used them. These languages were used to describe everyday objects and actions, as well as to create understandings of how those objects should be used and what actions meant. Creating such meanings day after day, year after year, made the language as well as the objects and actions it interpreted appear natural or obvious. While print increased the speed with which information was transmitted, the news of the New World was nearly always transmitted in vernacular languages.[11] Furthermore, vernacular languages were invariably used to describe the actions and means of possession. Sharing a language enabled people to make sense of the New World according to familar insights and meanings, making the language and gestures of expression of their fellow countrymen comprehensible. Sharing common cultural (everyday life) experiences and language allowed groups of Europeans to understand each other, even when they did not always entirely agree on the conditions for legitimately creating colonial authority.

If language and the gestures of everyday life were the cultural media through which European states created their own authority and communicated it overseas, law was the means by which states created their legitimacy. Law labels and separates the legitimate from the illegitimate; it defines the realm of the permissible and impermissible.

No nation ever sees its own law code as either arbitrary, or as culturally and historically constructed. Law codes operate in the rhetoric of right and wrong, removed from their own embedded cultural histories. Yet law codes and legal practices are not exempt from the arbitrariness of linguistic and historic cultural construction.

In the late Middle Ages, European law codes began to be composed in the language of the everyday. Where legal systems did not rely upon codes, customary understandings began to be compiled during the

---

11 The three notable exceptions were Peter Martyr, *De orbe novo*, (1530); Amerigo Vespucci, *Mundus novus* (1504); and the Latin edition of Theodor de Bry, *Americae pars I–XIII* (Frankfort, 1590–1634). All were also translated.

same period.[12] Using ordinary languages to define political concepts, including authority and power, made the ideas seem obvious, expressing concepts that either were or could be widely understood in each society. Using vernacular languages in codes and in court proceedings endowed each legal system's concepts and ideas with a sense of transparency and inherent rightness. Subjects or citizens of each European power could perceive their enactments of authority overseas as legitimate because they were grounded in the familiar ideas of power and authority expressed in their own everyday language. Whether dictated by formal authority or carried out on the basis of an implicit consensus, all Europeans relied upon implied cultural understandings of how legitimate political authority ought to be initiated. In so doing they based themselves upon familiar language and culture, as well as upon what they understood their own legal and cultural traditions to have established as legitimate. But because both language and mundane cultural existence differed dramatically from one European power to another, these very characteristics that rendered their own enactments of colonial power understandable, even legal, were the very factors that made it incomprehensible and apparently illegal to other Europeans of the same period. The transparency created by habitual use did not mean that either a given language's words or their meanings had the identical significance to those not so intimately familiar with that language.

Languages construct objects in culturally specific ways. The English expression *heathen land,* for example, makes it impossible for us to consider this expression as anything other than natural. Yet the expression cannot be translated literally into other European languages. It is awkward, even slightly incoherent, in French, Spanish, and Portuguese. In these languages, heathen can only modify a person and cannot be applied to an inanimate object such as land. The characteristic of English which allows heathen to be used to describe an inanimate object is unacceptable beyond the bounds of English. The codes by which languages circumscribe meaning for words are different. These differences cannot be argued with or reasoned against. They are simply correct only in terms of their own codes.

---

12 *Ordenações Afonsinas* (1444); *Las Siete Partidas del rey Alonso IX* (thirteenth century); England ironically began with the English language in the late sixth century, only to have it displaced by Latin in 1066. François I made French the language of the law courts, while compilations of regional customary law (in French) began in the thirteenth century. Ernest Glasson, *Histoire du droit et des institutions de la France,* 8 vols.(Paris, 1887–1903), 4: 14–167; Charles P. Sherman, *Roman Law in the Modern World,* 3 vols. (Boston, 1917), 1: 229–232. By the sixteenth century, English was increasingly being used in courts. Geoffrey Elton, *The English* (Oxford, 1992), 11, 37. Hugo Grotius, *Inleidinge tot de Hollandsche rechts-geleerdheid* (The Hague, 1631).

In 1492, Western European languages for the first time began to formalize their own (independent) standards for correct and incorrect meanings and syntax. Codifying rules for speaking and writing the language meant producing the first vernacular grammars.[13] Antonio Nebrija told the Queen of Castile that "language was the companion of empire,"[14] but overseas conquest also contributed to unifying languages. Fixing rules for expression permitted speakers of the same language from different regions to communicate with each other overseas effectively without the misunderstandings that grammatical differences create. But these vernacular grammars had an additionally important effect. Formally fixing rules for expression (syntax) *within* a language established each and every language as the sole authority upon itself. Latin syntax was no longer authoritative, only the vernacular's own rules.

Also in the sixteenth century, single-language vernacular dictionaries began to appear.[15] Such dictionaries defined the meanings of words only by reference to other words in the same language, thus reinforcing the idea that each language constituted a closed self-referential circle since all words could be defined using only other words of the same language. By the sixteenth century, no language's grammar or definitions of words was "right" in any absolute sense – each was only right regarding its own arbitrary conventions. Translation between languages therefore invariably confronted unforeseen difficulties.

All languages share an irreducible difference, which Jacques Derrida terms the supplement, something which always makes a word in one language ever so slightly different in another. Even cognate words for authority with Latin roots such as *possession* (*posse* [Port.], *posesión* [Sp.], *possesio* [Dutch], *possession* [Fr.]) conveyed slightly different constructions of the concept in each language. Yet these subtleties, often missed or misconstrued by translation, altered what was understood in each language as "possessing" the New World. Furthermore, these subtle linguistic distinctions were linked to substantive differences regarding how Europeans thought possession could and should be enacted. Two short examples will illustrate the point.

13 Jurgen Schafer, *Early Modern English Lexicography*, 2 vols. (Oxford, 1989); Aimar de Ranconet, *Thresor de la langue française*, 2 vols. (Paris, 1621); Robert L. Collison, *A History of Foreign-Language Dictionaries* (London, 1982), 61–73; F. Yndurain, "Relaciones entre la filología y la historia," in *La reconquista española y la repoblación del pais* (Zaragosa, 1951), 223–241; Antonio Nebrjia, *Comiença la gramatica que nuevamente hizo el maestro Antonio de Lebrira sobre la lengua castellana* (Salamanca, 1492); João de Barros, *Gramática da lingua portuguesa* (Lisbon, 1971). The first Dutch grammar and dictionary were produced in 1553. Geoffrey Parker, *The Dutch Revolt*, 2d ed.(London, 1985), 31, 36, 282n11.

14 Antonio de Nebrija, *Gramática castellana* (Halle, Belgium, 1909; orig. pub. 1492), f. 1.

15 Ibid.

In 1562 the Portuguese ambassador to Elizabeth's court lodged a formal protest against English trading in Guinea on the west coast of Africa, justifying an exclusive claim on the basis of Portugal's discovery, propagation of Christianity, and peaceful domination of the commerce of that territory for sixty years. He further complained that the English had placed an arbitrary interpretation on the concept of dominion and asked the queen to forbid her subjects to trade in Portuguese-dominated areas. "They [the English] decide that he [the Portuguese king] has no dominion except where he has forts and tribute . . . but as the words are dubious, he desires her [Queen Elizabeth] . . . to change them into such others [words] as may comprehend all the land *discovered* by the crown of Portugal."[16] The queen replied that "her meaning . . . is to restrain her subjects from haunting [frequenting] . . . land . . . wherein the King of Portugal had obedience, dominion, and tribute, and *not* [to prevent their trading] from all places *discovered*, whereof he had no superiority at all."[17] An annoyed ambassador responded that "his master *has* absolute dominion . . . *over all those lands already discovered.*"[18]

At the core of this exchange were fundamental cultural and linguistic differences between Portuguese and English. To the Portuguese ambassador the word *discovery* signified the establishment of legitimate dominion.[19] For the Portuguese, the concept of discovery was linked to the technology and knowledge which they had pioneered. They had invented the navigational skills, found the most efficient sailing routes to West Africa, and located the African groups willing to supply the goods most desired by the European market. Expressed in more modern terms, the Portuguese concept of discovery was the insistence that they held a patent on the technology – maps, sailing devices, and knowledge – of trading seaports, latitudes, and sea lanes – that they had invented.[20] The English crown refused to consider discovery, so understood, as a legitimate source of the right to rule. Responding with arguments derived from their own traditional cultural and linguistic meanings of the word discovery, Queen Elizabeth assumed that the Portuguese ambassador was talking about the

16 Replication of the Portuguese ambassador, June 7, 1562, in Joseph Stevenson, ed., *Calendar of State Papers, Foreign Series, of the Reign of Elizabeth, 1562* . . . (London, 1867), 77.
17 Answer to the Portuguese ambassador, June 15, 1562, ibid., 95.
18 Second replication of the Portuguese ambassador, June 19, 1562, ibid., 106 (emphasis added).
19 Portuguese sovereigns saw their stone pillars with crosses and the kings' arms "as a sign of how they saw said lands and islands . . . and acquired . . . dominion over them." Júlio Firmino Júdice Biker, *Collecção de tratados e concertos des pazes que o estado da India portuguesa fez com os reis e senhores . . . da Asia e Africa e oriental . . .*, 14 vols. (Lisbon, 1881–1887), 1: 55.
20 For a discussion of this, see Chapter 4.

meaning of the term in her own language.[21] The Portuguese ambassador made the same assumption about the English understanding. Literal translation of the same word but with different cultural import guaranteed that each side could remain convinced that the other was engaged in an outrageous violation of obvious principles.

Nearly two decades later, a similar dispute erupted between England and Spain, turning on mutually exclusive concepts of the legitimate means of establishing political empire. In 1580, the Spanish ambassador complained against Francis Drake's intrusions into territory claimed by the Spanish during his voyage around the world (1577–1580). The official chronicler of the reign of Queen Elizabeth, William Camden, reported that the queen responded by denying Spanish dominion over the territory in the following words: "[Spaniards] had touched here and there upon the Coasts, built Cottages, and given Names to a River or Cape which does not entitle them to ownership; . . . Prescription without possession is worth little."[22] In attacking the Spanish conception of their rights to the New World, Elizabeth relied upon the commonplaces of the English tradition: the idea that discovery was related to landing rather than sailing (touching on coasts); that naming did not entitle a state to ownership, that building cottages did not create ownership (only houses), and finally by quoting to the Spaniards a commonplace of medieval English law that "a man cannot by prescription [i.e., by declaration or decree] make title to land,"[23] a conception not shared by Spaniards or indeed by any other European power of the time.

The cumulative effect of these subtle differences in meanings was dramatic. Every European legal code defined the meaning (and history) of possession, dominion, lordship, and regal sovereignty differently. Symbolic actions or practices for instituting authority differed, frequently dramatically, from one European nation to another. This should not be surprising, for no two European powers shared the exact same cultural experience of everyday life, let alone the same language or legal code. No two powers had identical ideas as to how colonial power should be symbolically created, or indeed even over what it should be established. To ask whether colonial power should

21 The official legal statement of the Portuguese position was Justo Seraphim de Freitas, *De ivsto imperio lvsitanorvm asiatico* (Valladolid, 1625), a response to the publication of Hugo Grotius's *De mare liberum* (1608).

22 "Nec alio quopiam jure quam quod Hispani hinc illinc appulerint, casulas posuerint, sslumen [*sic*] aut Promontorium denominaverint quae proprietatem acquirere non possunt . . . cum praescriptio sine possessione haud valeat." William Camden, *Rerum Anglicarvm et hibernicarvm Annales regnante Elisabetha* (London, 1639), 328, translated as *Annals, or a History of the Most Renowned and Victorious Princesse Elizabeth, Late Queene of England*, 3d ed., by R. N. Gent (London, 1635).

23 Thomas Arnold Herber, *The History of the Law of Prescription in England* (London, 1891), 2. Similar sentiments are expressed in Robert Johnson, *Nova Britannia* (Amsterdam, 1969; orig. pub. 1609).

or even could control, land, water, minerals, wild animals, or people in the New World required a different response, depending upon the colonizing power.

While it may not have been possible to define what was distinctively English about political practices at home, it was possible to observe it overseas. When in an identical situation with other powers – creating empires in the Americas overseas – the differences between English and Portuguese customs appeared particularly salient. Moreover these differences appeared obvious to other Europeans.

Europeans in the New World characteristically referred to each other's practices as national ones. Englishmen referred to other European colonists' practices as French, Spanish, or Dutch. Groups of colonists did not appear to others as they saw themselves, that is, in terms of their own internal regional, linguistic, or status differentiation. To those outside, each group of European colonists appeared as a uniform group, identified by common language, political loyalty, and characteristic means of appropriating indigenous land, people, or goods.

While there were internal struggles within each national tradition – among local New World authorities, the crown, or chartered company, and private persons over who had or even could have ownership rights over each of these objects – these debates were carried on solely within the confines of each cultural tradition of legal ownership. Even internal criticisms of how colonial power was to be established derived from these same embedded cultural and legal systems. The internal critics of colonialism in each European society – Roger Williams in New England, Bartolomé de Las Casas in Spain, Adriaen Van Der Donck in New Netherland – never suggested that the cultural practices of another society were preferable or that another power's legal system targeted the correct object of colonial authority. Rather, every European critic of colonialism assumed that his own legal and cultural tradition was the only legitimate one and strove to find better means within that framework for justifying his own state's exercise of power over the New World.

Symbolically enacting colonial authority meant that ceremonies, actions, speeches, and records primarily targeted their fellow Europeans. It was above all their own countrymen and political leaders that colonists had to convince of the legitimacy of their actions, not indigenous peoples. When official guidelines for taking possession were lacking, actions had to be culturally persuasive across a broad spectrum of their home society. When centrally created, as Spanish and Portuguese enactments were, it was monarchs and political elites above all who had to be won over. While French colonists attempted to persuade natives – it was no less crucial to persuade their fellow Frenchmen of their success in convincing natives.

Internal criticisms of colonialism never led to the idea, common today, that all colonialism was either bad or wrong. Numerous European nations were engaged in colonialism and it is not surprising that even internal critics self-righteously understood their own position. But they were less accepting of their fellow Europeans' expression of colonial legitimacy.

We are accustomed to thinking of cultural boundaries as occurring between European powers and indigenous peoples, but they also existed between different European powers. Subjects and citizens of any European power understood each other not simply from the perspective of competition; they also interpreted what their counterparts in other colonizing nations were doing. Criticism of other powers at the time appeared in international conflicts, as well as in writings about each other.

Such challenges occurred time and again on the fringes of colonial domains. Dutch- and Englishmen clashed in Connecticut, the French and Spanish battled in Florida, all giving rise to military action, negotiating missions, and countless expressions of hostility and antagonism toward other European powers' expression of legitimacy.

Given the international competition over colonial empire, cultural differences were uncharitably interpreted, especially when political prestige and economic interests were involved. What is more surprising is that European participants in colonialism never tried to understand each other. No European power ever expressed curiosity about another's ceremonial practices or legal beliefs or sought to understand them on their own terms. These hostile expressions were rooted in profound misunderstandings of the actions and cultural premises behind practices initiating and maintaining colonial authority.

Commentaries about other Europeans' actions rested upon the erroneous belief that they understood what representatives from that power should be doing. Taking their own practices as the model, each set of Europeans was convinced that what the other Europeans were doing failed to perform some critical action. Such certainty rested upon the fundamental transparency communicated by their own cultural, legal, and linguistic system. Common vernacular language and shared everyday experiences created the assurance that their legal code, ceremonies, and other means of enacting colonialism were both obvious and right. Speakers of each language regularly assumed that their own definition of authority was the only one – and, at most, that other cultures' definitions were identical when they were merely similar. Considered from a Spanish, Portuguese, French, or Dutch legal or cultural system, for example, the English idea that fences and hedges demonstrated ownership was unconvincing. Outside England, the entire cultural, agricultural, and linguistic context was missing, and English landscape signs were wholly unpersuasive. Similarly, Spanish speeches (duly notarized) were incomprehensible to the English, as they were to the French and Dutch as well. The audience for critiques of other European colonial practices therefore was really only those sharing the same language, culture, and legal code. They inevitably viewed their denunciation of other states' colonial practices as devastating. Yet this perception of their criticisms as crushing occurred only to their fellow countrymen. Europeans from different states unfailingly responded with impatience and annoyance. The same factors that rendered each society's perception of its own cultural and legal practices as obviously valid also rendered others' practices as incomprehensible or simply irrelevant. The result of a shared cultural experience and common language was the confident assurance that their own legal position was inherently and wholly correct, their concept of dominion transparent and true.

This book treats all rationales and legitimation of the exercise of imperial political power as cultural constructions. These constructions have a certain logic with respect to the cultural, political, economic, ecological, and social history of each nation. They are entirely reasonable given national languages and particular histories. But they are also entirely "reasonable" *only* in the context of those histories. The same things that rendered them rational for subjects of one monarch or citizens of one republic were the very factors and experience that rendered them unfamiliar and alien to the subjects and citizens of another. This book attempts to show exactly why such convictions appeared reasonable to members of each European society, while failing to persuade others.

Chapter 1 begins with the actions most familiar to English-speaking readers, the almost anticeremonial English conceptions of possession. It describes the major means used to implement English colonial possession employing architectural objects and everyday agricultural activity. Chapter 2 contrasts anticeremonial English approaches with the usual French practices of staging a parade, sometimes elaborately conceived and staged, and seeking native consent.

By contrast, the central Spanish method of enacting colonialism was a ritualized speech addressed to the natives and demanding their submission to the Catholic crown of Spain. Unlike all other powers, the Spanish crown specified a text, the Requirement, which was to be read to assembled natives. Ceremonial gestures were less important than the speech, and notaries often certified that it had been delivered, for it was a formality that justified military action for failing to submit. Chapter 3 discusses the historical origins and implications of this practice.

Portuguese claims to the New World rested upon their claims to "discovery." Chapter 4 deals with the Portuguese claims to possession, first by examining the claims of discovery based upon technological and scientific achievement, especially astronomical knowledge about the world. Astronomers, mathematicians, shipbuilders, pilots, and others employed by the Portuguese invented the technological advances in ship design and navigation that made it possible for Europeans to sail across the Atlantic to the New World in large numbers and on a regular basis. They claimed that their technological achievements granted them a kind of intellectual property which in turn granted them right to a commercial monopoly in regions they had uncovered. This chapter describes the origins of the Portuguese scientific and technological achievement – discovery – and their claim to "possess" – historically the two most disparaged (and misunderstood) justifications in the English-speaking world.[24]

Finally, Chapter 5 concerns Europe's expert coastal sailors, the Dutch, who adopted Portuguese high-seas navigational expertise together with Portuguese claims of ruling a seaborne empire. While adopting virtually word for word the Portuguese title to a colonial empire based upon discovery the Dutch conception of discovery was tied more closely to written description and maps than to astronomical knowledge.

Previous comparative studies have missed both the range of cultural categories used to construct colonial authority – science, agriculture, commerce, biblical texts – and the extent to which the ongoing mutual evaluation and critique of both one's own and other nations' colonial practices were embedded culturally as well.

The beginning point of this history requires no explanation; it is the year of the first European ceremony of possession of the New World, Columbus's solemn declaration on San Salvador. Since the book examines originary colonial rites – actions by which Europeans initiated their political authority over natives, their natural resources, tradable goods, or lands – these actions of claiming principally occurred in the century and a half between 1492 and 1640. After 1640, Europeans progressively viewed New World peoples and resources as inherently theirs, revenue-producing or strategic pawns on the table of European political chess. Viewed thus, measures justifying supplanting indigenous authority came to be seen as a matter of historical record after 1640 as newer enactments of possession more often transferred resources from one European group to another.

The history of colonialism has been written in the recent past as intellectual cultures of dominant peoples, on the one hand, or as the history of resisting peoples, on the other hand. Intellectual histories

24 For example, see Wilcomb Washburn, "Dispossessing the Indian," in James Morton Smith, ed., *Seventeenth-Century America* (Chapel Hill, N.C., 1959), 17; Samuel E. Morison, *Portuguese Voyages to America in the Fifteenth Century* (Cambridge, Mass., 1940) 5–10. French historian Pierre Chaunu, *European Expansion*, 207–210, provides a more dispassionate view. For a further discussion, see Chapter 4.

focus exclusively on "high culture" literature and thus present only abstract ideas about colonial power. The difficulty with such an exclusive focus is that such writings can tell us about formal ideas, but not about the actions that instituted colonial power. Furthermore, ideas cannot provide us with the contemporary consequences or legacies of colonialism because they avoid considering the practices or mechanisms for enacting power.

While the histories of resistance tell something about how indigenous identity was preserved and defended under colonial rule, they tell us little about the cultural practices of power, only about the value of the struggle against it. Hence, such studies miss the cultural distinctiveness of regional struggles in the Americas because colonial power itself is undifferentiated, as are critical dimensions of those struggles themselves.

The recent literature studying the resistance of indigenous peoples to the imposition of colonialism has made the point that these cultures have made powerful efforts to sustain their identities despite external forces that have threatened to crush them. Throughout the Americas indigenous communities were devastated by disease and forced to reconstitute themselves out of fragments of their former cultural identities in the political presence of very powerful entrenched colonial forces. Because the mainland of the Americas experienced little of the successive replacement of different European forms of colonialism characteristic of coastal regions of Southeast Asia and the Caribbean, the legal and political systems of the Americas have far greater historical continuities with the earlier political forms of European colonial rule. Thus, the current situation of aboriginal peoples within nation-states of the Americas depends upon the ability to validate their identity in the world of political interests and to construct themselves in terms of categories of ownership, possession, and sovereignty defined by legal codes derived from those originally imposed by colonialism. Homogenizing colonialism by insisting that it is a single undifferentiated European project has thus prevented us from understanding how contemporary struggles by indigenous communities to preserve themselves have taken distinct political directions in different regions of the Americas. These directions, as will be argued at greater length in another volume, derive from national legal systems that are the heirs to separate colonial cultural and legal traditions.

There are powerful and enduring legacies of European colonial rule over the Americas, traces that are apparent in forms of mundane objects such as fences and hedges, names of streets and constellations, forms of state organization, where and how each American nation remembers the founding moment of its history. Colonialism's legacies remain with us today, largely invisible reminders of a past that began over five hundred years ago.

HOUSES, GARDENS, AND FENCES
SIGNS OF ENGLISH POSSESSION IN THE NEW WORLD

"On the 15. of December, they [the Pilgrims] wayed [weighed] anchor to goe to the place they had discovered. . . . And afterwards tooke better view of the place, and resolved where to pitch their dwelling; and on the 25 day begane to erect the first house for common use to receive them and their goods."[1] Thus, William Bradford describes the start of English colonization at Plymouth, Massachusetts, on December 25, 1620. Bradford's is a quotidian and matter-of-fact account of English possession of the New World. There was no ritual order of disembarkation, no solemn kneeling to claim the land,[2] no ceremonies upon landing, no crosses planted, nor even any handing over of turf and twig. No banners were described as unfurled, no solemn declarations made or recorded by the leaders of the expedition, as were characteristic of Spanish possession. Rather Bradford, like other Pilgrim writers, described the possession of the New World as guided by the most mundane decision "where to pitch their dwelling," where to erect "the first house."[3] A decade later John Winthrop would describe the Massachusetts Bay Colony's possession as beginning "by building an house there."[4] But the New England settlers were by no means the only English colonists to describe their settlement in the New World thus.

Farther south at Jamestown, some fourteen years before the Plymouth settlement's first founding, the Virginia colonists were finding a residence. George Percy described the English occupation of James-

---

1 William Bradford, *History of Plymouth Plantation*, ed. William Davis (New York, 1908), 105.
2 When Pilgrims reached Cape Cod on Nov. 11, 1620, and "fell on their knees and blessed the god of heaven," they did so in gratitude for safe deliverance from a dangerous voyage, not as a ceremony of possession. Bradford, *Plymouth Plantation*, 95.
3 "[They] resolved where to pitch their Dwellings; and on the Five and twentieth day of December began to erect the first House." Nathaniel Morton, *New Englands Memoriall* (New York, 1937; orig. pub. 1669), 22. "After our landing and viewing of the places . . . we came to a conclusion . . . to set on the main land . . . resolving in the morning to come all ashore and to build houses." *Mourt's Relation* (orig. pub. 1622), in Alexander Young, *Chronicles of the Pilgrim Fathers*, 2d ed. (Baltimore, 1974), 167–168.
4 John Winthrop, *The History of New England from 1630 to 1640*, ed. James Savage, 2 vols. (Boston, 1825), 1: 290.

town in equally mundane terms: "The Thirteenth day, we came to our seating [dwelling] place in Paspiha's country. The fourteenth day we landed all our men which were set to work."[5] George Popham's 1607 account described a choice of a place for settlement on August 18 and on the following day "the 19th of August, we all went to the shore where we made choice for our plantation."[6] Here as elsewhere the remarkable ordinariness of English possession comes through. When Englishmen returned in 1587 to find the site of the first settlement at Roanoke in ruins and abandoned, the first "order was given that every man should be employed for the repairing of those houses which we found standing, and also to make other new cottages for such as should need."[7] Repairing houses rather than ceremonially fixing symbols of European authority was the first order of work for the day.

While some of early efforts at colonization also planted crosses or read sermons, these actions were often omitted. But no English expedition ever omitted mention of setting up a house.[8] An early-sixteenth-century play wistfully observing the Spanish and Portuguese overseas empires regretted, "If they that be Englishmen/Might have been the first of all/That there should have taken possession   And made first building and habitation."[9]

That accounts of English occupation of the New World usually began by describing ordinary house-building activity is far from coincidental. While other sources of rights such as "discovery" have been subsequently alleged as the justification for English possession of the New World, the colonists themselves usually failed to use this argument.[10] Nor did most of the colonial advocates home in England at the

---

5 David B. Quinn, ed., "Observations gathered out of 'A Discourse of the Plantation of the Southerne colonie in Virginia by the English, 1606' by Hon. George Percy" (Charlottesville, Va., 1967), 161.

6 Alexander Brown, ed., *Genesis of the United States* (New York, 1964), 191–192.

7 "The Lost (Second) Colony," in Richard Hakluyt, *Voyages to the Virginia Colonies* (London, 1986), 144–145.

8 Popham read a sermon in 1607; Percy set up crosses at the Chesapeake and at the James River. Brown, ed., *Genesis,* 164, 191–192; Quinn, ed., "Observations," 10, 20. Thomas Yong planted "his Majesty's arms upon a tree" of the Delaware River in 1634. Albert Cook Meyers, *Narratives of Early Pennsylvania, West New Jersey, and Delaware, 1630–1707* (New York, 1912), 41. Thomas Gates had both a sermon and his commission read; "Letter of the Governor and Council of Virginia to the Virginia Company of London, July 7, 1610, in Brown, ed., *Genesis,* 402–413, esp. 407. Winthrop describes the Massachusetts Bay Colony as beginning in the same fashion, "by building a house there." Winthrop, *History of New England,* 1: 290.

9 *A New Interlude and a Mery of the Nature of Life* (ca. 1519), reproduced in Edward Arber, ed., *The First Three English Books on America* (Birmingham, Eng., 1985), xxi.

10 Seventeenth-century Englishmen were ambivalent about the right to title based upon "discovery." Sometimes the Cabot voyages were invoked defensively as a discovery but English rhetoric soon remade discovery into "discovery and planting." John Brereton, *A Briefe and True Relation of the Discoverie of the North Part of Virginia* (1602), in David B. Quinn and Alison M. Quinn, eds., *The English New England Voyages, 1602–1680* (London, 1983), 168, 175. More often the idea of entitlement

time. Instead, sixteenth- and early-seventeenth-century Englishmen usually constructed their right to occupy the New World on far more historically and culturally familiar grounds: building houses and fences and planting gardens. The king described how the founders of the Virginia Company "have been humble suitors . . . to make habitation and plantation,"[11] that is, to build houses (habitation) and plant gardens or crops (plantation.) Building the first house was critical to the initial stages of English settlement in the first place because of their cultural significance as registers of stability, historically carrying a significance of permanence missing even elsewhere in continental Europe.

The central characteristic of English society was, and still is, the village. "England is a land of villages," wrote geographer Brian Roberts. Even today there are an estimated thirteen thousand villages, many of which can document nearly one thousand years of continuous existence in the same place.[12] Parish boundaries in Lincolnshire, Berkshire, and Devon, for example, go back over a thousand years.[13] While the peculiar fixity of English settlement may owe something to its composition as an island nation without contiguous territory to expand into, there is a fixed and permanent character of English settlement that is missing elsewhere in Europe. Therefore, by establishing a house, an Englishman was assuming a model of fixed settlement that had lasted centuries. To build a house in the New World was for an Englishman a clear and unmistakable sign of an intent to remain – perhaps for a millennium.[14]

Houses also established a legal right to the land upon which they were constructed. Erecting a fixed (not movable) dwelling place upon a territory, under English law created a virtually unassailable right to own the place.[15] Deploying physical objects such as houses to establish

based upon discovery was criticized. See, e.g., J. Eric Thompson, ed., *Thomas Gage's Travels in the New World* (Norman, Okla., 1958); Wilcomb Washburn, "Dispossessing the Indian," *Seventeenth-Century America*, ed. James Morton Smith (Chapel Hill, N.C., 1959), 16–18, 26. Discovery became a central part of the rhetoric justifying English-language claims to the New World only in the nineteenth century – the 1823 U.S. Supreme Court decision in *Johnson v. MacIntosh*. Felix Cohen, *Handbook of Federal Indian Law* (Washington, D.C., 1942), 292.

11 Samuel Lucas, *Charters of the Old English Colonies in America* (London, 1850), first Virginia charter, Apr. 10, 1606, 1; second Virginia charter, Mar. 23, 1609, 12.

12 Brian Roberts, "Planned Villages from Medieval England," in Alan R. H. Baker, comp., *Man Made the Land: Essays in English Historical Geography* (Newton Abbott, Devon, 1973), 46–58.

13 H. R. Loyn, *Anglo-Saxon England and the Norman Conquest*, 2d ed. (London, 1991), 169.

14 Perry Miller's interpretation of the role of the "city on the hill" has been decisively critiqued by Theodore Dwight Bozeman, *To Live Ancient Lives: The Primitivist Dimension in Puritanism* (Chapel Hill, N.C., 1988), 90–115; Perry Miller, *Errand into the Wilderness* (Cambridge, Mass., 1956), 11, 158–159.

15 Even late in the eighteenth century, William Blackstone, *Commentaries on the Laws of England* (New York, 1968; repr. 1808 ed.), bk. 2, chap. 1, sec. 4, declares, "Even

title to land was a unique and remarkable characteristic of English law. All the other European legal systems that would come to the New World – French, Spanish, Portuguese, and Dutch – required either formal permission or written records to acquire title even to apparently unused land.[16] In English law, neither a ceremony nor a document but the ordinary action of constructing a dwelling place created the right of possession. The continuing presence and habitation of the *object* – the house – maintained that right.

In addition to houses, another kind of fixed object also created similar rights of possession and ownership. By fixing a boundary, such as a hedge around fields, together with some kind of activity demonstrating use (or intent to use, i.e., clearing the land), anyone could establish a legal right to apparently unused land.[17] As with the house, mundane activity rather than permission, ceremonies, or written declarations created ownership. The ordinary object – house, fence, or other boundary marker – signified ownership.

The English preoccupation with boundaries and boundary markers as significant markers of ownership characterizes the earliest English records of sales or gifts of land dating from 600 to 1080 A.D. Called perambulations, they contain highly detailed descriptions of physical objects around the boundaries as if described during a walk (ambulation) around the edges (perimeter) of a property. Even these earliest records note hedges as the second most common boundary marker.[18] By the early Middle Ages the cultural importance of boundaries was well established, widely understood, and utilized in acquiring property.[19] Boundaries around land – a fence (wooden stakes) or a hedge – established ownership in long-standing English practices and legal customs.[20]

brute creation . . . maintained a kind of permanent property in their dwellings. . . . Hence a property was very soon established in every man's house and home-stall."

16 For an analysis of the system closest to that of the English (also requiring use in order to establish ownership), see the appendix to Chapter 4.

17 In English towns, the boundaries of the commons were and still are inspected and annually marked by hammering new wooden stakes – the boundary markers. Alan R. H. Baker, "Field Systems in Medieval England," in Baker, comp., *Man Made the Land*, 59–68.

18 Trees were the most frequently mentioned boundaries. Oliver Rackham, *Trees and Woodland in the British Landscape*, rev. ed. (London, 1983), 44, 184–186. Spanish and Portuguese transfers of private property often included walks around the border, but it was the motion of walking rather than the visual identification of physical objects that were critical.

19 Baker, "Field Systems in Medieval England," 67. See also Howard L. Gray, *English Field Systems* (Cambridge, Mass., 1915); C. S. and C. S. Orwin, *The Open Fields* (Oxford, 1954). For the legal terminology associated with this action, see William Searle Holdsworth, *A History of English Law*, 12 vols., 2d ed. (London, 1937), 7: 59. Coppice woods in Anglo-Saxon times had earthen boundaries. Rackham, *Trees and Woodland*, 114. For the medieval increase in hedges, see ibid., 188.

20 English surveyor Ralph Agas, *A Preparative to Platting of Landes . . .* (1596), called specifying a boundary on a map as bringing "perfection to the woorke, and may in

From the fourteenth century onward, the fence or hedge acquired another significance as well: the principal symbol of not simply ownership, but specifically private ownership of land.[21] In many parts of medieval England a group of people often shared a collective interest in a plot of land. But during the fourteenth and fifteenth centuries, collective ownership increasingly gave way to individual private ownership. This social (later legal) process was called the enclosure movement. Formally an enclosure meant that collective owners were to exchange their shared rights in a large piece of land for private rights in a smaller piece. To establish definitive ownership of the smaller piece, it was bounded or marked on the edges. "Fence well therefore let your plot be wholly in your own power," wrote William Lawson, author of a popular book on gardening.[22]

The enclosure movement gained momentum during the sixteenth century by eliminating considerable shared or collective ownership, thus making a considerable number of people landless.[23] Hence, by the start of English colonization overseas, enclosing land by fences or hedges meant establishing specifically individual ownership. With few exceptions, the English created private property in the Americas. Even when settlements began with collective grants, lands were soon subdivided and passed into private hands.[24] Thus, fencing or enclosing was additionally critical to early colonists because it was the customary means of establishing private property. Englishmen shared a unique understanding that fencing legitimately created exclusive private property ownership in the New World.

time to come bee many waeis most necessarie and profitable." Quoted by Roger Kain and Elizabeth Baigent, *The Cadastral Map in the Service of the State: A History of Property Mapping* (Chicago, 1992), 4. Tabor claims that any barrier constituted a "fence" including ditches, banks, and walls; Grace Tabor, *Old-Fashioned Gardening* (New York, 1925), 186.

21 Tenants in common had begun to be eliminated in the fourteenth century by the process of enclosure. Joan Thirsk, *Tudor Enclosures* (London, 1959).

22 William Lawson, *A New Orchard and Garden* (London, 1618), 16. There are three early-seventeenth-century editions of this book. John Winthrop owned a copy, as did other leaders of Puritan settlement. Thomas Tusser, *Five Hundred Points of Good Husbandry*, ed. William Mavor (London, 1812; orig. pub. 1573), 200. "Ill husbandry loseth for lack of good fence; Good husbandry closeth."

23 Kain and Baigent, *The Cadastral Map*, 237; Joan Thirsk, "Enclosing and Engrossing," in H. P. R. Finberg, ed., *The Agrarian History of England and Wales*, vol. 4 (1500–1640) (Cambridge, 1967), 200–255; Thirsk, *Tudor Enclosures*, notes that open field farming had given way to enclosure in southern and eastern England by 1500, progressed considerably by that date in the Midlands, but leaving a fair part of central and much of northern England unenclosed.

24 Some *initial* forms of English settlement in New England were collective. "A town consisted of a trace of land with defined legal status granted to a *group* of settlers, so that New England settlement, at least initially, was . . . a communal venture." Kain and Baigent, *Cadastral Map*, 285–286; Neal Salisbury, *Manitou and Providence: Indians, Europeans, and the Making of New England* (New York, 1982), 142–143; Sung Bok Kim, *Landlord and Tenant in Colonial New York: Manorial Society, 1664–1775* (Chapel Hill, N.C., 1978), 41.

The types of fences could vary. In Rhode Island, English settlers employed Narragansett peoples in building stone fences.[25] More often, early English occupants of the New World used hedgerows, fences, and paling to surround their agricultural property. Hedgerows and fences were classic Anglo-Saxon and early medieval English methods of creating property boundaries; paling (sharp-pointed stakes placed close together) was the classic thirteenth-century English means of enclosing animals in a hunting park.[26] The variety of timber available for fencing in the New World soon made the fence the most popular form of enclosure.[27] As landscape architect V. R. Ludgate notes, sharp-pointed sticks placed close together were "undoubtedly the forerunner of the picket fence."[28]

When property was not fenced voluntarily, local and even royal officials demanded that English settlers put up fences. A Rhode Island Quarter Court in 1639 ordered "ther shall be suffcent fences, eyther hedge or post and raile, made about the Corne Grounds that shall be planted or sowne" on Rhode Island.[29] Among the first laws passed by the Virginia assembly (March 25, 1623) was the proviso that "every freeman shall fence in a quarter acre of ground before Whitsuntide" (September 8, 1623) – an injunction repeated again by the legislature in 1632, 1642, and 1646. "Every man shall enclose his ground with sufficient fences or else to plant."[30] At a later date, even the minimum height of fences was fixed at $4\frac{1}{2}$ feet.[31] Similar laws were imposed in the Connecticut River valley and the colony of Maryland.[32]

English officials at home were equally concerned with fencing. The Virginia Company sent instructions to Governor Francis Wyatt in

25 Daniel Gookin, "Historical Collections of the Indians in New England," in Massachusetts Historical Society, *Collections* (Boston, 1792), 1: 141–227, esp. 210.
26 V. R. Ludgate, *Gardens of the Colonists* (Washington, D.C., 1941), 7; Rackham, *Trees and Woodland*, 152–153, 184–196; John M. Gilbert, *Hunting and Hunting Reserves in Medieval Scotland* (Edinburgh, 1979), 82–87.
27 William Cronon, *Changes in the Land: Indians, Colonists, and the Ecology of New England* (New York, 1983), 130.
28 Ludgate, *Gardens*, 7. New World pales like picket fences often had a horizontal stay. The picket fence was a nineteenth-century creation in the shipbuilding towns of New England. Tabor, *Old-Fashioned Gardening*, 186, 189.
29 Carl Bridenbaugh, *Fat Mutton and Liberty of Conscience: Society in Rhode Island, 1636–1690* (Providence, 1974), 34; *Records of the Colony of Rhode Island and Providence Plantations* (Providence, 1856), 1: 76, 78, 90, 96.
30 Hening, *Statutes*, 1: 126, 199, 244, 332. In Mar. 1642 and Oct. 1646 the failure to fence was linked to liability for damage done by cattle.
31 Hening, *Statutes*, 1: 458, Mar. 1657.
32 See William Hand Browne, ed., *Proceedings and Acts of the General Assembly of Maryland*, vol. 1 of *Archives of Maryland* (Baltimore, 1993), 90 (Oct. 1640), for requirement for fencing. For similar height for fences in Virginia, see *The Laws of the Province of Maryland* (Wilmington, Del., 1978; orig. pub. 1718), 127–130. See also, Lyman Carrier, *The Beginnings of Agriculture in America* (New York, 1968; orig. pub. 1923), 167, 183.

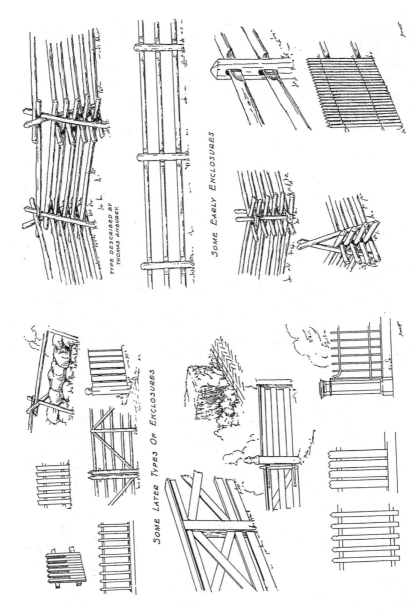

TYPE DESCRIBED BY
THOMAS ANDREY.

SOME EARLY ENCLOSURES

SOME LATER TYPES OF ENCLOSURES

Figure 1. Some early fences in the English New World. From V. R. Ludgate, *Gardens of the Colonists* (Washington, D.C., 1941).

1621 that company lands in Virginia were to be fenced.[33] After the demise of the Virginia Company, the king sent two successive (nearly identical) orders to the governors of Virginia ordering settlers to fence in land. Given the vast expanses of the New World and the impossibility of actually fencing in the entire domain claimed by an individual, the erection of a fence was sometimes ordered for a portion of the land to symbolize ownership. In his instructions to the governor of Virginia, King Charles ordered that every settler "be compelled for every 200 acres Granted unto him to inclose and sufficiently Fence . . . a Quarter of an Acre of Ground."[34] While fences were often rationalized in practical terms, such as protecting crops from predatory animals, it was clear they had political significance as well. Only in English colonies did officials – the crown, courts, local assemblies – consistently and regularly order fences to be erected.[35] The reason was that fences and other types of boundaries had legal significance. Fences created the presumption of ownership in medieval English law; their visible presence on the landscape physically indicated actual English occupation and communicated English rights. Furthermore, the fence kept cattle from destroying evidence of private property ownership, the act of possessing by planting.

Besides ordering fences to be erected, officials in the English colonial world often ordered another related action to private property – surveys. From the beginning, the Virginia Company of London employed surveyors and avidly sought information regarding the cartography of the country. "In 1616 when Virginia and the Bermudas were under nearly the same management, surveyors and commissioners . . . were sent out to both plantations," wrote Alexander Brown.[36] While official surveyors did not appear for several decades in

33 Hening, *Statutes*, 1: 115, July 24, 1621.
34 Warren M. Billings, *The Old Dominion in the Seventeenth Century: A Documentary History of Virginia, 1606–1689* (Chapel Hill, N.C., 1975), 56. The 1639 instructions were virtually identical to those given to Governor William Berkeley.
35 In colonial Brazil, fines were more common than orders for fences. Owners of aggresive cattle were given a month to get rid of them or face substantial fines (2,000 reais – the cost of the most valuable cows in the region) São Paulo (Feb. 10, 1590). If cattle or pigs caused damage to someone else's crops, the animals's owner would be fined for each head of cattle he owned (regardless of how few did the damage), plus pay damages to the owner of the plot (Apr. 14, 1590). When troops of horses and cows had entered at night and caused damage, the council of São Paulo simply ordered horses and cows not be permitted in the town henceforth (Jan. 26, 1598), *Actas da Câmara da Vila de São Paulo* (São Paulo, 1914), 1: 384–385, 395–397; 2: 37, 288–289. Prices are from Alcântara Machado, *Vida e morte do bandeirante*, 2d ed. (São Paulo, 1978), 54. Clearing roads rather than planting fences was more important to the town council of São Paulo. See, e.g., *Actas*, 2: 409.
36 Brown, ed., *Genesis*, 458; see also instructions for Governor Francis Wyatt, July 24, 1621, in Hening, *Statutes*, 1: 116; "Mr. William Claybourne a surveyor sent to survey the planters lands and make a map of the country."

Massachusetts, all colonies hired surveyors, usually in the initial phases of colonization.[37]

The surveyors' principal work throughout the colonial period of U.S. history consisted of formally appraising private property boundaries, a tradition that continued during the westward expansion.[38] Indeed surveying was originally justified in England on the grounds that it created more detailed descriptions of private boundaries.[39] Among other European colonizers the Dutch also sent surveyors, but to engineer the design of forts, rather than ascertain limits of private property.[40] The Swedes sent a surveyor in 1634, but to describe the political limits of a territory purchased from the Indians rather than to establish private property.[41] Private property boundary maps did not even appear in France until 1650.[42] No other European colony employed surveyors so extensively; no other European colonists considered establishing either private property or boundaries in the New World as central to legitimate possession.[43]

Affixing the symbols of individual ownership by planting fences and hedges was sometimes referred to by colonists as "improvements." While in popular speech today *improvement* merely means to make something better, the word first signified fencing in large tracts of previously unenclosed land. It originated with the enclosure movements

37 *Proceedings and Acts of General Assembly of Maryland*, 1: 59 (Feb.–March 1638–1639) for payment of the Maryland surveyor. Massachusetts did not appoint surveyors until 1682. William Penn, "Instructions" (1681), in *Memoirs of the Historical Society of Pennsylvania*, vol. 2 (Philadelphia, 1827), 213–221. See also Edward T. Price, *Dividing the Land: Early American Beginnings of Our Property Mosaic* (Chicago, 1995).

38 "Every private planters evident shall be surveyed and laid out in severall and the bounds record by the surveyors" (Sept. 1632). Hening, *Statutes*, 1: 197; John R. Stilgoe, *Common Landscape of America, 1580 to 1845* (New Haven, 1982), 99–107, 112. "In the midst of heated, complicated debate about the federal grid survey [private land ownership] they [Congressmen] neglected to mandate a system of 'artificial' roads." Ibid., 133. See also Norman J. W. Thrower, *Original Survey and Land Subdivision* (Chicago, 1966).

39 By the fifteenth-century, local English maps concerned "external problems of landed estates, showing how contiguous parcels of lands adjoined, setting out disputed rights or boundaries." Ralph Agas, in his 1596 treatise *A Preparative to Plotting of Landes and Tenements for Surveigh*, argues for maps of properties on the grounds that the bounds of each piece of land could be shown in greater detail on a map than in a book. P. D. A. Harvey, *Maps in Tudor England* (Chicago, 1987), 79, 91.

40 "Particuliere instructie voor den Ingenieur ende landmeter Cryn Fredicxsz," in A. J. F. Van Laer, trans. and ed., *Documents Relating to New Netherland, 1624–1626, in the Henry E. Huntington Library* (San Marino, Calif., 1924), 132; Svetlana Alpers, *The Art of Describing: Dutch Art in the Seventeenth Century* (Chicago, 1983), 148–149.

41 The survey was kept in the royal archives of Sweden. Reverend Israel Acrelius, "The Account of the Swedish Churches in New Sweden," in Myers, ed., *Narratives of Early Pennsylvania*, 61.

42 Kain and Baigent, *Cadastral Map*, 209–210.

43 The very different approach to boundaries in the Portuguese colony is explored in the appendix to Chapter 4 entitled "Portuguese and English."

of sixteenth-century England.[44] To "improve" the land initially meant to claim it for one's own agricultural or pastoral use by surrounding it with one of the characteristically English architectural symbols of the sixteenth century, the fence. Historian William Cronon writes that the fence "to colonists represented perhaps the most visible symbol of an *improved* landscape."[45] Even in the present-day United States, a fence is still legally an improvement.[46] Whether it enclosed the entire property or merely a portion it, the fence symbolized English ownership in a culturally powerful way.

Thus, Englishmen occupying the New World initially inscribed their possession of the New World by affixing their own powerful cultural symbols of ownership – houses and fences – upon the landscape. But while houses and fences registered ownership through fixed markers, there was a second way to secure possession. Ownership of land could be secured by simply using it, engaging in agricultural or pastoral activities. In the seventeenth and eighteenth centuries, improvement also referred to two activities repeatedly carried out on the same land: grazing (domestic animals) and planting. A New England colonist wrote, "Finding then no better way to improve them [estates than] to set upon husbandry [domestic animals]." "Gardening . . . I think ought to be applauded and encouraged in all countries," wrote William Temple. "[It] is a public service to one's country . . . which . . . improve[s] the earth."[47]

PLANTING THE GARDEN

"The second of July [1584] we found shoal water, where we smelt so sweet and so strong a smell, as if we had been in the midst of some delicate garden." Thus, did Englishmen describe their approach to the

---

44 *Oxford English Dictionary:* "To improve, to make one's profit of, to avail oneself of by using to one's profit. Especially used of the lord's inclosing and bringing into cultivation of waste land." A second definition, also obsolete, is "To turn land to profit, to inclose and cultivate (waste land); hence to make land more valuable or better by such means. . . . The ancient sense, or something akin to it, was retained in the 17th–18th centuries in the American colonies."

45 Cronon, *Changes in the Land*, 130. Governor Macquarie's report on his administration "teems with references to stone walls, brick walls, rail fences, pailing fences, stockades and undefined 'strong fences.' " Lionel Arthur Gilbert, *The Royal Botanic Gardens, Sydney: A History, 1816–1985* (Melbourne, 1986), 18.

46 "Improvement," *Words and Phrases* (St. Paul, Minn., 1959), 20: 491, 495. A fence fails to constitute an improvement only in railroad right-of-ways (493).

47 *Johnson's Wonder-Working Providence, 1628–1651*, 99; *The Works of William Temple* (London, 1757), 4 vols. "Upon the Gardens of Epicurus; or Of Gardening in the year 1685," 3: 195–237, esp. 231. Bridenbaugh described the planting of grass seed, the building of fences to keep cattle in, and the draining of marshes. Bridenbaugh, *Fat Mutton and Liberty of Conscience*, 31–34. Howard S. Russell, *A Long, Deep Furrow: Three Centuries of Farming in New England* (Hanover, N.H., 1976).

land of Virginia.[48] "The soil," they added, "is the most plentiful, sweet, fruitful, and wholesome of all the world."[49] Fifty years later John Winthrop would use a nearly identical expression describing "so pleasant a sweet air as did much refresh us, there came a smell off the shore like the smell of a garden."[50] "What pleasure can be more then . . . in planting Vines, Fruits or Hearbs in contriving . . . their Fields, Gardens, Orchards," wrote John Smith of New England.[51] George Wither would also describe New England as a garden, and James Rosier proclaimed the Maine coast as "a land, whose pleasant fertility bewarieth it selfe to be the garden of nature."[52]

Even before they began to settle abroad, Englishmen were predisposed to experience the overseas world as a garden. Richard Hakluyt's "Discourse on Western Planting" selectively appropriated earlier French writers' descriptions of Florida's agricultural abundance in order to advocate English colonialism; Walter Ralegh invoked the meaning of the name Florida for the same end.[53] Even other areas of the world – such as Asia – were seen through translated travel literature as portraying a garden.[54]

Spanish explorers and colonists were lured to the New World by tales, tall and true, of gold; the Portuguese were enticed by tales of spices and dyewoods; but the English, far more than any other group

---

48 Philip Amadas and Arthur Barlow, "The First Virginia Voyage," in Hakluyt, ed., *Voyages to the Virginia Colonies*, 66. For how this contributed to unrealistic expectations about the New World, see Karen Ordahl Kupperman, *Roanoke: The Abandoned Colony* (New York, 1984), 16–17.

49 Amadeus and Barlow, "First Voyage," 71.

50 *Winthrop's Journal*, ed. James Kendall Hosmer, 2 vols. (New York, 1908), 1: 47. The appreciation of the garden through these senses, particularly that of smell, was characteristic of garden literature of the period. Lawson, *A New Orchard and Garden*, 56–57.

51 John Smith, *Description of New England* (1616), in Barbour, ed., *Works*, 1: 347.

52 "Beside the benefit that shall arise . . . to order Nature's fruitfulnessse a while / In that rude Garden." George Wither, "To His Friend Captain John Smith," preface to John Smith, *A Description of New England* (1616), in Barbour, ed., *Works*, 1: 315; "Rosier's True Relation of Waymouths' Voyage, 1605," in Henry S. Burrage, ed., *Early English and French Voyages, 1534–1608* (New York, 1906), 388.

53 Hakluyt quotes sections of Jean Ribault's account of Florida. E. G. R. Taylor, ed., *The Original Writings and Correspondence of the Two Richard Hakluyts*, 2 vols. (London 1935), 2: 222. *The Works of Walter Ralegh, Kt;* vol. 2, *History of the World* (Oxford, 1829), 2: 68–69 (bk. 1, chap. 3). Had either man used Cabeza de Vaca's description of Florida's hostile natives and frequent bouts of hunger, they would have come to a different conclusion. Cabeza de Vaca's narrative was originally published in 1542 as *La relación que dio Alvar Núñez Cabeza de Vaca de lo acaescido en Las Indias en la armada donde yua por governador Pánfilo de Narváez desde el año de veynte y siete. . . .*

54 The quotation "Gardeynes frutes is there much gretter than in our landes of Europa" is taken from a book Edward Arber designated as the "first English book on America," which is in fact a skeletal outline of the Portuguese voyages to India and contains no references to the New World. The quotation refers to a site twenty leagues from what was, until 1520, the Portuguese capital in Asia. Arber, ed., *English Books*, xxiii–xxxv, esp. xxix.

of colonists, were tantalized by the garden.[55] They referred to their own activities in occupying the New World as planting the garden. To "plant in soiles most sweet, most pleasant, most strong and most fertile" is how Richard Hakluyt the Elder described potential colonization in 1584.[56] Why gardening and agricultural metaphors appealed so strongly to the English (and to them alone) is worthy of consideration.[57]

Early in the seventeenth century, the garden emerged as an art form for the English. Dozens of books from France and Italy on the aesthetics of gardening were translated, and works on the aesthetic appreciation of gardens were composed. The growing interest in the purely ornamental or aesthetic functions of gardens – a trend which has continued through the present day[58] – did not diminish the fact

55 For Spanish and Portuguese myths, see Beatriz Pastor, *Armature of Conquest* (Stanford, Calif., 1992); Sergio Buarque de Holanda, *Visao do Paraíso*, 5th ed. (São Paulo, 1992); Carl Erdmann, *A ideia da cruzada em Portugal* (1940). Many English-language writers have mistakenly assumed that the Spanish and Portuguese were looking for a heavenly "garden" in the Americas. The eminent Brazilian scholar, Sergio Buarque Holanda, criticized such readings of his own work by U.S. scholars as nationalist interpretations resulting from nothing more than "the popular image of an agrarian society." (i.e., the United States; x–xi). Only Columbus on his third voyage seems to locate Paradise in the New World (near the Orinoco). *Nuova Raccolta Colombina* (Rome, 1992), pt. 1, 2: 35–37. The inappropriate generalization from the English experience that Paradise was *physical setting* appears, for example, in John Prest, *The Botanic Garden and the Re-Creation of Paradise* (New Haven, 1981), 32. See Chapter 5, note 149, for more details.

56 Richard Hakluyt the Elder, "Inducements to the liking of the voyage intended toward Virginia" (1585), in Quinn and Quinn, eds., *English New England Voyages*, 181–182, and Richard Hakluyt, "Discourse of Western Planting," in Taylor, ed., *Two Hakluyts*, 2: 211–326. See also John Smith, "What hath ever beene the worke of the best great Princes of the world, but planting of Countries." John Smith, *Advertisements for the unexperienced Planters of New-England* (1631), in Barbour, ed., *Works*, 3: 276–277. The land needed only to be "cultured, planted and manuered by men of industrie, judgment and experience." *Description of New-England* (1616), in ibid., 333.

57 Even God appears as First Gardener in Francis Bacon, "Of Gardens," *The Essays, 1625* (London, 1971; orig. pub. 1625), 266, thus apparently sanctioning the English planting.

58 John Parkinson, *Paradisi in Sole Paradisus Terrestris* (London, 1629), is one of the first gardening treatises combining practical concerns with aesthetic ones. Bacon, "Of Gardens," 266–279, lays out the aesthetic principles of early-seventeenth-century gardens. The recent secondary literature on the aesthetics of gardens includes John Dixon Hunt, *Gardens and the Picturesque: Studies in the History of Landscape Architecture* (Cambridge, Mass., 1994); Douglas Chambers, *The Planters of the English Landscape Garden: Botany, Trees, and the Georgics* (New Haven, 1993); idem, " 'Discovering in Wide Landskip': 'Paradise Lost' and the Tradition of Landscape Description in the Seventeenth Century," *Journal of Garden History*, 5: 15–31; and Richard Bisgrove, *The National Trust Book of the English Garden* (New York, 1990). Even historical bibliographies on gardening tend to focus on the aesthetic dimensions. Blanche Henrey, *British Botanical and Horticultural Literature Before 1800*, 3 vols. (London, 1975), 1: 155, 169, omits (among others) Gervase Markham's enormously popular *Cheape and Good Husbandry.for the well-ordering of all beasts, and fowles, and for the generall Cure of their Diseases* (London, 1614). For the eighteenth century, see Henrey, *Botanical Literature*, vol. 2; Joan Bassin, "The English Landscape Garden in the Eighteenth Century: The Cultural Importance of an English Institution," *Albion*, 11 (1979):

that the garden had another, more basic and traditional meaning in English culture.

As early as perhaps the eighth century, Old English created the distinction between wild plants and those that were cultivated.[59] *Wild* in its broadest modern meaning signifies everything that is unrestrained – people, feelings, animals, plants. When applied to an animal, wild signified neither tame nor domesticated; when applied to plants, it signified uncultivated; the *Oxford English Dictionary* traces both uses back to the eighth century. The pair of terms *wild/cultivated* thus signified a critical difference between savage (uncontrolled) and civilized.

Beginning in the eleventh century, Englishmen began to erect a physical barrier – a fence or a wall – to separate the wild from the cultivated. This barrier defined an enclosed piece of land dedicated to the cultivation of flowers, fruits, or vegetables called a garden.[60] Barnabe Googe's enormously popular edition of Conrad Heresbach's *Husbandry* (1577) declared that "the first thing needful for a Garden is water. The nexte to that is enclosure."[61] But placing a boundary marker – an enclosure – between the wild and the cultivated also transformed the garden.

By acquiring a physical boundary, the English garden began to signify possession. While New World peoples most certainly cultivated crops, and their plots were sometimes described as "resembling" gardens, most native American agriculturalists did not wall or fence in their plots. The failure of most native Americans to use the fence to symbolize ownership convinced Englishmen that despite their resemblance to gardens, native plots did not create possession.

Since creating boundaries had long established legal ownership in English law and custom, the garden fence or wall transformed the garden into a symbol of possession. Thus, one of the most popular seventeenth-century essays on gardening stated somewhat ethnocentrically: "The use of gardens seems to have been the most ancient

15–32; Harriet Ritvo et al., *An English Arcadia: Landscape and Architecture in Britain and America* (San Marino, Calif., 1992).

59 "Wild," *OED*, defs. 1 and 2; later examples are under "garden," def. 5a.

60 The *OED*'s first quotation for "garden" is from 1028. Harriet Ritvo, "At the Edge of the Garden: Nature and Domestication in Eighteenth- and Nineteenth-Century Britain," in *English Arcadia*, 306, has the fourteenth century, in what must be a misprint. The most vivid seventeenth-century description is John Milton's: "Paradise . . . with her enclosure green / As with a rural mound the champaign [open country] head / of a steep wilderness, whose hairy sides / With thicket overgrown, grotesque and wild, / Access denied." These lines develop from the ideas of an enclosed garden whose function is to maintain the distinction between the wild and the cultivated. John Milton, *Paradise Lost* (New York, 1975), 4: 132–137.

61 Conrad Heresbach, *Foure Bookes of Husbandry,* ed. Barnabe Googe (Amsterdam, 1971; orig. pub. 1577), 50. More's Utopians had "large gardens inclosed" and "set great store by their gardens." Thomas More, *Utopia,* bk. 2, chap. 2, trans. Raphe Robinson (1551), rev. ed., (London, 1808), 2: 20–21.

and most general of any sorts of *possession* among mankind."[62] Yet the garden symbolized possession only in an English context and was age-old only if the eleventh century can be considered "ancient."

Thus, an early action of English colonists in the New World was planting a garden as a sign of possession. Shortly after building a house "a garden was laid off, and the seeds of fruits and vegetables not indigenous to the country were planted."[63] John Smith planted a garden "on top of a Rocke Ile" off the coast of Maine that provided salad greens in June and July. Settlers moving into the northern Connecticut River valley in 1636 carefully laid out gardens near the river as a sign of possession. Following orders from the king, Governor Berkeley of Virginia in 1641 required every settler with over two hundred acres to plant and enclose a garden.[64]

One solution to the inability to fence or bound every piece of land Englishmen claimed was planting and enclosing of a small portion of that land, a garden. As a sign of possession the garden represented the entire colonial ambition to possess the land by establishing a part of the project in a central and visible way. No other country used the garden in the same way, because in no other European country was the garden a symbol of possession.

While the garden itself represented the colonial endeavor in a fixed, visible form, Englishmen described themselves as "planting" the garden. According to the *Oxford English Dictionary*, "planting" originally meant a "setting in the soil so that plants might grow." In sixteenth-century English, planting meant setting or establishing anything that metaphorically resembled setting in the soil. In *Good Newes from Virginia*, the Reverend Alexander Whitaker declared that the English colony in Jamestown "hath taken better root; and as a spreading herbe, whose top hath been often cropped off, renewes her growth, and spreads her selfe more gloriously."[65] The action of the colonists in the New World was planting; the colonists were metaphorically plants in relation to the soil, and hence their colonial settlements were referred to as plantations.

Thus, when the English most commonly referred to their colonies in the New World as plantations, they were referring to themselves

62 ". . . and to have preceded those of corn or cattle," Temple, *Works*, 3: 207.

63 Quoted by Ludgate, *Gardens of the Colonists*, 1.

64 Smith, *Description of New England* (1616), in Barbour, ed., *Works*, 3: 334; Thomas, "Cultural Change," in William W. Fitzhugh, ed., *Cultures in Contact: The Impact of European Contacts on Native American Cultural Institutions, A.D. 1000–1800* (Washington, D.C., 1985), 111; Ludgate, *Gardens of the Colonists*, 3; Billings, *Old Dominion*, 56. Governor Berkeley refers to the act of "inclosing and fencing" as synonymous with "impaling," that is, putting up pales. While livestock was rarely fenced in during the early years of the colony, the garden was marked by the fence. Tabor, *Old-Fashioned Gardening*, 186–187.

65 Whitaker, *Good Newes*, 23.

metaphorically as taking possession.[66] Dutchmen also sometimes referred to establishing their colonies with the verb *to plant* (*planten*). But they did not describe themselves as planters or use the word *plantations* for their agricultural settlements, preferring instead either the word *colonies* (coloniën) for their settlements and *households* and *families* (*huysghesinnen*) rather than planters for themselves.[67] Dutchmen did not identitify themselves and their mission overseas as primarily agricultural.

Planting, whether the garden or the colony, signified more than simple farm labor. In 1580 Richard Hakluyt expressed the hope to "induce oure Englishmen . . . *to plant a Colonie* in some convenient place, *and so to possesse the country.*"[68] Planting signified what William Strachey described in 1612 as "actuall possession."[69] The content of "taking actual possession" was elaborated by John Cotton in 1630. It was a principle of natural law, he wrote, that "in a vacant soyle, hee that taketh possession of it, and bestoweth *culture* and *husbandry* upon it, his Right it is."[70] "Bestowing culture" meant not language or laws or rules for conduct as it might today. Rather it had a quite different meaning: farming and raising domestic animals, "husbandry," care taken in breeding and raising animals, cultivating herbs and fruits, planting the garden.[71] Thus, planting the garden involved neither simple physical

---

66 The English consistently refer to themselves as the "planters." Brown, ed., *Genesis,* 507. Letters patent to De La Warr, for example, refer to the colony "to be planted in Virginia," in ibid., 380, Feb. 28, 1610. In 1609 Robert Gray asked, "By what right of warrante can we enter into the land of these Savages, take away their rightfull inheritance from them, and plant ourselves in their places, being unwronged or unprovoked by them." Gray's answer was that Englishmen were entitled to "plant ourselves in their places." Robert Gray, *A Good Speede to Virginia* (London, 1609). For New England, examples include Francis Higginson, *New England's Plantation* (1630), and William Wood, *New Englands Prospect* (London, 1634).

67 *Van Rensselaer Bowier Manuscripts,* trans. A. J. F. Van Laer (Albany, 1908), 136–153; Issack de Rasière (1628), in idem, *Documents Relating to New Netherland,* 198.

68 This was his introduction to John Florio's translation of Cartier's first voyage. Taylor, ed., *Two Hakluyts,* 1: 164–165 (emphasis added).

69 William Strachey, *The Histories of Travell into Virginia Britania* (1612), ed. Louis B. Wright and Virginia Freund (London, 1951), 9–10. "No Prynce may lay clayme to any more amongst these new discoveryes . . . then, what his People have discovered, tooke actuall possession of."

70 John Cotton, *God's Promise to His Plantations* (London, 1630), rpt. in *Old South Leaflets,* no. 53, 3: 6 (emphasis added). John Winthrop's "The whole earth is the Lord's garden, and he hath given it to the sons of Adam to be tilled and improved by them." "General Considerations for the Planters in New-England" (1629), in Young, *Chronicle of the First Planters,* 271–278.

71 One of the most popular early-seventeenth-century books was Gervase Markham, *Cheape and Good Husbandry.* See also Sir Hugh Platt, *Jewel House of Art and Nature;* bk. 2, *Diverse new sorts of soyle not yet brought into any public use for manuring of both pasture and arable ground* (London, 1594). Lawson uses the phrases "Husbandman in the rights and culture of the ground" and "to have fayre and pleasant Orchards . . . is a chief part of Husbandry. . . . and Husbandry maintains the world," William Lawson, *A New Orchard and Garden* (London, 1618), preface. Lawson also has two other chap-

exertion nor mere aesthetic enjoyment; planting the garden was an act of taking possession of the New World for England. It was not a law that entitled Englishmen to possess the New World, it was an *action* which established their rights.

The idea that agricultural activity signified possession also has a distinctive English history. Agriculture like houses signified a kind of permanence. The boundaries of estates and the lines in which tenth-century Saxon fields were ploughed are sometimes identical to their boundaries and lines in the late twentieth century.[72] There were thus not only seven-hundred-year-old villages, but seven-hundred-year-old farms in early modern England as well. To Englishmen arriving in the New World, their agricultural activities were understood to demonstrate an intent to establish permanent settlement.

While "bestowing culture and husbandry" were often used to describe the actions by which Englishmen planted a colony and thus possessed the country, there was another even more common set of verbs to describe this activity: replenishing and subduing. "That [land] which lies common and hath never been replenished or subdued is free to any that will possesse and improve it," wrote John Winthrop.[73]

REPLENISHING AND SUBDUING

While occasionally invoked to refer to peopling a relatively unpopulated land,[74] replenishing and subduing were principally linked to techniques of English agriculture which Indians did not employ. Replenishing meant enriching the soil, either by planting grain or using a familiar English fertilizer.[75] "The ground they [natives] never fatten with muck dung or any other thing, neither plough nor dig it as we in

---

ters with "husbandry" in the title: "Husbandry of Hearbes" (chap. 8) and "Husbandrie of bees" (chap. 10).

72 Loyn, *Anglo-Saxon England*, 167; Orwin and Orwin, *Open Fields*, 29. "By 1200 much of the modern landscape [of England] was already recognizable . . . the proportions of farmland, moorland, and woodland were not enormously different from what they are now." Rackham, *Trees and Woodland*, 39. In Lawshall (Suffolk), 85% of the present hedges were already there in 1612; 62% of those in Conington (Huntingdonshire) were there in 1595. Ibid., 192.

73 *Winthrop's Conclusions*, 6; Winthrop, *History of New England*, 1: 290.

74 Richard Eburne in 1624 wrote, "When finding a Country quite void of people . . . we seize upon it, take it, possesse it, as by the Lawes of God and Nations, lawfully we may hold it as our owne, and so fill and replenish it with our people." Richard Eburne, *A Plaine Pathway to Plantations*, ed. Louis B. Wright (Ithaca, N.Y., 1962; orig. pub. 1624), 32; Sir William Alexander, *An Encouragement to Colonies* (1624), suggests that the lands are "practically barren, and can be filled on the injunction to go forth and multiply." Wright, *Plaine Pathway*, 141. Francis Bacon refers generically (without biblical referents) to planting a people. "Of Plantations," in idem, *Essays*, 198–204.

75 Richard Hakluyt described soil as "*replenished* with all kinds of grain." Taylor, ed., *Two Hakluyts*, 1: 164–165 (emphasis added).

England," wrote Thomas Harriot in 1585.[76] Collecting animal manure for fertilizer appears to have been the distinctively English preference (compost being preferred in continental Europe) and was referred to with great disgust by medieval Frenchmen.[77] Manures and their application were frequently the subject of commentary in both popular and aristocratic English gardening books.[78] Indeed the verb *to manure* in sixteenth-century English meant "to own," "to cultiviate," by hand as well as "to enrich land with manure."[79] Subduing – the use of implements – appears to have meant the use of the Anglo-Saxon plough drawn by oxen. Harnessing oxen to ploughs began in most of Western Europe sometime in the ninth or tenth centuries with its earliest evidence in Saxon England dating from the eleventh.[80] Both words referred to characteristically European and sometimes distinctively English methods of working the soil.

The use of these two terms was not accidental. They originated in the book of Genesis. The most popular biblical quotation in the English occupation of the New World – Gen. 1:28, "Multiply and *replenish* the earth, and *subdue* it"[81] – was often described as the "grand charter given to Adam and his posterity and Paradise."[82] Anglican Richard Eburne said:

> It was God's express commandment to Adam Gen[esis] 1:28 that
> he should fill the earth and subdue it. By virtue of which charter

76 Thomas Harriot, "Brief and True Report of the New Found Land of Virginia," in Hakluyt, *Virginia Voyages*, 116.

77 Loyn, *Anglo-Saxon England*, 166–167. Platt, *Jewel House*, bk. 2, 52, notes the disdain of Lombards for dung.

78 Gervase Markham, *Cheap and Good Husbandry*, 153; Platt, *Jewel House*, 33–38; Lawson, *Orchards and Gardens*, 4; Platt, *The Garden of Eden* (London, 1655), 33, 36, 38, 56–58, 65, 67–68, 77–79, 93, 107, 148–149, contains extensive instructions among others on the use of horse dung for peas and annis, fine powdered cow dung for strawberries, pigeon dung for strawberries, mixed cow and horse dung for apricot tree roots. Even John Parkinson, *Paradisi Sole*, 2–3, 461–462, 535–536, 550, describes in great detail which animals' manures should be used for which type of soil, as well as when to put dung in. Tusser, *Good Husbandry* (1573), 30–32. See also C. S. Orwin, *A History of English Farming* (London, 1949), 62; Donald Woodward " 'An Essay on Manures': Changing Attitudes to Fertilization in England, 1500–1800," in John Chartres and David Hey, eds., *English Rural Society, 1500–1800: Essays in Honour of Joan Thirsk* (Cambridge, 1990), 251–278.

79 "Manure," *OED*, verb form, § 1, 2, 3, respectively. "Let the main part of the ground employed to gardens or corn, be to a common stock; ... besides some spots of ground that any particular person will manure for his own private use." Bacon, "Of Plantations," 201.

80 Loyn, *Anglo-Saxon England*, 157–161.

81 Cotton, *God's Promise* (1630); Winthrop, *Conclusions*, 5; other similar injunctions from Genesis include Gen. 13:6, 11, 12; 24:21; 41:20 invoked by Robert Cushman, "Reasons and Considerations," in Young, ed., *Chronicles of the Pilgrim Fathers*, 244. Gen. 1:28 was used as late as 1722 by Solomon Stoddard (1643–1729), *An Answer to Some Cases of Conscience*, excerpted in Perry Miller and Thomas H. Johnson, eds., *The Puritans* (New York, 1938), 457.

82 Cushman, "Reasons," 244.

he and his have ever since had the privilege to spread themselves from place to place and to have, hold, occupy, and enjoy any region or country whatsoever which they should find either not preoccupied.[83]

Virtually identical language came from Puritan Robert Cushman. "If therefore any sonne of Adam come and finde a place empty, he hath liberty to come, and fill and *subdue* the earth there,"[84] a quotation which unites the concept of vacant land ("finde a place empty") to the concept of subduing the earth.

The scriptural rationale for expropriating native lands was also mentioned in well-regarded political writings and laws. John Locke invoked the characteristic English understanding of Gen. 1:28. "God and his Reason commanded him to subdue the Earth. . . . He that in Obedience to this Command of God, subdued, tilled and sowed any part of it, thereby annexed to it something that was his Property."[85] It was even incorporated into Massachusetts law between 1633 and 1637: "It is declared and ordered by this Court and authority thereof, that what lands any of the Indians in this jurisdiction have possessed and *improved*, by *subduing* the same, they have just right unto, according to that in Gen. 1. 28 and 9.1 and Psalms 115, 116."[86] The same sentiments appeared in garden literature as well. "When God had made man after his own Image . . . and would have him to represent himselfe in authoritie . . . he placed him in . . . a Garden and Orchard of trees and hearbs."[87] The security of the English faith that their planting practices alone guaranteed legitimate title to the land stemmed from their language. And none of these divinely inspired rationales were ever subject to critical light.

Englishmen found a scriptural authority for their occupation of the land in Genesis: "Go forth and multiply."[88] But this association of Gen. 1:28 and agricultural practices is a uniquely English proposition. As Jeremy Cohen has noted, in both Christian and Jewish medieval

83 Eburne, *Plaine Pathway,* 41.   84 Cushman, "Reasons."

85 John Locke, *Second Treatise,* § 36, in Peter Laslett, ed. *Two Tratises of Government,* (London, 1967). For a commentary on Locke's interpretation of Genesis, see James Tully, *A Discourse on Property: John Locke and His Adversaries* (Cambridge, 1980), 60, 65.

86 *Laws of the colonial and State Governments relation to Indians and Indian Affairs from 1633 to 1831 inclusive* (Washington, D.C., 1832). Psalms 107:39: "God prepareth a land to sow and plant in," so understood by Eburne, *Plaine Pathway,* 41.

87 Lawson, *New Orchard* (1618), 56.

88 Gen. 9:1. The other major scriptural justification was the idea that the English were God's chosen people. In 1609 Anglican preacher William Symonds invoked Gen. 12:1–3 to justify the settlement of Virginia. See also the 1609 sermon preached by Robert Gray, *A Good Speed to Virginia,* citing Joshua 17:14–18. "Why has thou give me but one lot, and one portion to inherit, seeing I am a great people?" Wright, *Religion,* pp. 90–93. John W. McKenna, "How God Became an Englishman," in Deloyd J. Guth and John W. McKenna, eds., *Tudor Rule and Revolution* (Cambridge, 1982), 25–43.

theology this verse of Genesis, "Be fruitful and multiply," was understood to refer only to human reproduction. The phrase was controversial in sixteenth-century Europe among Reformation leaders because it was understood everywhere else in Europe to justify human *sexual* activity. Reformation leaders used this passage chiefly to support their argument that God had ordained human reproduction. Thus, both Martin Luther and Philip Melanchthon (author of the *Augsburg Confession*) used this verse to attack the Catholic Church for its emphasis on celibacy – as contravening this natural, divinely-ordained order.[89]

The unique English connection of the phrase "Be fruitful and multiply and replenish the earth" to agriculture stemmed not from formal ecclesiastical tradition, but from Anglo-Saxon folk culture. In medieval folk ceremonies, Gen. 1:28 was ritually repeated as an incantation to cure infertile soil and animals. Together with the Lord's Prayer, the generic prayer for all healing rites, it was invoked in rituals to render soil fertile for grazing and harvesting. The biblical phrase was chanted at dawn over a patch of infertile ground from which the sod had been removed. The phrase was divided into four parts ("be fruitful," "and multiply," "and fill," "the earth") each accompanied by sprinkling the earth with a mixture of holy water and the products of the ground that were hoped to spring from it. The combination of incantation and ritual gesture were repeated several times over the field.[90]

While the Lord's Prayer was often recited in Anglo-Saxon curing rituals, Gen. 1:28 was used strictly for rendering land fertile again. Nowhere else in Western Europe was it so appropriated. Thus, in medieval England, and England alone, Gen. 1:28 became widely understood as signifying agricultural rather than human fertility.[91] The constant rehearsal of this specifically English interpretation of Gen. 1:28 in sermons and discussions of the text among Englishmen confirmed its transparency to other English speakers, unaware of how incomprehensible such an interpretation would have been to someone from another national tradition and how culturally specific their biblical interpretation was. As a result seventeenth-century Englishmen – Puritan, Catholic, and Anglican alike – shared an understanding of Gen. 1:28 as referring to improving the reproductive capacity of land using domestic animals and English farm implements to increase the yield of the soil.

Some modern scholars have argued that Gen. 1:28 is an invitation to the abuse of the earth and that modern ruthlessness to nature is

89 Jeremy Cohen, *"Be Fertile and Increase, Fill the Earth and Master It": The Ancient and Medieval Career of a Biblical Text* (Ithaca, 1989), 307–11.
90 Thomas Oswald Cockayne, ed., *Leechdoms, Wortcunning, and Starcraft of Early England,* 3 vols. (London, 1961), 1: 398–405.
91 Cohen, *"Be Fertile."*

rooted in this verse.[92] Seventeenth-century English colonists had no such modern qualms, unmistakably expressing the idea that it was "a good, or rather better than any wee possesse, were it [land] manured and used accordingly."[93] The initial failures of cattle to thrive or European crops to succeed failed to dampen this enthusiasm; English settlers were unfazed by initial falterings. However, if Gen. 1:28 justifies modern ruthlessness to nature, then this link is characteristically and uniquely English.

But this scriptural understanding and folkways were not simply a common cultural trait establishing individual or group identity. This locally significant meaning of Genesis justified English title to the Americas. It was invoked in the laws of Massachusetts and in countless writings by early English settlers and colonial advocates to express their understanding of how English dominion over the New World had been legitimately constituted. It continues to be invoked as the foundation of English property law. In the introduction to the volume on property in his *Commentaries on the Laws of England,* a work that is still cited in legal writings in England and throughout the English-speaking world,[94] William Blackstone invokes Gen. 1:28 to justify the principles of occupation of land carried out by Englishmen in the New World and elsewhere. Selecting Gen. 1:28 stemmed from a cultural familiarity created and repeated by field rituals and by sermons, which consistently reinforced the culturally unique English impression that Gen. 1:28 was connected to agriculture, and the actions involved in agriculture were connected to legal title. The idea that planting a garden established possession continued to operate in English possession-taking well into the eighteenth century.

In the course of exploring the South Pacific, Captain James Cook was ordered to take possession of islands he discovered. British Admiralty officials, however, seemed to have difficulty telling Cook just exactly what to do. On his first voyage they ordered him to take possession "by setting up Proper Marks and Inscriptions, as first discoverors and possesors." In 1772 they added that he was also "to distribute among the Inhabitants, some of the Medals with which you have been furnished to remin as Traces of your having been

---

92 Lynn White, "The Historical Roots of Our Ecological Crisis," *Science,* 155 (1967): 1203–1207. For Bacon's credo of man's domination of nature, see Neal Wood, *John Locke and Agrarian Capitalism* (Berkeley, 1984), 24; for other scholars, see Cohen, "*Be Fertile,*" 15–18.

93 John Smith (1631), in Barbour, ed., *Works,* 3: 276–277. "Manured" in this usage means "cultivated." See "manure," *OED,* § 2.

94 Blackstone, *Commentaries on the Laws of England,* 3: 2. The citation to Gen. 1:28 is the first footnote in the chapter on property. For examples of the recent use of Blackstone in two former English colonies, see Carol M. Rose, "Possession as the Origin of Property," *University of Chicago Law Review,* 52 (1985): 73–88 (United States), and Henry Reynolds, *The Law of the Land* (Ringwood, Vic., 1987) (Australia).

there."[95] And for Cook's final voyage on July 6, 1776, he was commanded also "to distribute among the Inhabitants such Things as will remain as Traces and Testimonies of your having been there."[96] While Cook undertook these actions, as requested, on his own initiative he also planted gardens and released a pair of domestic animals on the islands that he had reached. And it was subsequently these actions that Englishmen most frequently understood as indications that Cook had established English dominion over much of the South Pacific.[97]

An even more dramatic example of how culturally persuasive planting the garden was (despite official orders to perform another action) occurred during the British occupation of the Falkland (Malvinas) Islands. In the course of British occupation of the islands, the head of the expedition carried out several formal acts of possession, including affixing a plaque to a building. Then, just as the ship was about to leave, the ship's surgeon jumped off the ship and planted a few vegetables in a garden. When it came time for international negotiations with the Spanish, it was not those official actions, but the impromptu vegetable garden planted by the ship's surgeon that high-ranking English diplomats invoked as proof of the legitimacy of the English claim to the islands.[98] Neither the formal ceremonies nor even the actions of the expeditionary leader were as culturally persuasive even to official English diplomats as the planted garden.

Planting the garden was the principal metaphor for the occupation of the western United States during the eighteenth and nineteenth centuries. "The myth of the garden was already implicitly in the iridescent eighteenth-century vision of a continental American expansion," writes Henry Nash Smith. From Benjamin Franklin and Thomas Jefferson through the Homestead Act of 1862, the metaphorical understanding of settling the American West as planting a garden continued to be compelling, despite the challenges and contradictions to that image that the terrain itself presented.[99]

95 *The Journals of Captain James Cook;* vol. 1, *The Voyage of the Endeavor, 1768–1771,* cclxxxii (July 30, 1768). The action was repeated by the *Resolution;* see ibid., vol. 2, *The Voyage of the Resolution and Adventure, 1772–1775,* clxviii (June 25, 1772).

96 Ibid., *The Voyage of the Resolution,* ccxxiii.

97 *The Journals of Captain James Cook,* ed. J. C. Beaglehole, 3 vols. (Cambridge, 1955–1967). The settlement of Australia was begun by planting the famous "9 acres in corn" at Sydney in July 1788. See Gilbert, *The Royal Botanic Gardens, Sydney,* 11–12. Thomas Hariot, "Brief and True Report," in Hakluyt, ed., *Voyages to Virginia,* 135–136, described these actions as what should be done by the English.

98 The planting of a vegetable garden was referred to in 1765 as the start of English settlement by the English secretary of state for the southern department. See Julius Goebel, *The Struggle for the Falklands* (New Haven, 1927), 233–234. When abandoning the islands, they left a lead plaque affixed to a blockhouse rather than to a tree (410).

99 Henry Nash Smith, *Virginia Land: The American West as Symbol and Myth* (Cambridge, Mass., 1950), 123–132, 165–210, quoted on 124. For a similar observation about an earlier period, see Kupperman, *Roanoke,* 16–17.

The British style of enacting authority involved gardens, or at least a garden-variety imperialism. The very ordinariness of British acts of possession was notable from the very beginning. Yet despite links to possession, planting retained its remarkably mundane character. In seventeenth-century English, "garden" became a joking substitute for "commonplace."[100] But this ordinariness, its most striking feature, did not sever its connection to colonialism. Gardens of all sorts, even elaborate formal ones, often were connected to their original colonizing function.

Botanical gardens throughout Europe first collected plants from the vast new treasure house that was the New World; "The great age of the Botanic Garden followed the discovery of the New World," writes John Prest.[101] While Botanical gardens in England often appropriated American plants and used them to further colonial expansion, elsewhere,[102] such gardens in the colonies also function as an enduring legacy of a colonial system which took possession by planting a garden.[103] Botanical gardens in many of the former British possessions were erected where European agriculture was first planted. When the British took over the Dutch colony of Capetown, they turned a garden planted to grow crops to prevent scurvy among India-bound crews into the Municipal Botanic Gardens. A boundary hedge of almond trees and thorns planted around the property of the first governor became the site of the National Botanic Gardens under British rule. When British historians rewrote the history of the origins of the Cape colony the planting of the hedge became the start of settlement.[104] The site of the current Sydney Botanical Gardens is where the first "9 acres in corn" were planted in 1788.[105]

---

100 "Garden," *OED*, def. 5c.   101 Prest, *The Garden of Eden*, 1.

102 The British redeployed rubber and chichona from the New World to create agricultural plantations outside their native habitats in areas under English political control. Lucile H. Brockway, *Science and Colonial Expansion: The Role of the British Royal Botanic Gardens* (New York, 1979), chaps. 6 and 7. For the cultural construction of the botanical gardens as re-creating paradise (including both its order and medicinal knowledges), see Prest, *Garden of Eden*, 9, 42–46, 54–59, 88–90.

103 Colonial botanical gardens also functioned as local collection points. In Australia the Botanic Gardens at Canberra are dedicated exclusively to Australian plants. The gardens in Sydney and Melbourne have striking collections of plants imported from the immediate surrounding regions (outside Australia). On the history of some of these functions for Sydney, see Gilbert, *Royal Botanic Gardens, Sydney*, 26, 55; for their exportation to England and elsewhere, see ibid., 28, 34–38. In addition, the Sydney Garden served as proving grounds for the cultivation of imported English crops (45, 48). On other colonial botanical gardens, see Brockway, *Science and Colonial Expansion*, 75–76.

104 The hedge was actually planted eight years after the settlement was begun and had no formal connection with claiming the property. Mia C. Karsten, *The Old Company's Garden at the Cape and Its Superintendents* (Cape Town, 1951); Hermann Giliomee, *Die Kaap tydens die Eerste Britse Bewind, 1795–1803* (Pretoria, 1975).

105 Gilbert, *Royal Botanic Gardens, Sydney*, 11–12, 16.

The concepts of improvement, replenishing, and subduing signified a variety of actions: building fixed permanent residences on a piece of land, erecting fences, growing hedges, introducing domesticated animals, using the English fertilizer (manure) and ploughs. Sometimes these actions resulted in the creation of fixed architectural symbols; other times they did not. Sometimes they were merely actions repeatedly taken upon the land, namely, agriculture and husbandry. They all had in common the expression of colonial authority not through written texts or documents but through actions. Yet the ability to claim land merely through actions alone was not simply a colonial precept; it continues to operate even in the contemporary United States.[106]

In writing recently on contemporary U.S. theories of possession, legal scholar Carol Rose declared that "possession thus means a clear act, whereby all the world understands . . . [that a person has] an unequivocal intention of appropriating . . . to his individual use." She continues, "The tacit assumption that there is such a thing as a 'clear act,' unequivocally proclaiming to the universe one's appropriation . . . [is one] that the relevant audience will naturally and easily interpret as property claims."[107] Planting gardens and releasing domestic animals constituted such "clear acts" to seventeenth-century Englishmen. But at the root of this belief was a cultural construct.

Another way of expressing Rose's concept of a clear act is the popular English saying "Actions speak louder than words." It is the clear *act* that is said to establish ownership, the physical gesture or movement. But no other European language used in the New World seems to have this saying, let alone this belief. From this it is all too easy to conclude that if "actions speak louder than words," they speak only in English. Planting a garden, releasing a domestic animal, fencing in a plot, building a house did not express ownership to French audiences of the time for whom the ceremonial entrance was the counterpart of a clear act expressing possession. While Frenchmen also enacted their colonial authority through gestures and motions, the actions and gestures they used were entirely different. For the English, actions spoke louder than words; they spoke almost as loudly for the French. But the problem was that it was different actions entirely that spoke to each of the two cultures. A ceremony of planting a royal standard instituted French colonial possession the way that planting a fence or a garden did for the English. And if such acts as gardening, fencing, and building houses failed to express ownership to other Europeans, how could they possibly be expected to convey intentions and rights clearly to an

---

106 Simply by cutting and yearly removing grass, an individual in the contemporary U.S. can enact possession entitling him- or herself to ownership of the land. *Words and Phrases,* 20: 495–496.
107 Rose, "Possession," 76, 84.

audience of indigenous peoples with whom they shared neither language nor cultural tradition?

The assumption that clear acts are sufficient to convey property thus relies upon the existence of an audience that shares the cultural system in which actions speak. If the relevant audience is not culturally English, such actions no longer convey any clear message. For clarity depends not on the action, but on the community of interpreters. Actions can speak – that is they can signify clearly – only if there is a common cultural context which is shared by interpreters of the actions.

Yet all English colonists, government officials, and political theorists constructed their compatriots' actions – planting gardens, building fences and houses, and expressions of the labor theory of property – as universally clear acts – establishing possession. But such constructions were cultural, depending upon a local system of understanding Genesis, the fixity of population and agricultural settlements in England, and common legal understanding of how property rights in land were created and expressed (through fences, hedges, and other enclosures). None of these understandings existed among citizens or subjects of any other European power. Yet they were widely believed by Englishmen to have granted them the right to possess the New World. As culturally specific as the understandings of these actions were, their absence was used to deny indigenous peoples of the New World possession of their lands.

By contrast with the familiar practices of enclosing, fencing, and sheep raising, the Indians' practices were described by an accumulation of negatives. "And for the Natives in New England," wrote John Winthrop, "they inclose *noe* land *neither* have any setled habitation *nor* any tame cattle to improve their land by" (emphasis added). The phrase piles up native deficiencies, "*noe* enclosures," "*neither* settled habitation," "*nor* tame cattle," establishing a series of lacks that can be summarized at the end as the failure to "improve." No enclosure meant they had no fences, no settled habitation meant they had no fixed villages in the English manner, no tame cattle meant they had no reliable meat source or manure with which to replenish their fields. Lacking settled habitation (fixed permanent English villages), domestic animals, and fences, Indians (Winthrop and other Puritans reasoned) did not institute full dominion over their land: "And soe [these natives] have noe other but a naturall right to those countries," that is, one that could be extinguished by the arrival of those who had a civil right through the clear action of improvement,[108] – building fences, planting gardens, constructing houses – the English signs of possession.

---

108 Winthrop's argument (derived from Pope Innocent IV) that holding land in common created a natural (but not civil) right to land subsequently became known in U.S. law as "aboriginal title." William C. Canby, *American Indian Law in a Nutshell,*

Enacting colonial authority through physical action alone – clear acts as it would later be called – meant that no speaking was necessary because the actions were supposed to convey meaning in themselves. By contrast, the French also created authority through actions but, unlike the English, created it through ritualized, not mundane, action.

2d ed. (St. Paul, Minn., 1988), 256–260; Cohen, *Federal Indian Law,* 291–294; Monroe E. Price and Robert N. Clinton, eds., *Law and the American Indian* (Charlottesville, Va., 1983), 527–578; James Youngblood Henderson, "The Doctrine of Aboriginal Rights in Western Legal Tradition," in Menno Boldt and J. Anthony Long, eds., *The Quest for Justice: Aboriginal Peoples and Aboriginal Rights* (Toronto, 1985), esp. 191–198; Michael J. Kaplan, "Issues in Land Claims: Aboriginal Title," in Imre Sutton, ed., *Irredeemable America: The Indians' Estate and Land Claims* (Albuquerque, 1985), 71–86. Although Winthrop never acknowledged it, his argument derives from Catholic canon law. In his *L'apparatus ad decretalia* (cap. de voto), Pope Innocent IV wrote, "In the beginning everything was [held] in common by everyone, until usage, and the first men introduced the appropriation of one thing by one man, and another by another." Quoted in Alfred Vanderpol, *La doctrine scolastique du droit de guerre* (Paris, 1919), 226; *Winthrop's Conclusions,* 6–7.

2

CEREMONIES

THE THEATRICAL RITUALS OF
FRENCH POLITICAL POSSESSION

———————

Anchoring off a tiny uninhabited island at the mouth of the Amazon on July 24, 1612, a French expeditionary force led by Sieur (Lord) Razilly sent an emissary to ask the local inhabitants "if they continued in the same wish they had in the past to receive the French," while the bulk of the expedition remained on board and "awaited the resolution of the Indians." Responding as expected, the Tupi expressed "the affection that they had at being his [the French king's] subjects, [and] recognizing him as their sovereign Monarch."[1] Having thus secured the consent of the local inhabitants for both their initial landing and eventual goals, the emissary returned to the ship and on Sunday, July 29, 1612, writes Claude d'Abbeville, youngest of the four Capuchin monks on board, "Every one of us placed our feet on land."

Soon afterwards a tree was cut to make a cross while a hymn was chanted. The litanies of the Virgin Mary sung, the cross was then carried to a small hill near the port where it was fixed by the expedition's commander. Another hymn was sung as the cross and the island were solemnly blessed with holy water. The Lord of Razilly "named the tiny isle Saint Ann . . . and then the Cross was planted." But this procession, naming, and cross positioning failed to enact possession. Rather they were, as D'Abbeville reports, together "a sign of *happiness . . . to have arrived* and seen the signs of Jesus Christ so gloriously planted in this infidel land."[2] To take possession of the Amazon region would require an

1 Claude d'Abbeville, *Histoire de la Mission des Pères capuchins en l'isle de Maragnan et terres circonvoisins* (Graz, Austria, 1963; orig. pub. 1614), 56v–57v. Razilly, a distant relative of Richelieu, would later found the French colony at Acadia. Marianne Cornevin and Robert Cornevin, *La France et les français outre-mer* (Paris, 1990), 79–80. The settlement had been preceded by an earlier scouting expedition. For French political intrigues, see Pierre Pluchon, *Histoire de la colonisation française*, 2 vols. (Paris, 1991), 1: 68–69. In 1603 René de Montbarrot, named by the king as the lieutenant general of the region between Trinidad and the Amazon, sent two ships to the Amazon region, arriving in April 1604. La Ravadière was the commander of the expedition. For Ravadière's initial voyage, see Jean Mocquet, *Voyages en Afrique, Asie, Indes orientales, & occidentales* (Rouen, 1645). They traded hatchets, bills, knives, and glass beads of several colors, "desiring to know what profit they had brought a thousand trifles, as Gum, egret Feathers, and Parrots, Tobacco, and other Things which the Country afforded" (81).

2 D'Abbeville, *Histoire*, 59–60 (emphasis added).

41

even more elaborately staged theatrical ritual in which indigenous peoples participated as well. But before such an occasion, Frenchmen needed to reassure themselves of the "sincerity and good affection of the Indians."[3] That assurance manifested itself in a variety of forms. D'Abbeville wrote that they were "very well received by the Indians who caressed their bodies a thousand times," gestures that this French expedition assumed – as previous ones in Brazil, Florida, and Canada had – meant "the [natives'] happiness at their [the French] arrival."[4] Reaching the largest Tupi community in the region on Sunday, August 5, the newcomers received news that the Indians "have admitted the desire to see us."[5] After nearly six weeks of such exchanges of native approval, the French staged the first of two rituals of political possession. Like that miniature ceremony of arrival on the tiny isle of Saint Anne, its central elements were a procession and a cross-planting.

On September 8, 1612, an elaborately orchestrated procession began led by a

> gentleman carrying holy water, another bearing incense, a third the censer, after whom marched one [gentleman] carrying a very beautiful crucifix in his hands. . . . Two young Indian girls, children of the leaders, marched on either side of the crucifix carrying two candlesticks with the candles lit . . . These two young Indians were of the same age and the lord of Razilly had them dressed in the same livery . . . We other four religious, dressed in our white surplices followed the cross in order. And after [us] marched the sieur de Razilly, Lieutenant General for their Majesties, with all the nobility, each in his rank, the rest of the Frenchmen walking along with the Indians [dressed in celestial blue shirts with white crosses on the front and back] . . . [singing] the litanies of the Virgin Mary . . . . Having arrived at the . . . place designated to set up the cross, one of us began to sing the Te Deum Laudamus.[6]

With this the cross was placed in the ground. D'Abbeville's careful details create a slightly unreal atmosphere – almost a Hollywood staging – of the French parade. There are costumes (sky blue tunics with the fleur-de-lis, blue shirts with white crosses), music (sacred chants), props (incense burners [censers], crucifixes, candlesticks), and a large procession carefully ordered by rank. The culmination would be the visually dramatic moment of stationing a cross while surrounded by large groups of members from a Tupi tribe. Furthermore the entire scene was set five hundred kilometers east of the mouth of the

3 Ibid.
4 Ibid.; Mocquet, *Voyages*, 99; François Belleforest, *Cosmographie universelle*, 2 vols. (Paris, 1575), 2: col. 2193.
5 D'Abbeville, *Histoire*, 61.   6 Ibid., 85v–88.

Amazon, the river that tantalized all of sixteenth-century Europe with its enormous size and legends of riches.[7]

In preparation for this event, the Tupis had promised to embrace both Catholicism and an alliance with the French. Upon agreeing, they were informed:

> It was then necessary above all things to plant and display triumphantly the standard of the holy Cross, which serves as witness to each [Indian] of the desire they had to receive Christianity and a continual memorial to them and to all their posterity as to the reason why we [French] took possession of their land in the name of Jesus Christ.[8]

This meaning was reiterated during the ceremony itself:

> The Lord of Vaux . . . instructed [the Indians] why we were placing this cross, telling them that it was a testimony of the alliance that they [the Indians] were making with God and a solemn profession embracing our religion, renouncing entirely the evil Jeropetry [a local deity] who will never be able to survive in front of this holy Cross when it is blessed . . . . By means of [the cross] they obligate themselves first to abandon their evil ways of living, principally not to eat any more human flesh. . . . Secondly to obey our laws and all that their Father [the French priest] teach them; and finally to fight valorously under the glorious standard, and to die a thousand deaths rather than ever allow this holy cross to be torn out from here.

D'Abbeville reported "the Indians were very attentive to the discourse. . . . And the emotion that it produced inside them assured [us] that they voluntarily and willingly received and embraced all that was suggested to them. [They did so] since they had long desired to know the God we adored and to learn how they could serve and adore him."[9] In D'Abbeville's account the Tupis both understood and voluntarily accepted the conditions of Christianity; French speeches persuaded the natives whose emotional responses clearly registered approval. While striking many contemporary readers as unbelievable, such assurances were more credible to an audience which, like many European ones, was willing to be convinced that natives the world over willingly desired Christianity.

---

7 The French occupied the isle of São Luis de Maranhão.

8 D'Abbeville, *Histoire,* 85v.

9 Ibid., 87–88. "Silence and attentiveness" were evidently the appropriate responses on other occasions. During his second voyage to Canada (1535–1536), Cartier read aloud out of a prayerbook while the Iroquois "maintained a great silence and were marvelously attentive, and looking up to heaven and making parallel solemnities to those they saw us do." Jacques Cartier, *The Voyages of Jacques Cartier,* trans. H. P. Biggar (Ottawa, 1924), 166.

Following a blessing, a line of Frenchmen and Indians streamed forward to adore the cross; French officials in descending social order were followed by Indian leaders ranged by age grades.[10] Finally guns were fired "as a sign of rejoicing [and] the Sieur de Razilly named the place Fort Saint Louis in perpetual memory of Louis XIII, king of France."[11]

To Frenchmen the cross symbolized a religious alliance with the natives and reflected the latters' desire to "embrace their [French] religion."[12] However, it was also imperative "to make it known to them [the Tupis], that this [cross-planting] was not enough. They must also place the arms of France by the same means (for the purpose of obliging the French never to abandon them)."[13] Another ceremony was needed.

This final ceremony would plant a different symbol, the arms of France. Since "the cross was a sign of how we have taken possession of their land in the name of Jesus Christ," wrote D'Abbeville, the royal "standards were a badge and a remembrance of the sovereignty of the King of France, and as evidence . . . of the obedience that they [the Tupi] promised always and in perpetuity to His very Christian Majesty."[14] The last ceremony was to be a strictly political occasion.

Like all other French ceremonies in the Americas from the initial landing onward, indigenous consent had to be secured first:

> They [the Tupis] were given a month so as to consider this action carefully among them, and for them to think on it. For by this means they would render themselves subjects of His Majesty, and submit to his laws. This [impending action] was made public in all the villages, and they were given the day on which the ceremony would be held. . . . November 1.[15]

The last ceremony was held nearly four months after the arrival of the French in the Amazon. Given its fundamentally military and political purpose, both the participants' dress and musical accompaniment differed from preceding ones. First, all the Frenchmen dispersed throughout the native villages were assembled with their arms:

> They went off with tambors and trumpets [traditional military instruments rather than hymns] followed by all the Indians. The

---

10 D'Abbeville, *Histoire*, 88–88v.   11 Ibid., 89–90v.

12 Ibid., 85v. The statement does not indicate the religion; La Ravadière himself was Huguenot. See Pluchon, *Colonisation française* (Paris, 1991), 68.

13 D'Abbeville, *Histoire*, 159v. The identical division occurred in the ceremony in 1671 taking possession of region around Lakes Huron and Superior. "Plantant . . . la croix pour y produire les fruits du Christianisme, et l'Escu de France pour y asseurer l'autorité de Sa Majesté et la domination Française." Pierre Margry, *Découvertes et établissements des Français dans l'ouest et dans le sud de l'Amerique septentrionale, Mémoires et documents inédits, 1614–1754* 6 vols. (New York, 1972; orig. pub. 1876–1886), 1: 96–97.

14 D'Abbeville, *Histoire*, 100.   15 Ibid.

Figure 2. Tupi planting the cross near São Luis Maranhão. Courtesy of the John Carter Brown Library at Brown University.

procession marched to the lodging of His Majesty's Lords Lieutenant General, to fetch the standard of France [embellished all around the big golden fleur de lis] that the six aforementioned Indian leaders were to carry. The tambors and the sounding trumpets marched in front, followed by the French company. . . . The six said Principal Indians followed dressed in their blue shirts with the white cross on the front and back, carrying the said

Standard of France on their shoulders. The lords Razilly and de la Rivadière, Lieutenants General, marched after them. . . . Following them were a great multitude of Indians.[16]

Upon arriving at the place where the cross had been planted the Lord de Razilly addressed the Indians saying:

"You and we plant this standard of our King of France . . . to take possession of your land and subject it under his empire. . . . You have been notified long before today of the consequences of this action. Consider again before planting this standard and arms, if you want the King of France to be the master, and if you wish to obey those whom he sends to govern you. Because *after having given him the present that you are making of your land . . . it will no longer be the time to repent nor to revoke your promise once given.* If you chose to do this of your free will, just as you have proven up to the present, I will promise you that for his part, that this great king will never abandon you. . . . The Indians responded transported with pleasure and happiness that they had *always* desired to ally themselves with the French, and to be their friends, and that they will *never* default on the promise that they had made. . . . They put it [their territory] in his [Razilly's] hands so that he could present it to the king, humbly begging his Majesty to kindly accept the offer that they were making . . . in witness wherof [they said] we presently place this standard, where the same arms are. At that instant they themselves [the Indians] planted the standard and the arms of France, while the trumpets sounded, the tambors banged, and the cannons and muskets fired as a sign of joy and happiness, to the great contentment of the French and all the Indians.[17]

Addressing the Frenchmen first, the Lord de la Ravadière pointed out how "the Indians *themselves* placed this standard of France, placing their land in the possession of the king, declaring themselves all to live and die with us as true subjects and faithful servants of His Majesty. . . . After the planting was over everyone returned to his village."[18] With this final ceremony, French possession of the Amazon was completely and authoritatively established.

Planning and undertaking such an elaborate event to legitimate a European presence in the New World was highly distinctive. Few Europeans enacted such intricate ceremonies, and few French political and religious ceremonies were as elaborate as that staged near the mouth of the Amazon. But the same repertoire of gestures – holding a parade in which natives participated, planting a cross, gaining apparent indigenous consent – marked nearly all the peaceful French es-

16 Ibid., 160v–161.   17 Ibid., 161v–162v (emphasis added).
18 Ibid., 161–161v, 172 (emphasis added).

tablishments of power in the New World through the mid-seventeenth century.[19] While the Ravadière expedition in 1612 enjoyed the full backing of King Louis XIII, even a pirate ship drifting off course a hundred years before had performed the same gestures in establishing French authority overseas.

In 1503 a group of Norman sailors decided on their own initiative to try to duplicate the Portuguese feat of sailing to India. Bribing two Portuguese sailors to give them information on how to sail the South Atlantic 'round the Cape of Good Hope, they set sail on June 24, 1503. But the French ships were unable to reproduce the Portuguese voyage and found themselves blown onto the coast of Brazil, where they traded with a group of natives using goods they had hoped to sell in India. Deciding to leave "marks that Christians had arrived there," the members of the expedition settled on a wooden cross, thirty-five feet high. Uninformed by any official guidelines, unsanctioned by any public officials, this small group of Norman sailors decided to hold a "beautiful and devout ceremony" to plant the cross on a hill overlooking the ocean.

The first step they took was to organize a procession, led by the ship's captain, Paulmier de Gonneville, and hierarchically arranged by status. Like the official French ceremony in the Amazon, this group of symbolically paired French and Indian leaders were followed by the crew of the French ship, and trailing them, the remainder of the Indians. Like the officially sponsored events at the mouth of the Amazon, members of the parade were carrying a cross to be planted. Also like the ceremony in the Amazon, the procession was accompanied by music. "Trumpets sounded and drums" boomed; the ship's crew sang a litany; the cross was planted and guns were discharged.

The French sailors then distributed gifts to all the Indians present, "giving them to understand, as best they could, that they [the Carijó] were to preserve and honor the cross." As the French ship set sail, promising to return in twenty moons, "all the people [Carijó] gave a great shout, and gave to understand that they would preserve the cross well, making the sign of it with their two fingers."[20] While La Ravadière's royally authorized expedition performed a more elaborate ceremony, even pirates who landed by accident insisted upon a parade, dialogue, and exchange of presents and noted a symbolic gesture with a cross.

---

19 As will be discussed in the following pages, the mid-seventeenth century marked a change in French political thinking which rendered elaborate ceremonies less central than before.

20 *Campagne du navire l'Espoir de Honfleur, 1503–1505. Relation authentique du voyage du Capitaine de Gonneville et Nouvelles Terres des Indes,* ed. M. d'Avezac (Geneva, 1971; orig. pub. 1869). An excellent study of this account is Leyla Perrone-Moisés, *Vinte Luas: Viagem de Paulmier de Gonneveille ao Brasil: 1503–1505* (São Paulo, 1992). There is also an English translation (not used here) in John H. Parry and Robert Keith, eds., *New Iberian World,* 5 vols. (New York, 1984), 5: 22–27.

Similar ceremonial enactments were carried out by French Protestants arriving on the coast of Florida in 1562 and by French Catholics arriving in Martinique and Guadeloupe in the Caribbean in 1635. Jean Ribault, leader of the first expedition to Florida in 1562, describes how the Timucuas welcomed him, and how he furnished them with the distinctive French colors – blue cloth embroidered with the yellow fleur-de-lis in which to march while accompanying them to see the surrounding meadows and fields.[21] The next morning, after a procession of the "captayns, gentilmen, souldiers, and others of our smale troup," Ribault planted the first stone column bearing the French fleur-de-lis upon a small hill on the banks of the St. John's River (near modern-day Jacksonville).[22] The official possession of both Martinique and Guadeloupe in the Caribbean in 1635 were marked by the ceremonial planting of a cross, singing of hymns, and the assistance of the local chiefs in placing the arms of France on the cross.[23]

Unlike the English belief that fixing stationary objects such as fences, houses, and gardens transparently conveyed rights of possession, or that the actions of ordinary agriculture could do so, Frenchmen appear to have entertained the notion that a different set of actions – processions, cross-planting, and staging theatrical performances – transparently conveyed possession. The reasons for the ceremonial character of French possession lay deep within the French political tradition and within the uniquely French meaning of the word *ceremony*.

CEREMONY

In other European languages of the sixteenth and seventeenth centuries, ceremony connoted an empty formality, a mere gesture, or simple courtesy. The Dutch had three words for *ceremony*, two derived

21 René Laudonnière, *L'histoire notable de la Floride située es Indes Occidentales*, in *Les Français en Amérique pendant la deuxième moitié du XVIe siècle* (Paris, 1958; orig. pub. 1586), 50; Jean Ribault, *The Whole and Truer Discoverie of Terra Florida* (De Land, Fla., 1927; orig. pub. 1563), 66–72.

22 Ribault was unable to return to France and so his account was published in England. Ribault, *True Discoverie*, 76; Laudonnière, *Histoire notable*, 50–51. A picture of the river was engraved by Theodore de Bry in 1591 following Jacques le Moyne's drawing. See plate 2 in Le Moyne, *Brevis narratio eorum qua in Florida America provincia Gallis acciderunt* (Frankfurt, 1591). A second column was planted near Parris Island, South Carolina. Ribault, *True Discoverie*, 94–97.

23 "Eclatoient en signe d'une particulaire satisfaction & entière joye," June 27–29 1635, André Chevillard, *Les desseins de son Eminence de Richelieu pour l'Amérique* (Basse-Terre, Guad., 1973; orig. pub. 1659), 24–26. The fleur-de-lis was raised over a fort on Martinique, followed by litanies of Our Lady, cries of joy, and cannon fire (ibid., 25). "La croix fut plantée . . . ce qui est une marque de possession actuelle"; see "Memoire faict en 1637 pour l'afaire des Pères Récollectz," in Margry, *Découvertes et établissements*, 1: 7.

from locations where certain kinds of solemn behavior were customary: court (*hof-hoffelijk*) and shipdeck (*plecht-plechtigheid*). A third, *vormelijkheid*, means empty or outward formality for form's sake. In English the word connoted a kind of stiffness or awkwardness; in Portuguese it signified a religious occasion, but also excessive politeness or timidity. In Spanish *ceremonia* meant an affected gesture of obsequiousness, or an action done merely for appearances.[24] While sharing a core meaning of formal or solemn, in these other languages *ceremony*'s slightly pejorative overtones of awkwardness and affectedness resonated. Although it would acquire these same overtones in twentieth-century French, during the sixteenth century it lacked these derogatory connotations.[25]

In French the word *ceremony* had four unique meanings in contrast to other European languages. The first such significance was a procession, a meaning it continues to have. *Cortege, cavalcade, parade,* and *procession,* are all synonymous with *ceremony*.[26] To say the word *ceremony* implied a parade or procession, but only in French.

A second distinctly French meaning of *ceremony* referred to clothes used in carrying out the event.[27] The careful attention to special vestments – blue dresses with gold fleur-de-lis, blue shirts with white crosses – confirmed the true formality of the occasion.

A third uniquely French meaning of *ceremony* was *complicated*. While the opposite of ceremonial in English and Dutch was informal, the oppositve of ceremonial in French was simple, uncomplicated.[28]

Finally, beyond complexity, a procession, and a specified form of dress, *ceremony* in French alone signified order. To do something ceremoniously meant to do it according to the rules.[29] Rule-governed

---

24 *Por ceremonia* in Spanish means to do something merely for show or courtesy. Juan Corominas, *Diccionario crítico etimológico castellano e hispanico,* 5 vols., 2d ed. (Madrid, 1980), 2: 44; Real Academica Española, *Diccionario de la lengua castellana,* 2 vols. (Madrid, 1984), 1: 307; H. Michaelis, *Novo Michaelis, diccionarion ilustrado* (São Paulo, 1978), 1: 274; *Woordenboek der nederlandsche taal,* 27 vols. (The Hague, 1942–1993).

25 Alain Rey, *Dictionnaire historique de la langue française* (Paris, 1992), 2 vols., indicates that the derogatory connotations of *ceremony* are modern.

26 Paul Robert, *Dictionnaire alphabétique et analogique de la langue française,* 9 vols., hereafter cited as *Le Robert* (Paris, 1985). See "cérémonie," def. 2, 2: 447.

27 "Habit de cérémonie," *Le Robert,* def. 2, § 5, 2: 448. "The clothes, the lace, the ribbons, the wig and its curls are not an addition, supplement, ornament, or decoration of the body. It is the body that is multiplied . . . (acquiring) a power." Louis Marin, *Portrait of a King,* trans. Martha M. Houle (Minneapolis, Minn., 1988), 27–28.

28 *Le Robert,* 2: 448, gives "naturel" and "simplicité" as antonyms for "cérémonie." "Ils n'ont peu imaginer une nayfveté si pure et simple, comme nous la voyons pour experience; n'y ont pu croire que nostre societé se peut maintenir avec si peu d'artifice et de soudeure humaine." See "Des cannibales," Michel de Montaigne, *Essais,* ed. Andrée L'Héritier (Paris, 1964), 262.

29 Edmond Huguet, *Dictionnaire de la langue française du seizième siècle,* 7 vols. (Paris, 1925–1967). "Cérémonieursement" is "selon les règles" 2: 156. "Cérémonial" is "l'ensemble et l'ordre de succession des cérémonies établis par l'usage ou règles par

details – music, procession, costumes, and props – were far from constituting trivial excess. D'Abbeville's highly detailed descriptions confirmed the validity of French actions as a ceremony in the true meaning of the word, an occasion governed by an elaborate set of rules, including the order of the procession, the dress of the participants, and the sequence of events. The complexity of French ceremonies in establishing possession overseas reflected similar complexity in familiar political rituals – royal entrances and coronation ceremonies – creating and cementing the political power of French monarchs.

While many European monarchs had ceremonies to accompany their crowning, French kings and queens (until the mid-seventeenth century) held the most elaborate, rigidly governed rituals. Intricate rules controlled even the most minute of details for royal coronation and investiture – the names of the hymns to be sung, number of knocks on the king's door, the placement of candles during the procession, the color of the bishop's robe, the order in which clothes of certain colors were placed on the king.[30] But the need for such complexly ordered ceremonies came from a unique political tradition about the origin of French kingship.

According to French legend, an ampulla of holy oil was sent from heaven in the beak of a dove for St. Remi to baptize Merovingian King Clovis in 496. In subsequent historical tradition, this baptism instituted French kingship. Succeeding monarchs were anointed with the holy oil sent from heaven and preserved in the monastery of St. Denis. This anointing played a central role in fixing the monarch. Despite remaining in possession of the Capetian family for over three hundred years (987–1317), the right of each prince to succeed his father (upon his death) was not automatic.[31] The new prince's power had to be established by a public ritual of consecration.[32]

"The crown is not properly hereditary, because the new king is not the heir of his predecessor, nor does he succeed to his patrimony and goods . . . but he is the successor to the crown," wrote sixteenth-

---

une autorité pour celebre une solemnité" (def. 2) or "ensemble de formules, de règles" (def. 3, 2: 447).

30 Richard A. Jackson, *Vive le roi!: A History of the French Coronation from Charles V to Charles X* (Chapel Hill, N.C., 1984).

31 The right of succession was sustained through a variety of legal fictions including primogeniture, the Salic law, customary law, and a kind of heirship derived from Roman law and called *suitas regia*. Ralph Giesey, *The Juristic Basis of Dynastic Right to the French Throne* (Philadelphia, 1961), 12–25. The end of the Capetian reign is sometimes also given as 1328.

32 Giesey, *Juristic Basis*, 3–6; Marc Bloch, *The Royal Touch: Sacred Monarchy and Scrofula in England and France*, trans. J. E. Anderson (London, 1973), 37–43. Until 1180 the son was crowned during the father's lifetime, eliminating the interregnum. See also Elizabeth A. R. Brown, *The Monarchy of Capetian France and Royal Ceremonial* (London, 1991); and Ernest H. Kantorowicz, *The King's Two Bodies: A Study in Medieval Political Theology* (Princeton, N.J., 1957), which deals largely with English theory and has a brief treatment of French ceremonies (409–413).

century French political theorist Charles du Moulin in his commentaries on *La coustume de Paris*.[33] Sixteenth-century Protestant François Hotman in *De jure regni Galliae* and Catholic Jean Bodin in the *Six livres de la république* agreed with earlier writers that the kingdom of France had a "successive monarchy."[34]

The political consequences of a "successive" rather than a hereditary monarchy were considerable. According to Jean de Terre-Rouge (ca. 1420) a monarch was not technically bound by the debts of his predecessor.[35] Nor, according to Jean Bodin, was he bound even by the ordinances, letters patent, or privileges of his predecessor, since their automatic renewal would infringe upon the sovereignty of the king.[36] Anointing established the king's right to affirm or dismiss laws as he saw fit. No particular legal arrangement was enacted, only the principle upon which all political order rested, making the ceremony itself far more significant than for other European monarchies. In 1593 Guy Coquille wrote, "I believe that the ceremony of the anointing is necessary to obligate the king to the people and the people to the king by means of things holy and sacred."[37] Far from being an empty observance, the coronation ritual actually legitimated political power.[38]

---

33 Charles du Moulin, *Consilia quatuor, seu propositiones errorum in caussa France*, popularly known as *Coustume de Paris* (Paris, 1624; orig. pub. 1539), tit. 1, no. 62, tom 1, col. 26, quoted by André Lemaire, *Les lois fondamentales de la monarchie française* (Geneva, 1975; orig. pub. 1907), 77; Giesey, *Dynastic Right*, 26–29.

34 Francis Hotman in *De jure regni Galliae* asserted that the monarchy was neither hereditary nor patrimonial succession, but simple succession, regulated by law, and the custom of the kingdom. Quoted by Georges Pere, *Le sacre et le couronnement des rois de France dans leurs rapport avec les lois fondamentales* (Baagmeres-de-Bigorre, 1921), 124. See also his *Francogallia* (1586), chaps. 6 and 7, reproduced in *Constitutionalism and Resistance in the Sixteenth Century: Three Treatises by Hotman, Beza and Mornay*, trans. Julian H. Franklin (New York, 1969). Jean Bodin, *Les six livres de la République* (Paris, 1583), liv. 6, chap. 5, 973–1013. Lemaire, *Les lois fondamentales*, 62, 77, 172; Jean de Terre Rouge, appendix, in Francois Hotman, *Consilia* (Arras, 1586), art. 1, concl. 1–3, cited by Giesey, *Dynastic Right*, 12–13. A related formula, "substitution immémoriale," was fixed under Charles VI in the middle of the fifteenth century. Fifteenth-century chronicler Jean Juvénal des Ursin reprised the successive rather than hereditary monarch. Pere, *Le sacre et le couronnement*, 126.

35 This point is articulated by Jean de Terre-Rouge, *Traités*, in 1418 or 1419. Lemaire, *Le lois fondamentales*, 57. It is reiterated by Bodin, *République*, liv. 1, chap. 8, 159–160.

36 "Le Prince souverain est exempt des lois de ses predecesseurs"; "Les princes souverains bien entendus, ne sont jamais, serment de garder les lois de leurs predecesseurs, out bien ils ne sont pas souverains." Bodin, *République*, liv. 1, chap. 8, 131–132, 135. The only exception were the laws such as the Salic law, governing the establishment of the kingdom. Ibid., 135–137, 145.

37 Quoted by Lemaire, *Les lois fondamentales*, 290.

38 Regencies were potentially dangerous times because they represented a prolonging of this liminal period. Thus, the question of regency is examined at great length by writers such as Bodin, *République*, liv. 1, chap. 8, 125–128. Not long after consecration ceased to actually institute rule, and the French monarchy became quasi-hereditary in the mid-seventeenth century, the elaborate coronations and entrance ceremonies ceased. Lawrence M. Bryant, *Parisian Royal Entry – The King and the City in the Parisian Royal Entry Ceremony: Politics, Ritual, and Art in the Renaissance* (Geneva, 1986), 23.

Following the end of the 330-year Capetian dynasty a new dynastic family, the Valois, took over early in the fourteenth century and added a new element to coronation customs.[39] Elaborate processions began to mark the first entry of a new king into the important cities of the kingdom. Previously such ceremonial entrances had marked a city's recognition of a new local lord and had combined popular revelry with official recognition of the new lord's authority.[40] Adapting such ceremonies to fit fourteenth-century Valois entrances required replacing chaotic popular revels with an elaborate protocol of sights and sounds.[41]

Newly anointed Valois monarchs marched ito cities prominently displaying the golden fleur-de-lis, symbol of the French monarchy since the thirteenth century, on an azure background.[42] Crosses, censers, and candles were carried in these processions according to a sequence that became fixed by 1350 and would remain unchanged for the next three hundred years.[43] Equal care was devoted to chosing the order of the march and participants. Children were often present in organized groups. Nor were the processions silent. Cannon were fired, bells and trumpets played; arriving monarchs were often greeted with the ritual cry of coronation ceremonies, "Vive le roi!"[44]

In addition to arranging the sound, props, and marching order of participants, municipal officials also began to regulate the color of both observers' and participants' costumes. Only the king and five

39 Bryant, *Parisian Royal Entry*, 69–70, 76.
40 Ibid., 22–23, 76. Other major sources of the procession include military victory parades and ecclesiastical processions. Jacques Chiffoleau, "Les processions parisiennes de 1412," *Revue Historique*, 284 (1990): 37–76; Bryant, *Parisian Royal Entry*, 66–69; Bernard Guenée, *Les entrées royales françaises de 1328 à 1515* (Paris, 1968), 22–23; Sam Kinser, *Reinventing Majesty: Political Imagination and the Princely Entry (France and Western Europe), 1450–1650*, forthcoming.
41 Between 1350 and 1431 the form of the entrance ritual was relatively fluid, with formal organization and protocol developing from 1450 on. Bryant, *Parisian Royal Entry*, 77, 84, 99. Kinser argues in *Reinventing Majesty* that popular festivities abruptly ceased in 1550. "La tendance à transformer la simple fête de naguère en une parade bruyante et colorée est évidente dans tout le royaume." Guenée, *Entrées royales*, 12; Bryant, *Parisian Royal Entry*, 15, 17, 69–70.
42 Jackson, *Vive le roi*, 27–40. Bryant, *Parisian Royal Entry*, 113. The 1431 Parisian entry mentions a scepter, coronet, and ermine-trimmed cloak as well (ibid., 104). A crowned helmet appeared in the latter part of the fifteenth century, the seal in 1484. Bryant, *Parisian Royal Entry*, 104–107, 109, 113. According to French legend, God sent his angel down bearing the fleur-de-lis to Clovis. Despite its widely believed putative origin with Clovis's coronation during the sixteenth century, the fleur-de-lis (orig. *fleur de loys*) was first used as a decoration by Louis le Jeune for dressing his son Philip Augustus. The first French royal seal with lilies was designed in the reign of Louis VII (1223–1226). The fleur-de-lis was a polyvalent symbol, variously interpreted as representing the Trinity (Father, Son, and Holy Spirit) and the relation of the nobility and clergy (the two side petals) to Christianity. Anne Marie Lecoq, *François Ier imaginaire: symbolique & politique à l'aube de la Renaissance française* (Paris, 1987), 48–49, 398–390.
43 Bryant, *Parisian Royal Entry*, 69–70.
44 Chiffoleau, "Processions parisiennes," 66; Bryant, *Parisian Royal Entry*, 56, 58.

other officials could wear fur-lined red robes; citizens of Paris wore different colored garments than non-Parisians during the 1350 entry of Jean II into Paris; in 1358 Parisian townspeople were dressed in blue and red, in 1380 they wore green and white. By 1549 each of the Parisian guilds wore a distinctive set of colors.[45]

In the fifteenth century, entrance ceremonies came to be accompanied by elaborately staged plays or *tableaux vivants* presented on ornate stage sets near the bridges at the city entrance.[46] The central elements of theatrical rituals were united: color, music, stages, costumes, props, and processional order. In replacing the formerly rowdy receptions for newly crowned kings with disciplined theatrical spectacles and processions, municipal officials finally effaced all signs of popular revelry by 1550.

These ceremonial entrances into cities fulfilled additional direct political functions deriving from the time when local lords had used them to obtain recognition of their power. As historian Lawrence Bryant writes, "A major part of the ceremony of the king's entry consisted of the public confirmation of rights and privileges that his subjects had enjoyed under his predecessors."[47] Kings used ceremonial city entrances to sanction the powers of bureaucratic and ecclesiastical officeholders and to name new masters of guilds.[48] Even as such approval of secular officeholders came to be virtually automatic in 1483 (subject to payment of a substantial gift), kings continued to assert a right to confirm these privileges at their entrances.[49]

Speeches and receptions by municipal leaders also commonly established the allegiance of a particular city and its citizens to the crown.[50] Civic judicial officials customarily delivered these speeches in which they asked for the confirmation of the city's liberties and for the preservation of the rights of corporate groups and political orders.[51] Sometimes, as at the 1424 Parisian entrance ceremony, citizens swore a general oath of obedience and loyalty to the crown.[52]

The length of time that it took to prepare, rehearse, execute costumes, and organize festivities meant that sometimes considerable time lapsed between the death of the former king and the coronation of the new. It took five months after Henry IV's death to prepare the

---

45 Bryant, *Parisian Royal Entry*, 76, 84–85.   46 Ibid., 195–203.
47 Ibid., 42. Guenée writes, "D'abord simple fête, puis aussi spectacle . . . une entrée royale est de plus devenue à la fin du XVᵉ siècle un grand théâtre où le sentiment monarchique est de plus en plus exalté et la politique royale de mieux en mieux justifiéee." Guenée *Les entrées royales*, 29.
48 Granting pardons and remitting fines were also frequent activities. Bryant, *Parisian Royal Entry*, 23–40, 83.
49 Ibid., 45, 47. By the fourteenth century a form of present was customarily granted – sometimes money, sometimes art objects (ibid., 31–40).
50 Ibid., 75–79.   51 Ibid., 54.   52 Ibid., 83.

ceremony for Louis XIII.[53] The willingness to endure such a lengthy liminal period – despite widespread political anxiety – testified to the importance of performing the ceremony precisely.

Only when succession to the crown became an automatic dynastic right in the mid-seventeenth century did the importance of public ceremonies wane.[54] Anointing ceased being the moment at which power was established, replaced instead by the right of automatic inheritance. Elaborate rituals to reestablish political order were no longer needed and soon thereafter fell into disuse.

Still other elements of entrance ceremonies evoked religious processions held on saints' feast days. Priests marched in the entrance processions wearing vestments customary on those occasions. Many of the objects displayed were religious – incense, censers, candlesticks, as well as the cross. Exhibiting religious paraphernalia visually dramatized ecclesiastical or even divine sanctioning of the political process.

The semiotics of color and clothing, of food and form, placement and procession were connected in an explicit and meaningful way to the establishment of political order and stability. Governed by explicit codes, entrance ceremonies functioned as a kind of public announcement, made with words or speeches, and a necessarily elaborate panoply of colors, clothes, and procession of special objects. Entrance and coronation ceremonies visually demonstrated the legitimacy, stability and order of French political power.[55] When Frenchmen moved to take possession of the New World, they employed the visual effects, sounds, and gestures that they had long associated with creating legitimate royal power in France.

Clothing for Indian participants in French ceremonies was neither casual nor unimportant but was purposefully supplied by expeditionary leaders. "The beautiful blouses of sky blue on which there were white crosses in the front and on the back . . . the lords Lieutenant Generals had given them [the Tupis] to use in this and other similar solemnities."[56] Jean Ribault also arrayed indigenous participants in

53 Jackson, *Vive le roi*, 16.
54 Henry II had defined a group of men as "princes of the blood" in an ordinancy of 1576, but not until 1666 was the notion of a "substitution graduelle en la famille des Princes du Sang" established. The quotation is from Charles Loyseau, *Des offices*, in his *Oevures* (Paris, 1666), cited by Giesey, *Jurisitic Basis*, 37, 40. The ceremonial was replaced with a financial consideration. Bryant, *Parisian Royal Entry*, 49–50, 216–224. Bryant also argues that the ceremonial entrance's demise was produced by concentration of power in the monarch and the absence of a need to seek approval (208, 213). This concentration, however, became possible only when the monarchy could depend upon its intrinsic quality ("blood") for definition, and no longer needed confirmation of its authority by external agents.
55 On the political functions of processional aesthetics, see Chiffoleau, "Processions parisiennes," 72–73.
56 D'Abbeville, *Histoire*, 88–88v.

the symbolic colors of the French realm, clothing Indian participants in azure tunics embroidered with the golden fleur-de-lis.

The French New World ceremonies of possession were also carefully choreographed – from the order and hierarchy of marchers to objects carried by its participants. Specific gestures contributed to the "solemnity" of the occasion.[57] In 1612 Tupi Indians marched to the cross with their hands joined, knelt on their knees, adored it, and kissed it.[58] Thus, the choeographed theatrical ritual at home became associated with the enactment of order and legitimation of political power in the colonies. While New World ceremonies of possession could not match coronation or entrance rituals in complexity, some element of ceremony had to be present. To omit ceremony – or to lack it – would mean to abandon political rules.[59] In the words of the seventeenth-century French historian of the Caribbean, Jean-Baptiste du Tertre, "Ceremonies [were] necessary to render possession valid."[60] Therefore, despite only intermittent royal interest, sixteenth- and seventeenth-century Frenchmen used elements of monarchical ceremonies in rituals creating royal authority and legal order overseas just as they did in France.

While costumes and staging were critical to such ceremonies in France,[61] equally important were the sounds and gestures of the public. The expressions of joy at the king's arrival, the shouts of "Vive le roi," the theatrical gestures, as carefully channeled and directed as they had been, were nonetheless officially understood in France as manifestations of popular consent to new political rulers. Accustomed to interpreting such shouts and movements as manifesting consent, sixteenth-century Frenchmen presumed that the gestures and their meaning were universal.

Even Michel de Montaigne, the sixteenth-century proponent of cross-cultural criticism, assumed that body language was transparently and universally understood. "There is no movement [of the body] that does not speak, and in a language that is intelligible without instruction, and in one that is common to all," he wrote.[62] Noting indigenous body language thus figured prominently in nearly all French narratives of colonization. Descriptions of native peoples' body language usually

---

57 Pascal describes the "august apparel" of magistrates and physicians as "very necessary" to "attract respect toward themselves." *Pensées*, quoted in Marin, *Portrait*, 31.

58 D'Abbeville, *Histoire*, 88v.

59 One of the few sixteenth-century French critics of this position was Michel de l'Hôpital, who argued that the ceremony was a nonconstitutional solemnity, contributing only to the grandeur of the kingship. Jackson, *Vive le roi*, 213.

60 Jean-Baptiste du Tertre, *Histoire generale des Antilles habitées par les français*, 4 vols. (Fort de France, 1978; orig. pub. 1667–1671), 3: 312.

61 Jean Meyer, Jean Tarrade, Annie Rey-Godlzeiguer, and Jacques Thobie, *Histoire de la France coloniale des origenes à 1914*, 2 vols. (Paris, 1990), 1: 40.

62 Montaigne, *L'apologie de Raymond Sebond*, ed. Paul Porteau (Paris, 1937), 31.

figured prominently at two separate moments in French narratives: when characterizing native responses to their arrival in the Americas and, above all, when describing possession-taking ceremonies.

CONSENT: THE "CONQUEST BY LOVE"

In several of their journeys to the New World, Frenchmen claimed the region for the crown by planting a cross, a pillar, or a royal standard. In all of these cases, however, Frenchmen were careful to secure by means of physical gesture, an indication that the natives consented to the planting of the sign of possession. Sometimes acceptance was registered by indigenous participation. In the French expedition to the Amazon, the Lord de la Ravadière pointed out how "the Indians *themselves* placed this standard of France, placing their land in the possession of the king."[63]

> After they themselves had placed the cross as a sign that they desired to be children of God, they likewise planted with the French the arms and standards of France in the middle of their land, so that it be recognized among all other nations, that our most Christian king is the sovereign master and peaceable possessor.[64]

Even the Norman pirate captain Paulmier de Gonneville described the Carijó chief Arosca and his followers as "invited guests of honor" for his ceremonial planting of the cross. Whether as direct participants in the planting or in the ceremonies leading up to the planting, natives were often involved in the creation of French colonial rights. This frequent participation of the audience in the ceremony, like that of French citizens in the accession ceremonies of their monarchs, occurred exclusively in French political actions overseas. Even when placing a marker of possession without native help, Frenchmen recorded native involvement in a subsequent dialogue, exchange of gestures, or native ritual that ensured that the marker would be respected.[65]

In the first voyage of French colonization to the New World, Jacques Cartier placed the first French cross on the territory of Canada on July 24, 1534, kneeling before it with his companions, joining their hands in prayer. But in his journal Cartier was careful to note that although

---

63 D'Abbeville, *Histoire*, 161–161v, 172.   64 Ibid., 164.

65 Frenchmen also apparently held that such markers were respected. René Laudonnière believed the "signs and coats of arms of the King of France" supposedly planted by Giovanni da Verrazzano successfully convinced the Spaniards that the territory was French to such an extent that the Spaniards called the land "French Land." Laudonnière, *Histoire notable*, 38. This was wishful thinking on Laudonnière's part. Verrazzano was looking for a passage to Asia, and there is no mention in his account of any markers placed in the New World. Lawrence C. Wroth, *The Voyages of Giovanni da Verrazzano* (New Haven, 1970), 133–143.

the natives had not participated in the cross-planting, they had witnessed it. "We planted this cross before them on said point while they
[the Stadaconans] watched it being made and erected." Cartier noted
the natives' apparent approval in facial expressions. They "gave it [the
cross] several admiring looks by turning and looking at [it]."

Shortly after the cross had been raised, a chief approached the
French vessel in a canoe and crossed a finger from each hand and ges-
tured to the hilltop.[66] While that gesture could have simply mimicked
the representation of the cross, been an inquiry about its form, or any
one of a dozen other possible meanings, Cartier understood that the
chief was objecting to the placement of the cross. Furthermore, Cartier
assumed that the chief was objecting to Cartier's failure to seek the
chief's permission before erecting the cross – a standard procedure
that should have been followed by a Frenchman claiming the region
for his crown. Cartier understood that from his perspective a cross
should signify indigenous consent, and he had failed to secure it.

By pretending to give him an axe, Cartier tricked the chief into coming on board his ship to discuss the cross. He then gave the chief food
and drink, as well as gifts of a hatchet and knives. He then misleadingly
"explained" to the chief in French that the cross was not a sign of possession of the New World, but only a beacon to enable the French to
find their way back to the harbor to be able to trade with them in the
future. Presumably thus reassured, the chief returned to land. By noon
when the French departed, over thirty Indians came in canoes to the
ship, and according to Cartier, they gave their assent to having the
cross there, "making signs to us that they would not tear down the
cross." What gestures they made is unclear, but Cartier's interpretation
of them was sure. They accepted the presence of the cross, the emblem
of French colonization.[67] Thus, having achieved minimal indigenous
consent, a form of body language that would "speak" without need for
translation, Cartier continued his exploration of the Saint Lawrence,
without being able to land again near settlements, and set sail for
France three weeks later. Cartier's actions were not exceptional. Captain Paulmier de Gonneville also interpreted natives' crossed fingers
as relating to questions of political assent. He described the Carijós'
making the sign of the cross with their two fingers as giving "to understand that they would preserve the cross well."[68]

The most unusual consent to the French presence was granted on
the coast of Florida in the 1560s. Furnishing the local Timucuas with
the distinctive French royal colors – blue cloth embroidered with the
yellow fleur-de-lis – Jean Ribault marched around the surrounding

66 The French text is in Cartier, *Voyages of Cartier*, 64–65.   67 Ibid., 65–67.
68 *Campagne du navire l'Espoir de Honfleur, 1503–1505.*

meadows and fields[69] and, the following morning, placed the first stone column upon a small hill near modern-day Jacksonville.[70]

These markers were not crosses, but were similar to obelisks, a decorative object appearing for the first time in the king's 1549 entry into Paris.[71] Like the Portuguese monumental stone pillars (each a round column topped with a square block and above it a cross), the Florida obelisks were tall, made of white stone, and engraved with the arms of the crown, the initials of the reigning monarch, and the year.[72] (See cover.) Like the Portuguese markers, they also signaled a claim to dominion.

The Timucua peoples not only did not tear down the monuments the French left; they proclaimed their acceptance of one in a way that took even the French by surprise. When a second expedition under René Laudonnière returned in 1564, he and his company were shown their obelisk, now crowned with magnolia laurels, surrounded by offerings of corn and other produce, fragrant oils in vases, and bows and arrows.[73] The Timucua Indians assumed that the stone pillar left by Ribault was some kind of sacred object; Jacques Le Moyne believed that the Timucua "adored the column as an idol." This was not exactly what the French had had in mind. Leading the Frenchmen to the site, the Timucua approached it and kissed it reverently, insisting that Laudonnière do the same. A nervous Laudonnière apologetically relates how he felt obliged to treat the monument in accordance with the forms of worship the Timucua accorded it. "We did not wish to refuse them for this end – to draw them more and more into our friendship."[74] The natives obviously consented to the presence of the object, but the obelisk's meaning as a sign of political possession clearly had not been communicated.

While Englishmen acted as though the object itself – the house, the garden, or the fence – transparently conveyed possession, Frenchmen did not act as though crosses or pillars could inherently transfer rights; it was necessary to communicate the meaning of the object to the natives. While Frenchmen regularly interpreted native responses to

69 Laudonnière, *L'histoire notable*, 50; Ribault, *True Discoverie*, 66–72.
70 Ribault, *True Discoverie*, 76; Laudonnière, *Histoire notable*, 50–51.
71 The obelisk was inscribed with the desire for "firm peace and harmony" during his reign. The inscription is reproduced in Bryant, *Parisian Royal Entry*, 173.
72 Missing from the French version was the characteristic cross, the symbol of the crusade, which sat atop many of the Portuguese columns and was engraved on the side of others. Ribault, *True Discoverie*, 14, 109–111.
73 Laudonnière, *Histoire notable*, 87-88; *Voyages en Virginie et en Floride* (Paris, 1927). Jacques Le Moyne's drawing was engraved by Theodor de Bry in his printing of Le Moyne's *Brevis narratio* (1591), plate viii. The pillar is also crowned with flowers of all kinds and branches of rare trees. The cover illustration is a later picture from this engraving.
74 Laudonnière, *Histoire notable*, 88.

planting crosses or obelisks as a form of acceptance or even happiness at French actions, they presumed there had to be a discussion and an exchange of gestures about the object for its status as a marker of possession to be established. However, this incident with the Timucua obelisk demonstrates that an object, even one about which there had obviously been a communication of its importance, still failed to communicate in a clear manner. The Timucuas assimilated the "important" object into their own categories of importance, not the Frenchmen's. The transparent communication and understanding of political rights had not occurred.

Frenchmen often described indigenous consent as appearing in facial expressions, movements of bodies, and shouts. They also believed that what they construed as the natives' emotional states during these ceremonies communicated their agreement. At the ceremonial cross-planting on Martinique in 1635, one of the Frenchmen present noted that the natives "shouted as a sign of a special satisfaction and complete joy" at the ceremony of possession.[75] While they could have been making a noise customary at public ceremonies or expressing delight in the spectacular pageantry itself, the Frenchmen in the Caribbean understood the shouts to establish "joy" at the onset of French colonial rule.

Describing the arrival of the Huguenot colony in Rio de Janeiro, Nicolas Barré noted five to six hundred natives "made it known to us in their language that we are welcome, offering us their goods, and making signs of joy that we had come."[76] Twenty-three years later, sailors from a French ship plying the Atlantic coast used identical language to describe natives of another region of Brazil "conveying to us in their language that we are welcome, offering us their goods, and making signs of joy that we had come."[77] Paulmier de Gonneville in 1504 described the Carijó chief Arosca as "happy" during the ceremonial cross-planting, while the rest of the natives were respectfully "silent and attentive," thus interpreting facial expressions to signify both active and passive acceptance.[78] Both the cross and standard planting in the Amazon were interpreted as having produced feelings

75 "Eclatoient en signe d'une particulaire satisfaction & entière joye," June 27–29, 1635, Chevillard, Les desseins, 24–26.

76 Letter of Nicolas Barré, July 28, 1556, reproduced in Paul Gaffarel, Histoire du Brésil français au XVIᵉ siècle (Paris, 1878), 373–382, esp. 379. André Thevet, who was not present at the initial arrival, also described the joy of the natives, their "human" reception, and their admiration for the French. Thevet, Les singularitez de la France Antartique, ed. Paul Gaffarel (Paris, 1878; orig. pub. 1558), 27. He described the construction of the place of the fort on wholly pragmatic grounds (128).

77 The letter of the French expedition (1581) is reproduced in Gaffarel, Brésil français, 496.

78 Cartier described the Stadaconans in 1535 in almost identical language. They "maintained a great silence and were marvelously attentive." Cartier, Voyages, 166.

of happiness. "The emotion that it [the French leader's discourse at the cross-planting in the Amazon] produced inside them [the Tupi] assured [us] that voluntarily and willingly they received and embraced all that was suggested to them."[79] "The standard . . . embellished all around the big golden fleur de lis . . . was itself planted by the hands of the Indians with as much joy and affections as with the cross."[80] Interpreting natives' gestures, shouts, and apparent emotional states as signifying contentment with the French presence further confirmed belief in the assent of New World peoples to their colonial rule.

The word "joy" is repeated over and over in these accounts of native emotional states: by the French Dominicans on Martinque in 1635 in interpreting the Carib response, by the French Huguenot Nicolas Barré describing their reception by the Tupi in Rio de Janeiro, and by the Catholic noblemen and clergy in the Amazon. Paulmier de Gonneville used the word "happy" to communicate his understanding of the Carajós' response. That so many Frenchmen, encountering so many diverse peoples of the Americas, could have nearly always encountered joy should create considerable suspicion.[81]

In the first place, the joy which indigenous peoples reportedly expressed could as easily have been signs of pleasure at a new source of trade goods, a traditional expression of welcome, or genuine delight at the grace and pageantry of French ceremonies. But Frenchmen in the New World, regardless of religious affiliation or social status, interpreted native responses according to their own categories, as joy at the French arrival and political presence. Yet other Europeans encountering the same peoples rarely if ever described even similar actions as joyful. Portuguese encounters with the same coastal peoples of Brazil near Rio de Janeiro and the Amazon describe trading practices, mutual curiosity, and even dances. But they characterize the Tupis as "dancing and diverting *themselves*" rather than welcoming the Europeans.[82] Spanish encounters with the Timucuas whom Ribault met described them as "humble and obedient."[83] Frenchmen, how-

---

79 D'Abbeville, *Histoire,* 87–88.   80 Ibid., 164v–165.
81 Other colonists' reports of their reception were not nearly so consistent. Amadas and Barlow report joy in the natives' reception of them off the coast of Virginia in 1584, but Richard Grenville's voyage to the same region the following year does not contain such a report. Hakluyt, ed., *Voyages to the Virginia Colony,* 68, 82. The Carajó were a Guaraní-speaking coastal people, now extinct.
82 When Diogo Dias began to play the bagpipe and dance with them, "they laughed and enjoyed themselves greatly" but then became sullen and went away. William B. Greenlee, *The Voyage of Pedro Alvarez Cabral to Brazil and India* (London, 1938), 21.
83 Not surprisingly, "humble and obedient" was the kind of Indian that the Spaniards desired to encounter. Letter to the crown, July 22, 1571. Eugenio Ruidíaz y Caravia, *La Florida: Su conquista y colonización por Pedro Menéndez de Avilés,* 2 vols. (Madrid, 1893), 2: 237. For the Spanish desire to have humble and obedient subjects, see Chapter 3.

ever, consistently reported native joy as a response to their arrival. Cartier, Ribault, Laudonnière, Razilly, and D'Abbeville among others described indigenous peoples' physical gestures as registering overt approval at their arrival.[84] The reasons are not hard to decipher.

Such responses readily fit French expectations. In medieval and early modern France, the popular response to a king's post-coronation entrance into a city was customarily proclaimed as joyous. French accounts of the reception of the king invariably dwell upon the people's joy, which was understood to indicate assent to the new monarch.[85] Ceremonial city entrances were officially described as public demonstrations of people's loyalty and affection for rulers,[86] despite having been carefully organized by muncipal officials. Finally, the ceremonies were often called "joyous entries" and the king's prerogatives were officially termed a "right of joyous accession."[87] Interpreting natives' gestures as joyous at their arrival or possession-taking ceremonies, Frenchmen understood their presence in the New World as duly authorized, just as their fellow subjects' presence at officially staged joyous celebrations expressed the consent of Frenchmen to a new monarch.

Early in the sixteenth century, a French voyager to the New World, Jean Parmentier, had confidently declared that the French "would have gained the friendship and assured the allegiance of the people of these new lands without employing other arms than persuasion and good conduct."[88] D'Abbeville described his expedition as having created their "conquest not by arms, but by the cross, not by force, but by

84 "En effet les Paúoitigoueieuhak [an Algonkian-speaking group] nous invitèrent de les aller voir en leur pays . . . . Les capitaines de cette nation du Sault invitent nos Pères à faire quelque sorte de demeure parmy eux." Extract of letter of Pères Charles Raymbault and Issac Jogues to France (1640–1642), in Margry, *Découvertes et établissements*, 1: 46–47. An expedition to the Iroquois in 1656 "s'y établirent du consentement des Iroquois," (ibid., 1: 39); "Nos Pères, qui sont aux Hurons, invités par quelques Algonquins" (1640), 1: 49. See also Patricia Seed, "Columbus, Cartier, and Cabral: European Discourses of First Contact in Comparative Perspective," *Cultural Anthropology*, forthcoming.

85 The shouts of "Vive le Roi" at the entrance of Henry II signified that Parisians were making "publiquement confession de sa grandeur." *Entrée de Henry II*, 26, quoted in Bryant, *Parisian Royal Entry*, 58.

86 Ibid., 36.

87 Ibid., 21–50. Note by contrast the way in which the joyous entry was assimilated in Brabant, where the first joyous entrance in 1354 became a charter of rights (also called joyous entry) requiring consent of subjects for wars, treaties, coinage, and territorial concessions. By 1477 the official joyous entry included an explicit statement of the right of subjects to disobey a prince and refuse his service until he repaired his ways. Petrus Johannes Blok, *History of the Peoples of the Netherlands*, trans. Oscar A. Bierstadt and Ruth Putnam, pt. 1, *From the Earliest Times to the Beginning of the Fifteenth Century* (New York, 1970; orig. pub. 1898–1912), 281; Martin Van Gelderen, ed., *The Dutch Revolt* (Cambridge, 1993), xiv.

88 Jean Parmentier (pub. 1531), quoted by Henri Blet, *Histoire de la colonisation française*, 3 vols. (Paris, 1946), 1: 69.

love which has sweetly led them [the Tupis] to donate themselves and their country to the king of France."[89] Jean Bodin had characterized the relation of French monarchs to their subjects as rule "by love."[90] Rule by love as Bodin wrote, came from "the sympathy and harmony between king and people. . . . [for] people never surrounded a prince with greater reverence or a prince a people with greater love." The people do not love the prince. Rather love is the gift that the monarch bestows upon the people in return for reverence. By inverting the sequence in France and first bestowing "love" (charity) upon the natives in imitation of the monarch, Frenchmen had been met with the appropriate response – native reverence and grant of themselves and their lands to the crown.

While not adverse to using force if the "conquest by love" failed, French expeditions characteristically sought the initial authorization, or at least the appearance of approval, for their political authority over the New World. Understanding native gestures as intending to express joy at their arrival, and comprehending native participation in rituals of cross- or standard-planting as demonstrating formal consent, Frenchmen understood natives to have voluntarily and legitimately authorized their colonial governance.

No other Europeans so consistently sought the political permission of the natives in order to justify *their own* political authority.[91] Nor did other Europeans so reliably compose the history of expeditions to make it appear that the natives had invited European political domination. When choosing a place to live, the Pilgrims had by all accounts discussed a great many things. They considered the availability of fishing grounds, the location of woods, whether there was enough fresh water, if the soil was rocky, whether the land would be difficult to clear, whether the land was near a harbor, whether the site was adequate for placing artillery.[92] What they never discussed was coming to any agree-

---

89 D'Abbeville, *Histoire,* 164.

90 Jean Bodin, *Methodus ad Facilem Historium Cognitionem* (Amsterdam, 1650), 273, quoted in Bryant, *Parisian Royal Entry,* 192.

91 Dutch, Swedish, and sometimes English settlers solicited what they construed as *economic* assent by purchasing tracts of land to live on. The Portuguese believed that native participation in trading relationships with them demonstrated a form of *economic* consent, but native *political* consent seemed unnecessary to justify European dominion. Only Spaniards were also concerned to legitimate their rule over the New World by creating a political relationship with native peoples, but despite Las Casas's arguments they more often demanded submission instead of seeking an invitation. Todorov rightly saw the analogy to French political practice in *Conquest of America,* 168–182.

92 Bradford's and Winslow's journal (also known as Mourt's Relation) emphasizes the abundance of food and building materials, game, medicinal plants, and good soil yet describes, "What people inhabit here we yet know not." The chronicle is reproduced in Young, ed., *Chronicles,* 113–114, 143, 167–168; Nathanial Morton, *New Englands Memoriall* (New York, 1977; orig. pub. 1669), 17–18.

ment with the natives about where the latter would be willing to let them reside. Rarely did English expeditions in the Americas before 1640 negotiate such initial political consent; French expeditions, however, did so as a rule rather than as the exception.[93]

ALLIANCE

Consent paved the way for the specific political relationship that Frenchmen envisioned themselves creating with natives, namely, an "alliance." Jean Ribault related how he "made alyance and entered into amytie with them [the Timucuas of Florida]" just as his fellow countrymen would do later in the Amazon.[94] Before landing on the isle of Saint Anne, French leaders had ascertained the natives' desire for "remaining always friends and allies of the French."[95] Natives were often characterized as responding joyously to the alliance with the French. A leader of the French expedition to the Amazon in 1612 assured Tupi villagers that the French had come "to live and die with them as do good friends and allies, to defend them also and support them against their enemies."[96] "The Indians were transported with pleasure and happiness since they had always desired to ally themselves with the French,"[97] wrote Claude d'Abbeville.

In writing the history of the Huguenot expedition to Brazil in 1555, Jean Crespin related two different versions of when the alliance was created. When Villegagnon's expedition arrived in Guanabara Bay, it approached a region where French businessmen from Honfleur had been trading for some twenty-five years. Crespin wrote that these traders "arranged an alliance between them[selves and the Indians] that has endured to this day [1570] since it continued [for] all the years of the voyages."[98]

Crespin also said that a great number of inhabitants of the country "receive[d] them [the French] with warm welcome; giving them presents of foodstuffs of the land and other unique things, in order to negotiate a perpetual alliance with them."[99] André Thevet remarked in his *France Antarctique* that "the savages of the country [Cabo Frio,

---

93 Only the Roanoke (1585) and Maryland (1634) expeditions negotiated consent, but even on these occasions they did so far less elaborately than did the French. *A Relation of Maryland* (London, 1635), reproduced in Clayton C. Hall, ed., *Narratives of Early Maryland* (New York, 1910), esp. 73–74; Quinn, ed., *Roanoke Voyages*, 1: 192n.2.
94 Laudonnière, *L'histoire notable*, 50.   95 D'Abbeville, *Histoire*, 57v.
96 Ibid., 60–60v.   97 Ibid., 163–163v.
98 "Iceux composèrent entre eux une alliance qui dure iusques auiourd'hui, depuis l'on a continué tous les ans de la navigation." Jean Crespin, *Histoire des martyrs persécutez et mis à mort pou la vérité de l'Evangile* (Geneva, 1619), 401, reproduced in Paul Gaffarel, *Brésil français*, 415. The earliest edition listed by the Library of Congress is 1570.
99 Crespin, *Histoire des martyrs*, 436.

Brazil] . . . showed great regret [when we left] since they expected a longer stay and an alliance following the promise we made them upon our arrival."[100]

As with indigenous expressions of joy at the French arrival, Tupi hospitality and gifts – probably customary on greeting strangers – were treated as signs that the natives wanted to make a perpetual alliance.[101] In the only version of Cartier's journal printed in the sixteenth century, he supposedly reported that the natives thought the French "had come from far away to make an alliance with them."[102] Huguenot and Catholic alike, Frenchmen described the natives as seeking and eagerly embracing alliances with them.

Even the Norman pirate captain who had inadvertently landed on the coast of Brazil in 1504 improvised a symbol of a relationship based upon affiliation. On a cross planted on the coast, he had carved the words "Binot Paulmier de Gonneville has planted this sacred [palm] his [Norman] company and our [Carijó] descendents associating equally."[103] Paulmier de Gonneville envisioned an affiliation of the Carajós and "his company." Indigenous willingness to participate in an alliance signaled that the French had not conquered the land, but rather had been able to persuade the natives voluntarily to ally with the crown of France.

That the natives were portrayed as so eagerly seeking an alliance with the French in fact reflected what the French were seeking in the New World. From the very first letters patent for colonization of the New World, the crown suggested that Frenchmen were "to travel to reach said foreign country, to land and to go into it, and set these [countries] in our hand [i.e., our control, our authority] if possible by means of friendship or amicable terms."[104] The actual beginning of

---

100 Thevet, *France Antartique*, 121, 126, 127.   101 Crespin, *Histoire des martyrs*, 436.

102 François Belleforest, *L'histoire universel du monde*, (Paris, 1570), 2: col. 2193. This is actually an invention on Belleforest's part, clearly part of the editorial process which made Cartier's account palatable to sixteenth-century audiences. The more accurate statement that it was the French who desired the alliance would appear in taking possession of Lousiana. "From the 6th to the 10th of September (1719), Du Rivage was engraving on a post with the arms of the king and the Company. The day and year of the taking of possession [Louisiana colony], it was planted in the middle of the village. The savages asked me what it meant. I told them that it was to mark the alliance that we had made with them." Margry, *Découvertes et établissements*, 6: 297.

103 The Latin is cryptic: "Hic sacra Palmarivs Posvit Gonivilla Binotvs / Grex socivs Pariter, Nevstraqve Progenies." The translation given was suggested by my colleague Katherine Drew.

104 "Lettres patentes accordez a François de la Roque, seigneur de Roberval, Jan. 15, 1540," in *Collection de manuscrits . . . relatifs a la Nouvelle-France* (Quebec, 1883), 30–36. This language was repeated in the subsequent letter of Henry II, who merely added the phrase "placing them in our allegiance" at the end. "Edict of Henry II to sieur de la Roche, Jan. 12, 1598," in Marc Lescarbot, *Historie de la Nouvelle-France* (Paris, 1866; orig. pub. 1612), liv. 3, chap. xxxii.

the French colonization of Canada proceeded under the 1603 commission to the Lord (*sieur*) of Monts. De Monts was to "negotiate and develop peace, alliance and confederation, good friendship, connections and communication with said people and their princes. . . . To maintain, respect, and carefully observe the treaties and alliances you have agreed upon with them."[105]

While officially commanded to seek alliances, Frenchmen were also authorized to use force. The first charter permitted Frenchmen to conquer "if it comes to that by force of arms," and the Sieur De Monts's patent added that "failing this [securing peaceful alliances] you are to war upon them openly in order to . . . [secure] the establishment, maintenance, and preservation of our authority among them [the natives]." Frenchmen preferred to envision themselves to be creating a consensual colonialism that they termed an "alliance."

While an alliance signified an agreement voluntarily entered into by both parties, it did not necessarily imply parity. Jean Bodin divided friendly alliances into two categories: equal and unequal. Between identically endowed and equipped European powers, an equal alliance was possible. But between disproportionately endowed parties, whether in military might or in wealth, the relationship was unequal. Alliance simply ensured mutual obligation – even though the responsibilities differed substantially. According to Bodin the superior party usually supplied the weaker with military protection in exchange for respect and deference.[106] Yet because the alliances were voluntarily entered into, the term implied a distinct type of native political subordination; it did not automatically make natives French subjects.[107] In some overseas territories, such as the Amazon, all natives became French subjects, while in others, such as Canada, only Christianized natives became subjects. The political relationship termed an alliance implied the natives's duty of reverence to the crown, but not automatic obedience. While all Europeans from time to time formed partnerships with native peoples, only the French described the basis of their on-going political relationship to natives as an alliance, created by visible physical evidence of native consent.[108]

---

105 "Commission du Roy au sieur de Monts, Nov. 8, 1603," in Lescarbot, *Histoire,* liv. 4, chap. 1.

106 Bodin, *République,* liv. 1, chap. 7, 105–106. The relationship of alliance was slightly more equal than that Bodin believes exists between the monarch and his subjects. In a French state the people had to swear an oath to be faithful to the monarch and to observe his laws, but the monarch was not obliged to make a reciprocal oath, because he could only make an oath to God. Ibid., chap. 8, 143.

107 Ibid., chap. 7, 105–106; liv. 1, chap. 8, 143.

108 The Mohegans became allies of the English moving into Connecticut, and the Jamestown colonists allied with the Chickahominies. But these were not standard practices. I am grateful to Karen Ordahl Kupperman for supplying this information.

The theatrical rituals of French possession-taking also led to a different French cultural creation, ballet. Beginning at the end of the sixteenth century, a formal, highly specified vocabulary of movement called ballet emerged at the courts of Henri III and Louis XIV.[109] Ballet fixes an elaborate set of classifications for all of the positions and movements of the body. All of the motions are carefully proscribed; but so too are the positions of the body at rest. A set of labels attaches to every position of the face, of the arms, of the legs. Facing front to the right side on a diagonal has one label if the right foot is forward (*effacé devant*) another (*croisé devant*) if the left foot is forward. The precision of the steps, the positioning of the head, the direction the body faces, all ordered and controlled the natural motions of dance. Because highly regulated movement historically had created political order and instituted royal power both at home and overseas, it was logical that ballet debuted at the French court.[110]

Among the English the actions of taking possession and of establishing the cultural symbols of possessing land belonged to the realm of the everyday rather than the ceremonialized world. Ordinary acts of construction – cutting down wood, splitting logs, fitting them together – erected the cultural symbols of possession – buildings, houses, fences. The aesthetics of order and control expressed in English gardening and architectural structures resurfaced, but in carefully orchestrated theatricalized rituals produced for French audiences.

English- as well as French-speaking colonists were convinced that "actions speak," but the context and meanings of such acts differed dramatically. Englishmen considered that rights over property were obviously expressed through action, whereas Frenchmen characteristically understood body language to communicate political consent between peoples. Furthermore, English colonists believed their own actions in planting gardens and fields transparently conveyed their own rights of possession; the French found the actions of the natives in greeting them and participating in their ceremonies as unambiguously communicating their wishes to have the French rule over them. In both cases, Englishmen and Frenchmen were equally convinced that physical expressions or actions clearly established rights of possession. But the French believed that they understood the meaning of the Indians' actions; the English believed everybody else in the world

109 P. L. Jacob, *Ballets et mascarades de cour de Henri III a Louis XIV, 1581–1652*, 6 vols. (Geneva, 1968).

110 When royal entrance processions ceased to be held in the mid-seventeenth century, ritualized and stylized movement was shifted to the private theater of the court. Bryant, *Parisian Royal Entry*, 217. Focus upon the aesthetic aspects of movement increased in importance as dance ceased to create public political power.

(including the Indians) could understand the significance of what they were doing. The arrogance of English colonists about the transparency of their own actions was matched by the French colonists' conceit regarding their ability to interpret the natives' actions correctly.

Theatrical rituals often created French possession of the New World through carefully choreographed steps by costumed participants bearing carefully chosen props, accompanied by music, and culminating in the climactic moment of cross- or standard-planting. Even when such intricate ceremonies were not held, Frenchmen closely monitored the repertoire of gestures, facial expressions, and emotions on the faces of those who watched them enacting possession for signs of assent. French possession-taking ceremonies were more elaborate, lengthy, and rigidly structured than any other European power's.

Nearly all other European powers required only a few ceremonial elements – at most handing over turf and twig for the English, reading the Requirement for the Spaniards, taking astronomical measurements for the Portuguese, making maps and descriptions for the Dutch. Among the European powers, Spanish officials most resembled the French in their concern for due solemnity in establishing authority overseas but, unlike the French, often left its form up to individuals.

Ferdinand and Isabel merely ordered Columbus to take possession of new lands "with appropriate ceremony and words." No specific steps, motions, or gestures were specified, only a requisite degree of solemnity. Unoccupied territory was later claimed by crosses carved on trees or nopal cactuses, or by stones piled beside an ocean. Viceroy Antonio de Mendoza instructed an expedition to the north of Mexico to "take possession of it for His Majesty and make the signs and [written] documents that the case appears to require." In contrast with the elaborate ballets enacting French possession, Spanish ceremonies were often a theater of improvisation. Twenty years after Columbus's gestures, improvised ceremonies were only performed to claim uninhabited territory. If there were people, a specific ritual speech was required.[111]

Even the most elaborate French overseas ceremony required no set speech. Speeches and discussions frequently occurred, often centering on the meaning of the gestures being made. Indians were customarily informed that they were obligating themselves to the French

---

111 *Colección de documentos inéditos, relativos al descubrimiento, conquista y organización de las antiguas posesiones españolas en América y Oceania*, 42 vols. (Madrid, 1864–1884), 13: 325–328, esp. 327–328. The requirement is summarized in the instructions: "You will give the natives of the land to understand that there is God in heaven and the Emperor on earth, who exists to command and to govern all those who are obliged/compelled/to serve and be his subjects."

monarch or queried about the meaning of their gestures, for example, crossing the fingers (mimicking the sign of the cross). For the French, the motions, sequences of gestures, costumes, and above all physical actions, not words, enacted colonial authority. But for the Spanish it was the words that mattered. A highly formalized and stylized speech known as the Requirement had to be made when encountering indigenous peoples for the first time. The text of the speech was not a request for consent, but a declaration of war.

3

THE REQUIREMENT

A PROTOCOL FOR CONQUEST

On behalf of His Majesty, . . . I . . . his servant, messenger . . . notify and make known as best I can that God our Lord one and eternal created heaven and earth . . . God our Lord gave charge [of all peoples] to one man named Saint Peter, so that he was lord and superior of all the men of the world . . . and gave him all the world for his lordship and jurisdiction (*señorío y jurisdicción*). . . . One of these Pontiffs . . . made a donation of these islands and mainland of the Ocean Sea to the Catholic kings of Spain. . . . Almost all who have been notified [of this] have received His Majesty and obeyed and served him, and serve him as subjects . . . and turned Christian without reward or stipulation . . . and His Majesty received them . . . as . . . subjects and vassals. . . . . Therefore I beg and require you as best I can . . . [that] you recognize the church as lord and superior of the universal world, and the most elevated Pope . . . in its name, and His Majesty in his place as superior and lord and king . . . and consent that these religious fathers declare and preach . . . and His Majesty and I in his name will receive you . . . and will leave your women and children free, without servitude so that with them and with yourselves you can freely do what you wish . . . and we will not compel you to turn Christians. But if you do not do it . . . with the help of God, I will enter forcefully against you, and I will make war everywhere and however I can, and I will subject you to the yoke and obedience of the Church and His Majesty, and I will take your wives and children, and I will make them slaves . . . and I will take your goods, and I will do to you all the evil and damages that a lord may do to vassals who do not obey or receive him. And I solemnly declare that the deaths and damages received from such will be your fault and not that of His Majesty, nor mine, nor of the gentlemen who came with me.[1]

1 There are multiple texts of the Requirement. *Colección de documentos ineditos relativos al descubrimiento . . . en América y Oceanía* (hereafter cited as *CDI*), 43 vols., (Madrid, 1864–1884), 20: 311–314; Antonio Herrera, *Historia general de los hechos de los Castellanos,* dec. 1, liv. 7, cap. 14 (Madrid, 1935), 3: 170–172; José Toribio Medina, *El descubrimento del Océano Pacífico* (Santiago, 1920), 2: 287–289; Bartolomé de Las Casas, *Historia de las Indias,* 3 vols. (Mexico, 1986), lib. 3, cap. 57; for Peru, Diego Encinas, *Cedulario indiano,* ed. Alfonso García Gallo (Madrid, 1946), 4: 226–227; for Panama, Manuel Serrano y Sanz, *Orígenes de la dominación española: estudios históricos* (Madrid, 1918), 1: 292–294; Gonzalo Fernández de Oviedo, *Historia general y natural las Indias,* 5 vols. (Madrid, 1959), 3: 28–29. Lewis Hanke translated the Requirement in his *History of Latin American Civilization,* 2 vols. (Boston, 1973), 1: 93–95.

This speech, called the Requirement (*Requirimiento*), was the principal means by which Spaniards enacted political authority over the New World during the era of their most extensive conquests (1512–1573). Read aloud to New World natives from a written text, the Requirement was an ultimatum for Indians to acknowledge the superiority of Christianity or be warred upon.

Unlike French practices of seeking an alliance and watching the faces and gestures of indigenous peoples for signs of assent, Spaniards created their rights to the New World through conquest not consent. While English rules governed the planting of fences, gardens, and houses, and French rules governed the conduct of ceremonies, Spanish rules governed the procedures for declaring war.

To initiate a war that results in legitimate political dominion over the conquered, the procedures for launching it must be carefully proscribed by the same political authorities that will later claim to have established lawful dominion. To establish the right to rule by virtue of conquest means that all the soldiers, captains, and leaders in battle must follow the political steps they have been commanded to undertake. For what is at stake is not simply their own personal control over a region, but the legitimate government of an entire state. To omit the rituals would be to jeopardize the establishment of legitimate dominion. Hence, it was not necessary for soldiers or their leaders to find the rhetoric or logic of the declaration of war compelling or convincing. It was only necessary that they observe its protocol, as they had been commanded to do.

The threat of warfare contained in the Requirement was one of the most distinctive features of Spanish colonialism. No other European state created a fully ritualized protocol for declaring war against indigenous peoples. Warfare against native peoples was, for the most part, a decision made by local communities, governor-generals, or confederations of towns, undertaken by a consensus or decision by European settlers inhabiting the Americas. Official consent was sometimes required, but formal procedures for initiating war against natives were rarely dictated and equally rarely observed. Only Spaniards carried with them a protocol created on the orders of their king, and which they were directed to read before launching an attack.

Because it was constructed and ordered implemented by the Spanish crown, the Requirement defined the formalities for launching a war in political terms. It set the aims of the warfare not as mere surrender, but as submission to Catholicism and its legitimate representatives, the Spaniards. The Requirement was thus both a military and a political ritual. But as a ritual for declaring war it was uniquely Spanish, having no parallel in any other European culture. Other Europeans found both its method of implementation and its demands

unfamiliar; many prominent Englishmen, Frenchmen, and Dutchmen mocked it. Walter Ralegh derided it, as did Michel de Montaigne
and the Dutch writer Johannes de Laet.[2]

Even the eminent Spanish Dominican Bartolomé de Las Casas wrote
that when he heard the Requirement he did not know whether to laugh
or to cry.[3] When read at full speed from the deck of a ship at night before a daytime raid, when read to assembled empty huts and trees,
when muttered into thick Spanish beards, the way the Requirement
was implemented strikes many even today as absurd as the text itself.

The apparently preposterous character of the text includes the form
of the demand and its substance. It "requires" that indigenous peoples
of the New World acknowledge the church as superior of the world
and therefore consent to have priests preach to them. It contains an
equally mystifying promise that such submission will result in Spanish
soldiers leaving "your women and children free," not compelling anyone to turn Christian. But this was not an entirely free choice. If they
failed to acknowledge the superiority of Christianity, they could be
warred upon "everywhere and however" possible. Finally, there is the
incredible disclaimer that by rejecting this demand all the deaths and
devastation caused by the Spanish attack were the fault of the natives
for rejecting their demands. There is, on the surface at least, nothing
more absurd than a demand that a community of natives to whom the
text was being read (assuming, of course, they understood sixteenth-
century Spanish) acknowledge the "church as lord and superior of the
world" or else be warred against and "subject[ed] . . . to the yoke and
obedience of the Church and their Highnesses." The Requirement of-
fers limited options – either accept Christian superiority voluntarily,
or we will impose submission at the point of a sword or a harquebus.
Being told they will not be "compel[led] to turn Christian" by a full
complement of Spanish soldiers armed to the teeth with the very lat-
est in sophisticated European weaponry created a further apparent absurdity.[4] It was not merely the text itself that created the absurdity, but
the context in which it was delivered.

What appears ludicrous is most often what is unfamiliar. And de-
cidedly alien to most of Christian Europe were the practices of Spain's

2 Michel de Montaigne, "Des Coches," in *Essais*, ed. Pierre Villey, 3 vols. (Paris, 1965),
3: 169; Joannes de Laet, *Nieuwe Wereldt* (Leiden, 1630), 1–2. Ralegh writes, "No
Christian prince, under the pretence of Christianity only, and of forcing of men
to receive the gospel . . . may attempt the invasion of any free people not under
their vassalge; for Christ gave not that power to Christians as Christians." Walter
Ralegh, *History of the World in Five Books*, 8 vols. (Philadelphia, 1820; orig. pub.
1614), 6: 122.
3 Las Casas, "Cosa es de reir o de llorar," in *Historia de las Indias*, lib. 3, cap. 58, 3: 31.
4 This is Montaigne's critique of the Requirement's claim that the Spaniards came in
peace. "Que quand à estre paisible, ils [les Espagnoles] n'en portoient pas la mine."
Montaigne, "Des Coches," in *Essais*, 3: 169.

longest imperial rulers – Moslems. The Requirement most closely resembles the unique ritual demand for submission characteristic of the military version of an Islamic jihad. While the term *jihad* means only "struggle," it has been subject to a variety of controversial interpretations. Not all its meanings involve armed force; some scholars argue that it does not even primarily signify armed contest, yet historically it has had such a meaning. When used to imply combat, jihad (struggle) was a specific kind of warfare. It was neither a border raid nor skirmish,[5] but a form of warfare ordained by God and practiced by Moslems in the early years of Islam.[6] On the Iberian peninsula in particular, jihad meant fighting according to proper legal principles.[7]

While not the original form of Spanish authority in the New World, the Requirement was the most enduring. Designed by the eminent Spanish legal scholar Juan López Palacios Rubios in 1512, it was created as a result of a crisis in the earlier forms of enacting Spanish authority in the New World.

During their first two decades in the New World, Spaniards ventured little beyond the narrow confines of the Caribbean to which Columbus had led them. Experimenting with a variety of forms of political authority over the New World, the Spanish crown's goal of legitimate dominion suffered a setback in 1511 when it was attacked by the Dominican friars of the Caribbean island of Hispaniola. In a fiery sermon denouncing the religious and political practices of the leaders of Spain's wealthiest overseas colony, the Dominican fathers forced the crown itself to a critical reevaluation of the procedures it had been following to guarantee legitimacy of its own rule.[8]

Inviting a legal opinion from Palacios Rubios and a leading expert on church law – Fray Matías de la Paz – the crown received new advice on how best to establish its authority. In Palacios Rubios's response – supported by Paz – was a section describing how the crown might legitimately constitute its rule.[9] This section was transformed into an official statement – the Requirement – which all Spaniards were required to read before subjecting New World peoples to the

5 These are more usually identified as *razzia*. An excellent history of Moslem–Christian border skirmishing is James F. Powers, *A Society Organized for War: The Iberian Municipal Militias in the Central Middle Ages, 1000–1284* (Berkeley, 1988).

6 Ibn Khaldun, describes two kinds of "holy and just wars": those the religious law calls holy and "against seceders and those who refuse obedience." Khaldun, *The Mugaddimah: An Introduction to History*, trans. Franz Rosenthal, ed. and abr. N. J. Daood (Princeton, N.J., 1967), 123–124.

7 Federico Corriente, *El léxico árabe andalusí según P. de Alcalá* (Zaragoza, 1988), 38.

8 For a critical history of this episode, see Patricia Seed, " 'Are These Not Also Men?': The Indian's Humanity and Capacity for Spanish Civilization," *Journal of Latin American Studies*, 25 (1993): 629–652.

9 Juan López Palacios Rubios, *De las islas del mar océano*, and Matías de la Paz, *Del dominio de los reyes de España sobre los indios*, trans. Augustín Millares Carlo (México, 1954), 36–37, 250–252.

crown of Castile. Reading the Requirement thus became the mechanism which enacted Spanish political authority over the peoples of the New World. Its historic roots lay in the history of another early conquest – that of the Iberian peninsula itself.

In the century following the death of the Prophet Muhammad (632), Islam expanded rapidly eastward and westward, conquering Syria and Iraq, Egypt and Spain. Like the Spaniards in the New World, the Arabs were relatively few, and their enemies numerous. They fought in small bands, often on horseback, and defeated well-equipped armies tens and hundreds of times their own size.[10] Only a handful of Moslem warriors defeated a population of 2.5 million Christians on the Iberian peninsula.

Rapidly finding themselves in control of a vast territory stretching from Baghdad to Toledo, and from Aden to Zaragosa, the leaders of the eighth-century Arab empire were militarily ill-equipped to defend a territorial whole. Flooding the area with Arab settlers (or Berbers in Al-Andalus) was impossible, given the relatively small size of the conquering population. What it could and did devise most effectively was a policy of ruling over conquered people, a great many elements of which would be imitated by the Spaniards in their conquest of the New World.

From its early years on, Islam did not separate political from religious rule. "Government and religion are two brothers, neither can stand without the other" was a popular saying from the second or third century of the Islamic empire.[11] However, Moslems soon came to disagree among themselves regarding the details of this relationship. After a theological and leadership succession dispute similar to that splitting Eastern from Roman Christendom, Shi'a and Sunni Islam diverged. Spain, the western edge of the Islamic world, remained Sunni.

Substantial differences also soon emerged within Sunni Islam over jurisprudence (*fikh*), how best to govern an Islamic community. Roughly two to three hundred years after the death of the Prophet, there emerged four distinctive traditions referred to by the names of their founders: Ḥanafī (Abū Ḥanīfa), Shāfi'ī (Idris al Shāfi'ī), Ḥanbalī (Aḥmad b. Ḥanbal), Mālikī (Mālik b. Anas).

Each of the schools are currently dominant within different parts of the Islamic world and have distinctive characteristics. The Ḥanafites are the only ones to permit the recitation of the Qur'an in a language

---

10 J.J. Saunders, *A History of Medieval Islam* (London, 1965), 39–57, 82–94; Hugh Kennedy, *The Prophet and the Age of the Caliphates: The Islamic Near East from the Sixth to the Eleventh Century* (London, 1986), 57–69.

11 The quote is from a collection of maxims on statecraft dating from the seventh to the ninth centuries of the Christian era. Bernard Lewis, *Islam: From the Prophet Muhammad to the Capture of Constantinople*; vol. 1, *Politics and War* (New York, 1987), 1: 184.

other than Arabic; they dominate India and countries formerly part of the Ottoman Turkish Empire. Shaf'ites follow a systematic deductive procedure for legal rulings and dominate Egypt, Syria, South Arabia, and Indonesia. Ḥanbalites, formerly influential in Iraq, Egypt, Syria, and Palestine, are now confined to Whahhabi in central Arabia.[12] But by the early ninth century most of Moslem Spain had embraced the earliest school of jurisprudence based upon the teachings of Mālik (d. Medina 795), noted for its emphasis upon ritual and religious dimensions of legal life.[13]

In addition to separate traditions of governing a community of believers, each school evolved slightly different legal procedures for launching a jihad. Mālikī jurisprudence was and is noted for two distinctive characteristics in this area: its emphasis on a legal ritual for initiating a jihad (a summons), and its liberal treatment of defeated peoples. Spaniards would adapt both features in governing the New World. To illustrate distinctive Mālikī characteristics in launching a jihad and treating subject peoples, I will use the writings from the great twelfth-century Andalusī Mālikī scholar Ibn Rushd, known in the West as Averroes.

Ibn Rushd (Averroes) summarized Mālikī jurisprudence on jihad in his legal handbook *Bidāyat al-Mudjtahid.*[14] The first critical step in launching a jihad is that a messenger must be sent announcing one's intentions to the enemy.[15] For some Islamic schools of law, the mere

12 "Fikh," *Encyclopaedia of Islam.* Gustave E. Von Grunebaum, *Medieval Islam: A Study in Cultural Orientation,* 2d ed. (Chicago, 1954), 153.

13 Abdel Magid Turki, "La veneration pour Mālik et la physionomie du Mālikisme andalou," in *Studia Islamica,* 33 (1971): 41–65. Mālikite jurisprudence replaced the earlier jurisprudential forms beginning at the end of the reign of the Umayyad ruler 'Abd al Raḥmān I. The major criticism of Mālikī jurisprudence came from Ibn Hazm in the eleventh century. Maḥmūd 'Alī Makkī, *Ensayo sobre las aportaciones orientales en la España musulmana* (Madrid, 1968), 87–106, 134–149, 183–186. See also Mālik b. Anas," *Encyclopaedia of Islam.*

14 Averroes was born in Córdoba (Spain) in 1126 and was a judge, physician, and philosopher. He died in Marrakesh in 1198. In *Bidāyat al-Mudjtahid,* he comments on all the minor differences in practices regarding waging a war among all the major branches of Islam present on the Iberian peninsula. An English translation is *Jihad in Mediaeval* [sic] *and Modern Islam,* trans. Rudolph Peters (Leiden, 1977). Mālik's own work (*Kitāb al-Jihād*) is in *Muwaṭṭa' Imam Mālik,* trans. Muhammad Rahimuddin (Lahore, 1980), 198–213.

15 Averroes, *Bidāyat al-Mudjtahid,* 20. While the sending of a messenger was not the custom in all Islamic communities, it was always the characteristic of the Malekite school. Ibn Abī Zayd al-Qayrawānī, *La risala ou épître sur les éléments du dognme e de la loi de l'islam selon le rite malekite,* trans. Leon Bercher (Algiers, 1975), chap. 30; see also al-Māwardī (d. 1058), ibid., 76, 119; Ibn Hudhayl (d. 1399). The Hanafite school does not insist upon the summons. Edgard Weber and Georges Renaud, *Croisade d'hier, dijad d'aujourd'hui* (Paris, 1989), 118. Some scholars have argued that the attribution of the summons to Muhammad is apocryphal. See Benjamin Kedar, *Crusade and Mission: European Approaches Toward the Muslims* (Princeton, N.J., 1984), 37n91. However, it was adopted early in Islam and used on the Iberian peninsula from the beginning of the Arab conquest.

existence of the faith of Islam or a prior summons at a much earlier date was a sufficient message to the unbelievers. But the Mālikī school of jurisprudence paid far greater attention to ritual than did other schools.[16] Hence, Islamic rules on the Iberian Peninsula insisted strictly upon the official sending of an announcement – sometimes called by other schools a "double summons."[17] Like the Requirement, it was a public ritual, addressing itself in a highly stylized form to the unbelievers.

According to Averroes, an enemy must have heard the announcement of the new religion (Islam) following the injunction of Q. 17:15, "We have not been accustomed to punish until We have sent a messenger."[18] The person sent to announce the new religion (or to punish unbelievers) was called a messenger; the Arabic term Averroes used is *rasūl*.

The use of the term *messenger* to send a declaration was distinctively Islamic and characteristic of all its schools of law. In classical Greek warfare, the person sent with terms and conditions for declaring warfare was customarily a *keryx* (singer), in Roman warfare a *fetial* (one who places), later a legate, and in medieval Western warfare an ambassador. In classical Western traditions there were complex protocols for the treatment of ambassadors.[19] The word *messenger* in Western warfare signified a mere runner and had no special political significance.

But the word *messenger* had special significance in Islam. The prophet Muhammad described himself a messenger of God (*rasūl Allāh*) indicating his role in announcing a new religion. Similarly when conveying the notification of the new religion prior to a jihad, the Prophet described himself both as the messenger of God (*rasūl Allāh*) and a messenger (*rasūl*) bearing news of the new religion to non-Moslem rulers.[20]

---

16 O. Saidi, "The Unification of the Maghrib Under the Almohads," in D. T. Niane, ed., *Africa from the Twelfth to the Sixteenth Century*, vol. 4 of *General History of Africa*, 8 vols. (Berkeley, 1981–1993), 17–18.

17 Ibn Abī Zayd al-Qayrawānī (Mālikite jurist of the tenth century), *La risala*, chap. 30; Halīl ibn Isḥāq (fourteenth century), *Il "Muhtasar": Sommario del diritto malechita*, trans. Ignazio Guidi, 2 vols. (Milan, 1919), 1: lib. 8, no. 3; Robert Brunschvig, "Ibn 'Abdalh'akam et la Conquête de l'Afrique du nord par les Arabes," *Etudes sur l'Islam Classique et l'Afrique du Nord* (London, 1986), 11: 108–122. For contrast, see L. W. C. Van Den Berg, *Principes du droit musulman selon les rites d'about Ḥanīfa et de Chaʿfīʿi*, trans. R. de France de Tersant and M. Damiens (Algers, 1896), 225–226. See also Ann K. S. Lambton, *State and Government in Medieval Islam* (Oxford, 1981), 214; Albrecht Noth, *The Early Arabic Tradition: A Source-Critical Study*, trans. Michael Bonner (Princeton, N.J., 1994), 161.

18 Averroes, *Bidāyat al-Mudjtahid*, 20.

19 Yvon Garlan, *War in the Ancient World: A Social History*, trans. Janet Lloyd (New York, 1975), 44–50, 58–59; Alberico Gentilli, *De legationibus libri tres*, trans. Gordon J. Laing, 2 vols. (New York, 1924); Cornelius Van Bijinkershoek, *De foro legatorum liber singularis* (Oxford, 1946).

20 On the role of Muhammad or his messenger in summoning non-Moslems, see, e.g., the hadith in Al-Bukhārī, *The Translation of the Meanings of Sahih al-Bukhārī*, trans.

The representative of the Islamic state announcing the new religion was invariably termed messenger (*rasūl*). This is the identical term used by all texts of the Requirement to describe the envoy of the Spanish state proclaiming the new religion – Christianity – as a messenger.[21]

The task of the Islamic messenger was to deliver a very specific demand. According to Averroes, the envoy must first "summon them to conversion to Islam."[22] The word *summon* in Arabic (*daʿā*) means to "invite," "call for," "implore," "demand."[23] Its Spanish translation is the verb *requerir*.[24] Hence, the words of address to the natives of the New World, "I implore and summon you," express the two central meanings of the Arabic verb *daʿā*. Since it is the verb *requerir* in this statement that gave this text its name in Spanish – the *Requerimiento*, or Requirement – the title of the document signifies inviting people to accept a new religion, a Catholic summons to God.

In the Iberian Islamic tradition, the purpose of the summons was to invite the other person to accept Islam. According to Islamic tradition, the Prophet Muhammad would write to those against whom he was starting a jihad, "Now then, I invite you to Islam [surrender to Allah]."[25] The word *islam* itself means "submission" (sometimes translated "surrender"). Submission signifies a recognition of superiority. According to Islamic tradition, Muhammad used the word *aslim* (submit to Islam) in his summons.

The core of the Spanish requirement was also a summons to acknowledge a superior religion. It likewise insisted upon submission: "I implore and summon/require [you] . . . to recognize the church as

Muhammad Muhsin Khan (Beirut, 1985), 4: 116, 117; *Ṣaḥīḥ Muslim*, trans. ʿAbdul Ḥamīd Ṣiddīqī (Beirut, 1972), 3: 969, 971. For a classic hadith with both terms, see *Bukhārkī*, 4: 121. Muhammad also described himself as the slave of God.

21 For the use of this form to the Byzantines, see Marius Canard, "Les relations politiques et sociales entre Byzance et les Arabes," *Dumbarton Oaks Papers*, no. 18 (Washington, D.C., 1964), 33–56. For examples of the use of *mensajero*, see Serrano y Sanz, *Dominacíon española*, 1: 293; *CDI*, 20: 311; Medina, *Descubrimento*, 2: 288; Herrera, *Historia general* 3: 170.

22 Averroes, *Bidāyat al-Mudjtahid*, 20. In the hadith collection of Al-Bukhārī, "The invitation to Islam is essential before declaring war." See *Al-Bukhārī*, 4: 116. For another example, see Lewis, *Islam*; vol. 1, *Politics and War*, 228.

23 This is the word used in the hadith collections: *Al-Bukhārī*, 4: 116–117, 121, 123, *Ṣaḥīḥ Muslim*, 3: 971. It appears in this sense in Q. 24:24, 52, and 40:12. Hans Wehr, *A Dictionary of Modern Written Arabic*, ed. J. Milton Cowan, 3d ed. (Ithaca, N.Y., 1971), 282–283. It is also sometimes transcribed as *daʿwa*.

24 Reinhart Dozy, *Supplément aux dictionnaires arabes* (Beirut, 1981), 444–446. The other Arabic verb meaning the same thing is *wajaba*. Pedro Alcalá, *Arte para ligeramente saber a lengua arabe* (Granada, 1505), uses *daʿā* to mean "requerir que hagan justicia, llamar al que a de venir, citación, demanda." Corriente, *El léxico árabe andalusí*, 66. Covarrubias, *Tesoro* (1611), gives as synonyms for *requerir* – intimar, advertir, avisar.

25 *Al-Bukhārī*, 4: 121; *Ṣaḥīḥ Muslim*, 3: 971, the phrase is translated as "I extend to you the invitation to accept Islam." A 633 letter to the Persian kings, an example of a summoning to submission in English, is in Lewis, *Politics and War*, 228.

owner and superior of the universal world." This meaning is virtually identical to what Moslems understood by "surrendering to Allah," namely, acknowledging the superiority of Islam.

Neither in mainstream Islam nor in mainstream Catholicism was conversion supposed to take place immediately, much less at the point of a sword.[26] "The objective of the jihad . . . was not fighting per se, but the proselytization of unbelievers," writes Majid Khadduri.[27] In a Qur'anic verse recited by Muslims after Friday prayers, this position is explicit: "There is no compulsion in religion."[28] In another verse (Q. 49:14) the Qur'an points out that God does not want instant professions of belief, since faith cannot be coerced. Hence, an immediate profession by unbelievers would not be credible. Therefore, Muhammad said that he first wanted submission, recognition of the *superiority* of the religion of truth (Islam). "The desert Arabs say, 'We believe.' [You] Say, 'Ye have no faith; but ye (only) say, 'We have submitted our wills to Allah,' for not yet has Faith entered your hearts.' "[29] Those who surrendered to Moslems in a jihad were thus to recognize the superiority of Islam. Belief would come later.

The Arabic language itself differentiates between believers and those who have merely submitted. *Muslim* means one who submits, *mu'min*, one who believes. Those of the Islamic faith refer to each other as believers, *mu'min*, rather than *muslim*, those who have surrendered. This principle of uncoerced conversion in Islam was recognized by none other than Bartolomé de Las Casas. Writing in a treatise that would remain unpublished until this century, he wrote, "Muhammad forced no one to join his belief . . . so long as they remained subject . . . he forced them no further."[30]

This was just what those targeted by the Spanish Requirement in the New World were obligated to do. The Qur'anic phrase "no compulsion

---

26 This is one of the principal caricatures of Islam in anti-Moslem polemics, dating back to the ninth century. Kedar, *Crusade and Mission*, 24–25. See e.g., the famous anti-Muslim tract of Ricoldo of Montecroce (1243–1320), a Dominican missionary in Bagdhad, summarized in J. Windrow Sweetman, *Islam and Christian Theology* (London, 1955), pt. 2, 1: 116–159, esp. 130, 141–142.

27 Majid Khadduri, "International law," in Khadduri and Herbert J. Liebesny, eds., *Law in the Middle East: Origin and Development of Islamic Law* (Washington, D.C., 1955), 355.

28 Q. 2:256; Ayatullah Sayyid Mahumud Taleqani, "Jihad and Shahadat," in Mehdi Abedi and Gary Legenhausen, eds., *Jihad and Shahadat: Struggle and Martyrdom in Islam* (Houston, 1986), 51.

29 *The Meaning of the Holy Qur'an*, trans. Yūsuf Alī (Washington, D.C., 1991), 1343. Another translation reads, "The Bedouin say, 'We have attained to faith.' Say [unto them, O Muhammad]: 'You have not [yet] attained to faith'; you should [rather] say, 'We have [outwardly] surrendered' – for [true] faith has not yet entered your hearts." *Message of the Qur'an*, trans. Muhammad Asad (Gibraltar, 1980), 794–795.

30 Bartolomé de Las Casas, *The Only Way*, trans. Francis Patrick Sullivan, S.J. (Mahwah, N.J., 1992), 147. A recent edition is *De unico vocationis modo*, ed. Paulino Castañeda Delgado and Antonio García del Moral (Madrid, 1988).

in religion" was echoed almost literally in the Requirement – "We shall not compel them to turn Christian." The Catholic Requirement demanded only that the natives had to submit immediately, to outwardly surrender by acknowledging the superiority of Christianity – "recognize the church as ruler and superior of the universal world." In the Christian as well as in the Islamic summons, individuals did not have to attain the faith instantly – but like those confronted by a messenger of Allah, they had to promptly accept the superiority of the new religion. In the Requirement as in the summons to Islam, refusal to acknowledge religious superiority was the moment of truth, for in both cases rejection justified war.

The Mālikī summons to Islam threatened those who did not surrender with warfare. Averroes explained, "If they consent to that [summons], accept it and refrain from [attacking] them. But if they refuse it, then invoke the help of Allah and attack them."[31] The words of the Requirement are very similar: "But if you do not do it [acknowledge the superiority of Christianity and admit Christian preachers] . . . with the help of God, I will enter powerfully against you, and I will make war everywhere and however I can." The central idea of the Requirement – summoning people to acknowledge a superior religion or be attacked – is thus the same as the core of the summons as understood in the Islamic legal tradition of the Iberian peninsula.

The request to acknowledge a superior religion or be attacked which characterized both the Islamic summons and Catholic Requirement was highly unusual in classic Western warfare. The procedures for initiating engagement in classical Greek and Roman warfare also began with a declaration of intent to attack and demand for surrender. The terms of capitulation, however, never took the form of "submission" to the superiority of an alien religion. Roman and Greek forms of warfare required subordination to superior political and military forces without acknowledging a worthier faith.[32]

While Moslem rulers often demanded various forms of publicly deferential behavior, including distinctive dress, the Qur'an itself demanded only one special form of submission.[33] To recognize the superiority of Islam concretely signified a ritual humiliation. To show that they had been shamed by an Islamic conquest, the defeated were required to pay an annual tax called *jizya*.[34] This aim is explicitly laid

31 Averroes, *Bidāyat al-Mudjtahid*, 20; Hadith with this language is in *Al-Bukhārī*, 4: 115. See also Lewis, *Politics and War*, 228.

32 Garlan, *War in the Ancient World*, 47–50.

33 Dolores Bramon, *Contra moros y judios* (Barcelona, 1986); Halīl ibn Isḥāq, *Il "Muhtaṣar,"* 1: liv. 8, no. 23. See also Paula Sanders, *Ritual, Politics, and the City in Fatimid Cairo* (Albany, N.Y., 1994), 29–31.

34 This is founded upon an interpretation of Q. 9:29. Hanna E. Kassis, *Concordance of the Qur'an* (Berkeley, 1983), 263, translates it as "until they pay the tribute out of

out in the Qur'an. The verse Q. 9:29 states, "Fight those who believe not in Allah . . . nor acknowledge the religion of truth . . . until they pay the jizya [poll tax] with willing submission and feel themselves subdued [belittled]."[35] The purpose of the poll tax (*jizya*) was thus a personal form of ritual humiliation directed at those defeated by a superior Islam. The Arabic word *wa-hum ṣāghirūn* (to feel themselves subdued) comes from the root *ṣ-gh-r* (small, little, belittled, or humbled).[36] Since its object was personal humiliation, it was therefore a personal tax.[37] It was not paid on land, property, or trade goods. It was demanded of those people who submitted but refused to become Moslems.

Payment of jizya created an economic motive for Islamic states *not* to have subject peoples convert immediately, since upon conversion they would no longer be liable for payment of the poll tax.[38] Hence, Islamic rulers did not want quick conversions for either economic or religious reasons ("no compulsion in religion").

In most schools of Islamic jurisprudence, jizya was collected only from believers in monotheistic religions – Jews, Christians, Zoroastrians – often called collectively "people of the book." On the Iberian peninsula, conquering Moslems imposed jizya upon Christians and Jews.[39]

hand and have been humbled." Pickthall translates it as "until they pay the tribute readily, having been brought low." *The Meaning of the Glorious Koran*, trans. Mohammed Marmaduke Pickthall (London, 1930), 148. For Mālik on jizya see his *Muwaṭṭa'*, 212, 141–142, esp. n134.

35 Q. 9:29 (Yusuf Alī translation). In Averroes the translation is as follows: "Find those who believe not in Allah nor in the last day [the day of Judgment] nor hold forbidden that which has been forbidden by Allah and his apostles nor acknowledge the religion of truth [Islam] even if they are the people of the book until they pay the poll-tax (*jizya*) with willing submission and feel themselves subdued [belittled]." Averroes, *Bidāyat al-Mudjtahid*, 20. Subsequent Western (not Muslim) scholarship has argued that the poll tax was an eighth-century invention (see Julius Wellhausen, *The Arab Kingdom and Its Fall* [Beirut, 1927]) or that it was an adaptation of Byzantine and Sassanian revenue systems. Daniel C. Dennett, *Conversion and the Poll Tax in Early Islam* (Cambridge, Mass., 1950), and F. Løkkegaard, *Islamic Taxation in the Classic Period* (Copenhagen, 1950). In any case, it was in existence by the time of the conquest of Spain and introduced their by Moslem conquerors.

36 S. M. Hasan-uz-Zaman, *Economic Functions of an Islamic State* (Leicester, 1990), 70, also uses the related expression "being brought low." See also Lewis's transcriptions of the seventh-century peace terms in *Politics and War*, 239–241. Later examples are in Arthur Stanley Tritton, *The Caliphs and Their Non-Muslim Subjects* (London, 1970), 227.

37 Ibn al-Fuwaṭī (1167–1247), *Al-Ḥawādīth al-Jāmiʿa*, translated in Norman A. Stillman, *The Jews of Arab Lands: A History and Source Book* (Philadelphia, 1979), 180. Other forms of jizya subsequently evolved within law. See Khalīl Ibn Isḥāk (fourteenth century), *Précis de jurisprudence musulmane selon le rite mālekite*, trans. M. Perron, 4 vols. (Paris, 1849), 2: 292–295, but these were less frequently used on the Iberian peninsula.

38 "Jizya-paying people who became Muslims should be exempted from jizya." Mālik, *Muwaṭṭa'*, 142.

39 On Christians as *dhimmī*s in Spain under Moslem rule, see Evariste Levi-Provençal, *Histoire de l'Espagne musulmane*, 3 vols. (Paris, 1950–1953), 1: 225–239, and Reinhart Dozy, *Histoire des Musulmans d'Espagne jusqu'a la conquête de l'Andalousie par les Almoravides (711–1110)*, 3 vols. (Leiden, 1932) 1: 317.

But the Mālikī school differed from all other schools of jurisprudence. Either more tolerant of unbelievers or more interested in the jizya income they would produce, Mālikī law allowed believers in any non-Muslim faith who submitted to Islam to pay tribute.[40] Hence, *any* unbelievers subdued by Moslems fighting a jihad could be required to pay a poll tax.

What distinguished jizya historically from the Roman form of tribute is that it was exclusively a tax on persons, and on adult men. Roman "tribute" was sometimes a form of borrowing as well as a tax. It could be levied on land, landowners, and slaveholders, as well as on people. Even when assessed on individuals, the amount was often determined by the value of the group's assets and did not depend – as did Islamic jizya – upon actual head counts of men of fighting age.[41] Christian Iberian rulers would later adopt similar taxes during their reconquest of the peninsula.

Up until the eleventh century, Christian victories against Moslems were small; warfare resembled frontier raiding. In 1085 Christians conquered Toledo, their first major Islamic city. Faced with the problem of ruling large Moslem communities, the king of Castile turned for advice to a Portuguese Arab convert to Christianity, Siznado David, who suggested that he accord defeated Moslems the same treatment as Christians had been granted under Islam: payment of a head tax and protections for Moslem communities. Taking his advice, Castilian monarchs began to require defeated Moslems (and Jews) to pay a humiliating annual tax to Christian representatives – just as Moslem rulers had demanded one from them. This head tax, called tribute (*tributo*) was subsequently required in most of the other Iberian Christian kingdoms.[42] This custom would carry over to the conquest of the New World.

40 Averroes discusses the positions of Shāfiʿī and Abū Thawr (d. 854), founder of a school which lasted only a few centuries, who both maintained that these were the only people from whom poll tax could be collected. Mālik says that polltax may be collected from any polytheist. Averroes, *Bidāyat al-Mudjtahid*, 2; Mālik, *Muwaṭṭaʾ*, 142n134; Ibn Ishāk, *Jurisprudence musulmane*, 2: 290–292. See also Brunschvig, *Etudes sur l'Islam classique*, 11: 108–122; R. Dozy, *Histoire des Musulmans d'Espagne*, 1: 140–143; Cahen, "Djizya," in *Encyclopedia of Islam*, 2d ed. This is also born out by the 1505 *Léxico árabe andalusí* of Pedro Alcalá in which *jizya* is defined as "tributo de infieles" (34).

41 Claude Nicolet, *Tributum: Recherches sur la fiscalité directe sous la republique romaine* (Bonn, 1976); Andre Deleage, *La capitation du Bas-empire* (New York, 1975, repr. 1945); Walter Goffart, *Caput and Colonate: Towards a History of Late Roman Taxation* (Toronto, 1974); Erich S. Gruen, *The Hellenistic World and the Coming of Rome*, 2 vols. (Berkeley, 1984), 288–295. Nor was tributary subjection the only way Romans related to conquered people. Romans granted lands to defeated Terivingi (Goths) in 375. Peter J. Heather, *Goths and Romans*, 332–489 (Oxford, 1991), 122–123.

42 Jean-Pierre Molénat, "Mudéjares, cativos e libertos," in Louis Cardaillac, ed., *Toledo, séculos XII-XIII: Muçulmanos, Cristãos e Judeus: o saber e a tolerância*, trans. Lucy Magãl-

In 1501 Queen Isabel declared that her aim was to impose a tax she called tribute upon New World natives. The Indians were "subjects and vassals" of the crown, she declared, and as such "are to pay us our tributes and rights," sentiments that would be repeated again and again in instructions for ruling the New World.[43]

While Isabel stated that Indians would render tribute just "as we are paid by our subjects residents of our kingdoms and lordships," she did not suggest the same tax. While Spaniards paid indirect taxes to the crown, New World natives were to pay direct per capita taxes, "tribute, each one, every year," the customary formula of jizya-inspired Moslem and Jewish tribute payments to Christian rulers.[44]

In 1518 the crown first defined a specific gender and age structure for those owing tribute. Each married male Indian over the age of twenty was to pay a head tax of three pesos a year, unmarried men one peso.[45] Similar gender and approximate age ranges would be established for initial tribute collection in every region that Spaniards subdued in the New World. Because the ages at which men were mustered to fight (or became economically productive) depended upon the tribe, the age at which men first paid tribute varied by region, just as it had under jizya. Also like jizya, tribute payments excluded men too lame or infirm to fight.[46]

Like jizya and its Christian-derived form, tribute, the tax on Indians was securely established throughout the empire as a personal tax. Mexican viceroy Martín Enríquez observed in 1575 that tribute "is personal and not by estates."[47] The eminent seventeenth-century authority on Spanish politics, Juan Solórzano noted that "tribute is not

haes (Rio de Janeiro, 1992), 101–102. The architect of the policy, Sisnando Davídiz, was a native of Coimbra. Alexander Herculano, *História de Portugal*, ed. José Mattoso, 4 vols. (Lisbon, 1980), 2: 304n37; Ramón Menéndez Pidal and E. García Gómez, "El conde Mozárabe Sisnado Davídiz y la política de Alfonso VI con los Taifas," *Al-Andalus*, 12 (1947): 27–42. Subsequent examples include Sepúlveda (1076), Cuenca (1177), and the policies of Jaime I in Valencia. Robert Burns, in *Jaume I i els valencians del seglo XIII* (Valencia, 1981), 1: 149–236. The rationales were pragmatic and political rather than religious, but functionally the same.

43 "Instrucción a Nicolás de Ovando, September 16, 1501," in *CDI*, 31: 15–16. Vassals in medieval Spain (unlike other parts of Europe) were those who paid money to the crown. "Instrucción a Cortés, June 26, 1523," *CDI*, 9, 167–172; "Instrucción a Luis Ponce de Leon, juez de residencia de la Nueva España, Nov. 4, 1525," *CDU*, (the continuation volumes of *CDI*), 9: 219; *Recopilación de leyes de los reynos de las Indias*, 3 vols. (Madrid, 1791), lib. 6, tit. 5, ley 1 (1523, 1573). See also C. H. Haring, *The Spanish Empire in America*, 2d ed. (New York, 1952), 263–264.

44 "Instrucciones to Nicolás de Ovando, Sept. 16, 1504," *CDI*, 31: 16. For its uniqueness see José Miranda, *El tributo indígena en la Nueva España durante el siglo XVI* (México, 1952), 37.

45 Miranda, *Tributo indígena*, 37–38, 41–42.

46 Ibid., 250. In 1578 the ages for tribute-payers in New Spain was eighteen to fifty, but after the end of the sixteenth century the age at which payments began was twenty-five.

47 Ibid., 151.

owed by the lands, possessions, or estates of the Indians."[48] Rather payment of tribute "is equally divided by head [count]."[49]

Unlike taxes paid by other Spaniards, Catholic Spanish monarchs also explicitly and repeatedly made the connection between military defeat and the payment of tribute. They declared that conquered peoples pay tribute: "Indians who are pacified and reduced to our obedience . . . pay tribute."[50] Payments were declared to be in "recognition of lordship" or "superiority."[51] Conquistadores frequently demanded that the crown not permit anyone other than a conqueror to receive tribute.[52] Tribute symbolized not simply vassalage but subjugation, and was a consequence of military defeat.

Payment of tribute was often rationalized, as jizya had been, as a contribution by indigenous peoples to their military defense. Solórzano wrote, "It is just and necessary that the same Indians contribute something . . . to aid the expenses of defending them and protecting them in peace and war."[53] Finally, the way in which this tax was collected from New World "subjects and vassals" closely resembled the way such jizya revenues (and their Christian counterparts) had been collected in Spain.[54] As with jizya, leaders of the conquered communities were responsible for the collection of this tribute and turning it over to Spaniards, whether an *encomendero* or crown official.[55]

While the crown never entirely succeeded in capturing all such payments for itself, tribute obligations constituted the economic basis of Spanish colonial rule over indigenous peoples of the New

48 Juan de Solórzano Pereira, *Política indiana*, 5 vols. (Madrid, 1972; orig. pub. 1647), lib. 2, cap. 19, no. 45.
49 Ibid., lib. 2, cap. 19, no. 36.
50 *Recop.*, lib. 6, tit. 5, ley 1 (Ordenanzas 1523, 1573); ibid., lib. 6, tit. 5, ley 2. Sometimes they are placed in encomienda, in ibid., lib. 6, tit. 8, ley 1 (1509, 1580), leyes 3, 4.
51 "Instrucciones a Hernán Cortés, June 26, 1523," *CDI*, 9: 167; "Instrucciones a Ponce de Léon," *CDI*, 9: 24; "Instrucciones a Rodrigo de Figueroa," 1518, *CDI*, 23: 332; "Instrucciones a los frailes jerónimos," 1516, *CDI*, 23: 310.
52 Miranda, *Tributo indígena*, 180.
53 *Qur'an*, Ali trans., 445n1282; Solórzano, *Pol. ind.*, intro., pt. 3. A sixteenth-century rationalization that it was in payment for the costs of teaching them the faith was rejected by Solórzano in the seventeenth century. Miranda, *Tributo indígena*, 147–148.
54 "La razón del vasallaje que de vos es por los dineros que vos dieron, de los que el Rey dio a ellos," "Crónica de Alfonso X," in Cayetano Rossell, ed., *Crónicas de los reyes de Castilla* (Madrid, 1919), 29. In 1575 Philip II declared, "In recognition of our vassalage, those who do not pay the ordinary tribute should pay something." *Recop.*, liv. 6, tit. 5, ley 9.
55 Miranda, *Tributo indígena*, 266–268, 279, 345–348; Ibn Ishāk, *Jurisprudence musulmane*, 2: 290–291. The leader was also supposed to ensure that the members of the community generally showed proper deference to Moslems. The duties of such a leader in a fourteenth-century Egyptian Jewish community are remarkably similar to those demanded of the New World leaders. See Stillman, *Jews in Arab Lands*, 271–272.

World.[56] This tax was the central unique economic feature of Spanish dominion over New World peoples. No other colonial power imposed a per capita tax on indigenous peoples, let alone one initially levied on men of fighting age.

Even a subsequent modification of New World tribute collection followed medieval Iberian precedent. Under the Christian rule, wealthy conquered communities (usually Jewish) paid tribute in cash, but poorer ones (often Moslem) paid with their labor. In the New World, the monetary or in-kind tribute payments were commuted to a work obligation in poorer areas.

The fiscal basis of the Spanish state – its economic interest in indigenous people – aimed at their preservation – since they were a source of income. Islamic states, however, had not explicitly counted the numbers of jizya-payers. Spanish officials and even conquerors did so.[57] Surveys of the numbers of tributaries for the purpose of informing the crown were first proposed by Charles V in 1525 and actually implemented throughout the Americas beginning in the 1530s. Mexico undertook its first state-ordered inquiry in 1531–1532; Yucatán pursued its first in 1549, as did Peru.[58] While these surveys could also have been used to track the number of indigenous men of fighting age in the New World, their primary function seems to have been to count the number of men and thus identify and/or fix the level of income for the crown.[59] These censuses of tribute payers were repeated thereafter on a continuing, albeit irregular, schedule (in 1528, 1536, 1563, and 1596), thus creating state-run population surveys in the Americas as a result of economic (and perhaps originally military) interests of a colonial state.[60]

56 The very first settlers in the Caribbean had imposed a form of per capita tax upon the natives of the New World; conquistadores tried to make themselves the principal direct beneficiaries. But as the Spanish crown moved to take authority for colonization out of the hands of private Spaniards (beginning with control over labor), it also moved to redirect tribute toward state coffers. Haring, *Spanish Empire*, 263–264. Miranda briefly traces the history of political struggles over tribute in New Spain in *Tributo indígena*, 45–48; María Angeles Eugenio Martínez, *Tributo y trabajo del indio en Nueva Granada* (Sevilla, 1977).

57 Head counts were initially tallied by some of the conquerors to divide up labor. Cortés counted indigenous inhabitants in 1522–1523; Antonio Carvajal carried out a similar count in Michoacán in 1523–1524; Pizarro attempted to do so in 1538. Peter Gerhard, *A Guide to the Historical Geography of New Spain* (Cambridge, 1972), 28–29; David Noble Cook, *Demographic Collapse: Indian Peru, 1520–1620* (Cambridge, 1981), 76.

58 Gerhard, *Historical Geography*, 29–30; Borah and Cook, *Population History*, 2: 16; Cook, *Demographic Collapse*, 76.

59 *Recop.*, liv. 6, tit. 5, ley 21, pt. 2. For the *cédula* of May 26, 1536, see Miranda, *Tributo*, 93–94. Surveys also kept track of the amount of tribute being obtained by its principal economic rivals, the Spanish settlers. For modifications by oral declarations, see ibid., 281.

60 Spanish censuses of indigenous people surveyed them far more often than did other European censuses. Portugal and the city state of Florence both had censuses

The massive epidemics of the sixteenth century produced a precipitous decline in royal revenues from indigenous peoples. This led to a broadening of the categories of people liable for the New World jizya, people traditionally never subjected to its pressures. Women, and eventually blacks as well, were added to the tribute lists.[61] Additionally, the deaths of indigenous people from disease were lamented – by Charles V as a disservice to himself – in part because it was his *economic* interests that were being ill served by the epidemics that devastated the population of the Americas in the sixteenth century.[62]

While the payment of jizya or tribute was intended as a form of humiliation, as well as an economic burden, its payment traditionally gave rise to political compensations. From the earliest Islamic conquests, communities that acknowledged the superiority of Islam by paying the poll tax were called *dhimmī* communities (*ahl al-dhimma*).[63] According to the *Encyclopaedia of Islam*, "[Up]on the conquest of a non-Muslim country by Muslims, the population which does not embrace Islam and which is not enslaved is guaranteed life, liberty, and, in a modified sense, property."[64] These guarantees were the Moslems' "covenant" or "obligation" to the dhimmīs. Other political privileges granted dhimmīs included the right to retain their own forms of government, elect their own leaders, and transmit property to each other according to the traditions of inheritance and sale characteristic of their own communities.[65] These were the terms of the surrender of Christians to Moslems in 713 A.D. on the Iberian peninsula.[66]

Beginning with the conquest of Toledo, Spanish Christians began to conquer large prosperous Moslem communities whose economies they wished to preserve. Following Siznado Davíd's recommendation,

early in the fifteenth century, but did not repeat the counting and surveillance periodically. Vitórino Magalhães Godinho, *Les découvertes* (Paris, 1990), 35; David Herlihy and Christiane Kaplisch, *The Tuscans and Their Families: A Study of the Florentine Catasto of 1427* (New Haven, 1985). France did not have its first population census until 1694 when a poll tax was introduced. Jacques Revel, "Knowledge of the Territory," *Science in Context*, 4 (1991): 139.

61 The changes occurred in the 1560s and 1570s. *Recop.*, lib. 6, tit. 5, ley 7; lib. 7, tit. 5, leyes 1 and 2.

62 Real cédula à Hernán Cortés, 1523, in Diego Encinas, *Cedulario indiano* (Madrid, 1945; orig. pub. 1596), 2: 185.

63 Muhammad was reported to have said, "Accept Islam, God will give you double the reward." While conversion to Islam itself was a reward, mere submission also was grounds for a reward as well. *Ṣaḥīḥ Muslim*, 3: 971. While Islamic scholarship stresses the rewards, Jewish scholarship dwells on the disabilities. See S. D. Goitein, "Actual and Legal Position of the Jews Under Arab Islam," in his *Jews and Arabs: Their Contacts Through the Ages* (New York, 1964).

64 "Dhimmī," *Encyclopaedia of Islam*. See hadith on this subject in *Al-Bukhārī*, 4: 124, 182, 186; Mālik on this subject, *Muwaṭṭa'*, 312.

65 "Dhimma," *Encyclopaedia of Islam*, 2: 958–959; *Encyclopaedia of Islam*, 2d edition, 2: 227–231; Khadduri and Liebesny, eds., *Law in the Middle East*, 335–336.

66 The text is in Eduardo Saavedra, *Estudio sobre la invasión de los árabes in España* (Madrid, 1892), 128–130.

Castilian Christians began to offer these Moslem communities the same political privileges as Christians had been proferred. Calling the Moslem and Jewish tribute-paying communities *aljamas* (after the Arabic word for community), defeated Moslems (and Jews) were allowed to reside in their own communities, govern themselves according to their own laws, and transmit property according to their own traditions, just as Christians had been permitted under Islam.[67]

Christian monarchs habitually referred to the usually urban Moslems who were allowed to retain their own political, religious, and legal traditions in exchange for submission as their "subjects and vassals."[68] In the text of the Requirement, natives were told that they would be received by the crown "gladly and graciously and would order them treated as were Our other subjects and vassals."[69] But New World peoples were not to be treated as Spaniards; rather they would be treated as the other royal subjects who had capitulated to Spanish military force.

The status of Indians who surrendered to the Spanish crown were virtually identical to *aljama* status. Indians not enslaved by Christians were guaranteed life, liberty, and, in a modified sense, property. If they submitted, the Requirement read, "His Majesty and I in his name will receive you . . . and will give you many privileges and exemptions." Among these privileges and exemptions granted indigenous peoples were the right to collective and individual ownership of their property – both their lands and their personal possessions. Such protections were reiterated by Spanish monarchs including Philip II, who ordered that "the Indians . . . should not be injured in their persons, or goods."[70] No other European power formally guaranteed all

---

67 José María Lacarra, "La repoblación del Valle del Ebro," 66–71; José María Fonts Ruis, "La reconquista y repoblación del Levante," 94, 109, 114–115; J. González, "La reconquista de Castilla y Andalucia," 195–196, all in *La reconquista española y la repoblación del pais* (Zaragosa, 1951). Such guarantees by Christian kings were more likely for urban dwellers.

68 Miguel Angel Ladero Quesada, *Castilla y la conquista del region de Granada* (Granada, 1987), 80–97. The Christian Iberian practice of accepting defeated Moslems as subjects while at the same time guaranteeing their own jurisprudence produced conflicting lines of authority. The same conflicts emerged in the New World, where indigenous peoples were simultaneously subjects of their own communities and subjects of the crown of Spain. This Christian tradition, however, differed somewhat from Islamic practice. Members of the community of protected ones (ahl' al-dhimma) were *not* subjects of the Muslim state. Only Muslims could be subjects of a Muslim state. Jews and Christians were subject only to the leaders of their own community. Thus, it is the Spanish modification of the Islamic tradition that was applied in the New World.

69 Serrano y Sanz, *Dominación española*, 1: 293. The parallel question in Islam of the privileges of the converted relative to the conquerors was controversial early in Islamic history. Noth, *Early Arabic Historical Tradition*, 150–161.

70 *Recop.*, lib. 4, tit. 1, ley 2 (Ordenanza of Philip II no. 27 [1573]); José María Ots Capedequi, *El estado español en las Indias* (Mexico, 1941), 141–145, 176–177.

Indians' rights to own their own land, a tradition of treatment of conquered peoples dating back to the first Caliphs.[71]

The second major characteristic of Islamic ahl al-dhimma and the Christian aljamas was the right of community members to dispose of goods – to sell, transmit, or inherit them – according to their own customs, guarantees that were extended to New World indigenous peoples. The final major characteristic of aljamas was the right to be judged according to their own community's laws. In 1542, the Spanish crown made this a centerpiece of its own legislation regarding indigenous peoples: "Lawsuits among the Indians are to be decided summarily and according to their usage and custom."[72]

Other less central privileges and disabilities characteristic of the Iberian dhimmī/aljama were transferred as well. Upon conversion to Islam, dhimmīs received special rights regarding marriage. In the New World, upon conversion indigenous peoples were exempted from strict kinship limitations in marrying.[73] Dhimmīs' legal testimony received lesser weight in Spanish Christian courts, as did Indians' testimony in Spanish courts.[74] The Spanish crown called this separate political community not *aljama* but "the republic of the Indians" (*república de indios*). These New World "republics" elected their own leaders, and transmitted property according to their own codes.

The Spanish crown re-created these communities in the New World in circumstances nearly identical to those in which the category dhimmī originated in Islam. Small armies with local allies subdued vast territories governed by huge bureaucracies. Conquering armies were tiny compared with the vast largely agricultural, defeated populations. Those who submitted during Moslem conquests – generally the sedentary agricultural people of Iran, Syria, and Spain – became dhimmīs, and were allowed to remain near the crops they grew or the goods they produced. While the reasons for protecting large numbers of sedentary agricultural peoples may have been as pragmatic as ideological, the end result was the same: the initial protection of con-

---

71 'Umar is reported to have written to the conqueror of Egypt, "Leave the land (to its original owners) so that those who come afterwards can undertake military campaigns from its yield." Ibn 'Abd al-Ḥakam, *Futūḥ Miṣr*, 88: 4–10, quoted in Noth, *Early Arabic Historical Tradition*, 83.

72 New Laws, art. 25, in "Las leyes nuevas, 1542–1543," ed. A. Muro Orejón, *Anuario de Estudios Americanos*, 2 (1945): 809–836; Francisco Morales Padrón, "Las leyes nuevas de 1542–1543," *Anuario de Estudios Americanos*, 15 (1959): 561–619. An English translation is *The New Laws of the Indies for the Good Treatment and Preservation of the Indians*, trans. Henry Stephens (London, 1893). In the seventeenth century, the rewards for submission continued to be elaborated by Spanish authorities: exemption from the requirement to labor and from tribute for ten years. *Recop.*, lib. 6, tit. 5, ley 3 (1607, 1618).

73 "Dhimmī," *Encyclopaedia of Islam*.

74 Ibid. The most comprehensive study of this phenomenon in the New World is Woodrow Borah, *Justice by Insurance* (Berkeley, 1983).

quered agricultural peoples and their forms of production. Large sedentary agricultural populations of the Americas such as the Nahua and Inca empires were likewise allowed to keep their own lands, to retain indigenous forms of government, and to transmit property according to their own rules.

Ironically Spanish treatment of sedentary conquered peoples in the New World replicated the earlier Islamic designation of al-dhimma far more consistently than Christian kings had done on the peninsula. When Christian rulers wanted to obtain Moslem lands and forms of production, they expelled the Moslems from their territory. Only when they desired to keep agricultural and other systems operating did they grant Islamic communities *aljama* privileges.[75] Unable to flood the New World with settlers, Spaniards did not initially seek to displace settled agricultural indigenous peoples from their lands, as did the English.[76] Subjected to the Christian religion and its representative, the crown of Castile, natives under Spanish rule had their lands and property safeguarded. Indigenous peoples of the Americas became New World dhimmīs.

Both in Islamic Spain and the Catholic New World, the autonomy guaranteed subject communities upon surrender inevitably eroded under pressure from the dominant power.[77] But the initial commitments to conquered peoples – protection of property and persons and a degree of political autonomy – were similar. In both systems these peoples were called protected because captives were not sold after a military defeat. Thus, one of the fundamental protections was against the common practice of enslaving defeated enemies.[78]

In ḥadith and Islamic jurisprudence, no specific consequences (beyond war) were mentioned if a people failed to submit.[79] While slavery was a common fate of the defeated in the early years of Islamic

---

75 In the first half of the thirteenth century, Castilian rulers preferred to push the Moslems out. Reyna Pastor de Togneri, *Del Islam al Cristianismo: En las fronteras de dos foramaciones económico-sociales* (Barcelona, 1975), 127. So too did thirteenth- and fourteenth-century Valencia. Fonts Ruis, "La reconquista y repoblación," 94–100, 122–123; Jean Pierre Dedieu, "O refluxo do Islão espanhol," in *Toledo, séculos XII-XIII*, 43–44. See also Thomas Glick, *Islamic and Christian Spain in the Early Middle Ages* (Princeton, N.J., 1979), 163.

76 On the Iberian peninsula, they did seek to retake lands and property from Moslems, thus ironically making the practice in the Americas closer to the Islamic original than the Christian copy. But unlike the English, the Spaniards proceeded by granting incentives to Moslems to abandon property to Christians. See Ladero Quesada, *Castilla y la conquista*, 81, 87, 95–96.

77 Glick, *Islamic and Christian Spain*, 170–171; John Boswell, *The Royal Treasure: Muslim Communities Under the Crown of Aragon in the Fourteenth Century* (New Haven, 1877), 108–164; Lacarra, "Repoblación del Valle del Ebro," 71–72; James Lockhart, *The Nahuas After the Conquest* (Stanford, Calif., 1992), 14–58; Susan Kellogg, *Law and the Transformation of Aztec Culture, 1500–1700* (Norman, Okl. 1995).

78 *Al-Bukhārī*, 4: 182.

79 Averroes, *Bidāyat al-Mudjtahid*, 20; Lewis, *Politics and War*, 228.

expansion, this soon dwindled into insignificance.[80] On the Iberian peninsula, however, during the medieval era Christian and Moslem Spaniards routinely enslaved each other as prisoners of war.[81] The Spanish Requirement was specific in laying out the alternatives to accepting dhimmī status. If the natives refused the summons, then the Spaniards would "take your persons, your wives and children and will make them slaves . . . and will take your goods, and will do to you all the harm and damage that we can."[82] Nomadic Indians who refused to submit, and who instead carried on persistent guerrilla campaigns on the frontiers, were often enslaved.

At the close of the Requirement, an unusually worded disclaimer appears. In the Catholic summons the messenger announces, "And I solemnly declare that all the deaths and damage that result from this [attack] will be your fault and not that of His Majesty nor me, nor of the lords who come with me."[83] In the practice of summoning to conversion reported to have been followed by Muhammad himself, leaders of other nations were informed that if they rejected the call to Islam, then any damage to their subjects which followed would be their responsibility. Following the invitation to surrender, non-Muslim leaders were to be warned. "But if you reject this invitation of Islam, you shall be responsible for misguiding the people."[84] In other words the refusal to accept Islam/Catholicism was the fault not of the messenger of God/Allah, but rather those who refused to accept it and their leadership.

The basic, often misunderstood core of the Requirement was an Islamic-inspired summons to submit to a superior religion, allow its agents to proselytize, or to face a military attack. Since such conduct did not fit the classic profile of just war in the Christian tradition, this often led to considerable incomprehension by traditional Christian observers both inside and outside Spain.

The Requirement was a ritual, a protocol for conquest. Whether Spanish conquerors believed in it or found it personally compelling or convincing was irrelevant. What mattered was that the political and religious leaders of their society demanded its implementation. Rituals do not automatically create community or signify an interior

80 Bernard Lewis, *Race and Slavery in the Middle East: An Historical Enquiry* (New York, 1990), 6–9.
81 In 1488, the Castilian crown sold over three thousand captured Moslem inhabitants of Málaga into slavery. Ladero Quesada, *Castilla y la conquista*, 76.
82 Serrano y Sanz, *Dominación española*, 1: 294.
83 Ibid.
84 This is repeatedly attributed to Muhammad in the ḥadith collection of al-Bukhārī and a slightly different version in *Ṣaḥīḥ Muslim*. The latter has, "Upon you will be the sin of your subjects." *Al-Bukhārī*, 4: 115, 121; *Ṣaḥīḥ Muslim*, 3: 971. The exact meaning of the term *people* is disputed. Some scholars say it means cultivators or subjects; others say it refers only to Jews, Christians, or Persians.

state of belief. Rituals are requirements and, in this case, formal political protocols that had to be followed to legitimate Spanish political rule over the indigenous people of the New World. They were persuasive to political leaders of Spain, and hence had to be executed by conquerors desiring official recognition. But beyond the fundamental character of the demand – acknowledge religious superiority or be warred upon – there was a further element of Islamic inspiration.

When debating Christians and Jews in medieval Spain, Moslems often sought to show that Islamic beliefs merely continued Christian and Jewish ones.[85] To show that Islam's concept of jihad simply extended existing Christian and Jewish traditions on warfare, medieval Moslems frequently cited the text of Deuteronomy, a practice that continues to this day.[86] Composed as if spoken by Moses, Deuteronomy was well-known to Moslems since Moses is one of the five major Prophets (Abraham, Noah, Moses, Christ), along with Muhammad.

The biblical passage that Moslems considered (and still consider) to best express the Islamic demand for submission or war is Deuteronomy 20:10–16, which describes the capture of certain fortified towns by the Jewish people on the way to the Holy Land.[87] The text in a standard modern Jewish translation is as follows:

> When thou drawst nigh unto a city to fight against it, then proclaim peace unto it. And it shall be, if it make thee answer of peace, and open unto thee, that all the people that are found therein shall become tributary unto thee, and shall serve thee. And if it will make no peace with thee, but will make war against thee, then thou shalt smite every male thereof with the edge of the sword, but the women and the little ones, and even the cattle, and all that is in the city, even all the spoil thereof, shalt thou take for a prey unto thyself; and thou shalt eat the spoil of thine enemies which the Lord thy God hath given thee. Thus shalt thou do unto all the cities which are very far off from thee. . . . Howbeit of the cities of these peoples that the Lord thy God giveth thee for

85 Q. 3:146.
86 For uses of Deuteronomy in Muslim–Christian polemics, see Erdmann Fritsch, *Islam und Christentum im mittelalter: Beiträge zur geschichte der muslimischen polemik gegen das Christentum in arabischer sprache* (Breslau, 1930). Among Andalusian Islamic minorities, see Ibn Hazm, *Al-Fiṣal*, summarized in Sweetman, 178 and esp. 224 (Spanish edition by Miguel Asín Palacios, *Abenházem de Córdoba* [Madrid, 1928]). For the validity of the Old Testament generally in Islam, see Q. 3:65–110; for Moses in particular, Q. 2:285. See also Abraham I. Katsh, *Judaism in Islam: Biblical and Talmudic Backgrounds of the Koran and Its Commentaries* (New York, 1954), 134–136.
87 *Encyclopaedia Judaica* (Jerusalem, 1972), 5: 1583. In the Jewish tradition, the attack on these the Hittites, Amorites, Canaanites, Perizzites, Hivites, and Jebusites – the enemies of Israel – was commanded by God for the recuperation of the Holy Land.

an inheritance, thou shalt save alive nothing that breatheth, but thou shalt utterly destroy them.[88]

While Moslem interpreters sought to stress the continuities between jihad and this passage,[89] conventional medieval Jewish and Christian commentators failed to see it this way.

Jewish commentaries on these verses from the start of the Christian era through the late Middle Ages interpreted it in three important ways.[90] A code of second-century descriptive rules called the Mishnah Torah saw in this and related passages the distinction between wars commanded by God and those which He permitted. A collection of readings from the first seven centuries of the Christian era called the Midrash sees this passage only as historically descriptive.[91] Finally, the great Iberian Jewish commentator Moses Maimonides (1135–1204) interpreted this passage of Deuteronomy as a requirement that peaceful conditions be offered first, but did not see the demand as couched in religious terms. Furthermore, the terms of submission by a captured town were largely to include physical contributions to the war effort, building walls, and fortifying strongholds.[92] He, like other Jews of his time, was strongly opposed to conversion. In other words, from the birth of Christ to the end of the Middle Ages Jewish scholars under-

---

88 *The Holy Scriptures According to the Masoretic Text* (Philadelphia, 1917). The Jerusalem Bible translates the phrase as "forced labor," rather than tribute, but the Vulgate, the edition of the Bible most commonly in use in early-sixteenth-century Spain, says in Latin "tributo."

89 For the link to jihad, see Weber and Reynaud, *Croisade*, 80; Abedi and Legenhausen, eds., *Jihad and Shahadat*, 3–5; C. G. Weeramantry, *Islamic Jurisprudence: An International Perspective* (London, 1988), 145–146. Christian–Jewish debates did not discuss this dimension of Deuteronomy, only Christian–Moslem ones. Antonio Pacios Lopez, *La disputa de Tortosa*, 2 vols. (Madrid, 1957), 1: 371, 2: 612.

90 *The Talmud of Babylonia*, Tractate Sotah 44a–b, Tractate Sanhedrin 20b; Mishnah Sotah 8:1–7. There is also Midrashim, *Sifre: A Tannaitic Commentary on the Book of Deuteronomy*, trans. Reuven Hammer (New Haven, 1986), Piska 190–205, and *Maimonides' Commenary on the Mishnah Tractate Sanhedrin*, trans. Fred Rosner (New York, 1981) 8–10, 23–24.

91 General introductions are *The Mishnah: A New Translation*, trans. Jacob Neusner (New Haven, 1988); Neusner, *Invitation to Midrash: The Workings of Rabbinic Bible Interpretation* (New York, 1989).

92 Moses Maimonedes, *Mishnah Torah*, trans. Philip Birnbaum (New York, 1967). Maimonedes's commentary on Deut. 20 is in Kings 6 and 7 in which he says that no war is to be waged without first offering peace – whether it is an optional or a religious war. If the inhabitants respond peaceably, "They shall do forced labor for you and serve you – The tax imposed upon them consists in being prepared to serve the king physically and financially, as in the case of building walls and fortifying strongholds, or constructing a palace of the king and the like" (325). The procedures for starting a war are quite different. He writes in Kings 7 that regardless of whether it is a religious war or an optional war, "a priest is appointed to address the troops, and is anointed with anointing oil." Jewish commentators do not describe the consequence as slavery. Rashi allows destruction of a city granted by God, but mentions nothing about slavery. *Pentateuch and Rashi's Commentary on Deuteronomy* (London, 1934), 103.

stood Deuteronomy as either describing the past, distinguishing between wars commanded and permitted by God, or justifying mobilizing conquered peoples to work for the war effort. Neither eventual conversion nor submission to a superior religion played any role in Jewish interpretations.

Outside of the Iberian world, Christian theologians and canon lawyers did not use the Old Testament to justify Christian methods or aims of warfare. Christians customarily amalgamated the *New* Testament with classical Roman texts to produce justifications of warfare based centrally upon "protection," "defense," and "avenging insults,"[93] intimating that Christians were merely responding defensively to threats created by someone else. (Christianity thus covertly introduced and legitimated the popular idea of revenge as a justification for war.)[94]

While the dominant trend within medieval Christianity envisioned warfare as merely defensive, a less influential group of theologians and canonists beginning in the eleventh century accepted the use of force for religious purposes.[95] But they commonly cited the New Testament verse of Matthew 22, "Compel them to come in" (Compelle eos intrare), a phrase first used when a prominent missionary to the Slavic region called upon Henry II of Germany to compel conversions in 1008. Other Christian writers subsequently invoked this phrase (including the Spaniard Juan Ginés de Sepúlveda) to justify the use of military force to secure conversions.[96]

Neither Jewish interpreters nor Christians from outside the Iberian peninsula invoked Deuteronomy to justify war that sought eventual conversion. Yet the originator of the Requirement, Palacios Rubios,

---

93 Frederick H. Russell, *The Just War in the Middle Ages* (Cambridge, 1975), 16–17, 63–68; Villey, *Croisade*, 34; Jonathan Riley-Smith, *The First Crusade and the Idea of Crusading* (London, 1986), 145–146. See also the language in Gratian, *Decretum*, in *Corpus juris cannonici*, 2 vols. (Graz, 1959), 1: 894–895. Only medieval Iberian preachers, influenced by Islam, ever invoked Deuteronomy. Canonists and theologians – even Iberian ones – did not.

94 Riley-Smith, *First Crusade*, 56–57. Another view of violence was that it was connected to "love," whereby the use of force was rationalized as an expression of Christian "charity." Still another popular tradition saw crusaders carrying out God's will, almost as if divinely ordained. Ibid., 27, 118.

95 In 892 a king of France forced a defeated Viking to chose between death and baptism. Crusaders repeatedly offered Jews the choice between death or conversion in northern France and Germany; Raymond Pilet offered Muslim peasants in northern Syria the same choice. Kedar, *Crusade and Mission*, 62, 68. Massacres of Moslems effected forced conversions following the Norman conquest of Muslim Sicily (52). Nor was it merely renegade Christians who employed violence and even death threats to force conversion; prominent political and religious leaders did so as well. Pope Gregory I praised military wars that made possible preaching to subjugated pagans. Bernard of Clairveaux, writing in 1147, called on German Christians to "utterly annihilate or surely convert" the Wends (70).

96 Kedar, *Crusade and Mission*, 68.

cited precisely this section of Deut. 20:10–16 as his biblical authority for drawing up the text. This passage was also widely understood in sixteenth-century Spain as being the Requirement's biblical justification.[97] But it was neither Jewish nor Christian understandings of this text as historical descriptions that Palacios Rubios and other sixteenth-century Spanish jurists employed.

In the words of the requirement's originator:

> The natives of the island may justly defend themselves from the Christians until they discover the truth, having it explained to them how the care of the whole world, and the power over it resides in the Pope, who has made a donation and concession of the province in which they live to His Majesty, whom they must obey as the divine trustee of the Church. And thus they are obliged to admit the preachers of our faith to explain the mysteries [of the faith] to them in detail. And if after a prudent time limit they decide not to do so, they may be invaded and conquered, reduced by force of arms, have their possessions seized, and their persons placed in slavery, because war, on the part of the Christians is justified.[98]

This unique Iberian understanding of Deuteronomy most likely resulted from familiarity. Iberian Christians were the only Western Europeans exposed to extensive Moslem proselytizing which had sought to convince Christians that their beliefs on war were continuous with Moslem ones. "Muslim authors asked their Jewish and Christian neighbors for information and discussed religious issues with them. . . . They relied heavily on oral contacts" for knowledge of the Christian Bible and Jewish Torah.[99] Over the centuries Moslems had acquainted Christians with their interpretation of this passage in Deuteronomy as a source for a ritual style of declaring war. Therefore, when adopting these phrases to justify Spanish warfare in the New World, Palacios Rubios and Matías de la Paz were not consciously invoking Islamic precedent. Instead they were merely using a familiar understanding – widely shared by their fellow Spaniards – of an Old Testament text – whose origins they, like many in their society, were not familiar with. But there were others in Spain who were aware of this heritage.

The Islamic origin of the central, unfamiliar features of the Requirement was remarked upon by sixteenth-century Dominican friar Bartolomé de Las Casas. He repeatedly insisted that the wars of conquest fought by Spaniards in the New World were Islamic in inspiration. "Those who war on infidels [nonbelievers] mimic Muhammad,"

---

97 Palacios Rubios, *De las islas del mar océano*, 36–37.
98 Ibid.
99 Hava Lazarus-Yafeh, *Intertwined Worlds: Medieval Islam and Bible Criticism* (Princeton, 1992), 119, 121.

he declared.[100] Such wars were inspired by "the Mohammedan procedures that our Spanish people have had since [Muslims] entered these
lands."[101] His famous attack on the Requirement in his *Historia de las
Indias* (unpublished in his lifetime) points in the direction of its Islamic inspiration. Almost his first comment on the Requirement asks
what would happen if "Moors or Turks came to make . . . the same requirement. . . . Did the Spaniards show superior proof by witnesses
and truer evidence of what they declared in their requirement . . .
than the Moors showed of their Muhammed?"[102] Despite its erroneous
assumption that Muhammad was a God, as Christ was, rather than a
prophet, Las Casas understood that the Requirement's principles were
Islamic. Indeed, much of Las Casas's polemical attack on military
means of conquest can be understood as an attack upon what he understood to be Islamic-inspired ways of conquering and justifying the
conquest of the New World.[103]

Las Casas also indicated other unusual dimensions of the Requirement that he found odd in a Christian document – the omission of the
Trinity and the unusual emphasis on the role of Saint Peter instead
of Christ.[104] Yet these also betrayed traces of its Islamic origin. The
Requirement neglected to mention the Trinity – three persons in a
single God – and equally oddly never mentioned Christ, the second
person of the Trinity. Yet if its origin were Islamic, such an omission
would be unsurprising. Islam has a single unitary God and is strongly
opposed to Trinitarian doctrines. The prominent place of Saint Peter
and the pope in relationship to the Church may well have appeared to
Las Casas as similar to the role of the caliph (khalīfa) as successor to
the authority of the Prophet.[105]

The Requirement was neither the standard Western or Catholic declaration of war nor the orthodox Islamic summons to surrender to Allah – but a new form, a hybrid, one which contained mixed within a

100 " . . . also those who urge war to subdue infidels as a prior condition for preaching
the faith." Las Casas, *The Only Way*, 147, 164.
101 *Historia de las Indias*, lib. 3, cap. 155, 3: 361. This is also the theme of *The Only Way*.
102 *Historia de las Indias*, lib. 3, cap. 58, 3: 28.
103 "Porque sería ir a predicar la fé como Mahoma, que mandó dilatar su secta por vía
de armas." Bartolomé de Las Casas, *Aquí se contiene una disputa o controversia*, repr.
in Lewis Hanke and Manuel Giménez Fernández, eds., *Tratados* (Mexico, 1965;
orig. pub. 1552), 265; Las Casas, *Brevísima relación*, in ibid., 21.
104 Las Casas, *Historia de las Indias*, lib. 3, cap. 58.
105 While the caliphate is not the same as the papacy, it may well have appeared that
way to Las Casas. The role of caliph was initially religious, political, and military (like
the medieval popes), but both eventually lost their military roles. When the caliphate went into decline, it functioned much as the fifteenth-century papacy – without miliary power – but with the capacity to invest local political leaders' political
and military ambitions with moral authority. "Khalīfa," *First Encyclopaedia of Islam
and Encyclopaedia of Islam*, 2d ed.; David Santillana, "Il Concetto di Califfato e di
sovranità nel diritto musulmano," *Oriente Moderno*, 4 (1924): 344–345.

single utterance two styles, two belief systems. According to Mikhail Bakhtin, a hybrid is "an utterance that belongs by its grammatical [syntactic] and compositional makers to a single speaker but that actually contains mixed within it two utterances. . . . There is no formal . . . boundary between these utterances. . . . The same word will belong simultaneously to two languages, two belief systems that intersect in a hybrid construction."[106] Those "two different linguistic consciousnesses, separated from one another by an epoch, by social differentiation, or by some other factor . . . [become] unconsciously mixed."[107]

Like many Spaniards, the inventors, supporters, and users of the Requirement did not deliberately copy Islamic models. As Montgomery Watt writes:

> Few northern Spaniards or other western Europeans realized the Islamic provenance of many elements in this culture, and so they had no difficulty in combining acceptance of the culture with opposition to the religion. In this way Spain gained a culture which had important Arabic elements, even though she came more and more to assert her Catholic identity and deny her indebtedness to the Arabs.[108]

As political enemies, medieval Spaniards created a political discourse for themselves in which "Moslem" functioned as the inverse of "Christian." A recent critic of the Arab and Christian chronicles has pointed out that the images and representations of Christianity and Islam in the Spanish chronicles of reconquest were often mirror images of each other.[109]

Since enemies, even mirror-image ones, deny each other's legitimacy, traditional Islamic customs could not be acknowledged as a model for Spanish political authority. To recognize Islamic influences in Spanish political practices would mean to challenge their legitimacy as Las Casas did. Hence, Islamic precedent and customs could not be consciously cited as authoritative in the sixteenth century. But through hybrid, apparently Christian forms such as the Requirement, unacknowledged Islamic expressions could enter the dominant discourse.[110]

106 M. M. Bakhtin, *The Dialogic Imagination*, ed. Michael Holquist, trans. Caryl Emerson and Michael Holquist (Austin, Tex., 1982), 304–305.
107 Ibid., 358, 360. In an "organic hybrid," "two socio-linguistic consciousness, two epochs," are unconsciously mixed. Ibid., 360.
108 Montgomery Watt, *The Influence of Islam on Medieval Europe* (Edinburgh, 1972), 48–49.
109 Ron Barkal, *Cristianos y Musulmanes en la España medieval (El enemigo en el espejo)* (Madrid, 1984).
110 Homi Bhabha, "Signs Taken for Wonders: Questions of Ambivalence and Authority Under a Tree Outside Delhi: May 1817," in Francis Barker, Peter Hulme, Margaret Iversen, and Diane Loxley, eds., *Europe and Its Others*, 2 vols. (Colchester, 1985), 1: 96–97. Bhabha considers hybridity "a form of subversion" (154, 156).

While conceived when Spain's sole possessions were a handful of islands in the Caribbean and a few tiny coastal settlements in South America, the Requirement proved to be an enduring means of creating political authority. It was used to legitimate dominion over large native empires in the Americas as expeditiously as it had over a small number of Caribbean outposts.[111] But while the Requirement was persuasive to the crown and much of the political elite of sixteenth-century Spain, doubts and concerns about it existed. A degree of unease continued among some highly placed Spaniards, most likely stemming from the many overt resemblances of the Requirement to Islamic practice.

While hesitations and reservations about the suitability of the Requirement were voiced and debated at the highest levels of Spanish power, interestingly enough, neither the crown nor its officials were willing to repudiate it. The Requirement was retained unaltered for more than twenty years, even after a debate over its suitability, because, reservations aside, it remained culturally persuasive across an important spectrum of Spanish political officials.[112] Persistent official unease, however, eventually yielded two changes, the first a series of rhetorical distinctions. In 1573 Spanish officials forbade the use of the term *conquest*, requiring the neologism *pacification* to describe military efforts against indigenous peoples.[113] *Pacification* removed the association with the word *struggle* (jihad). In addition, the formal title of the "Requirement" was eliminated. After 1573 the formal summons to Christianity was to go by a different name – an "Instrument of Obedience and Vassalage," thus severing the linguistic association between *requirement* and *daʿa*.[114] Despite eliminating words such as *requirement* and *conquest* which were uncomfortably close to Arabic *daʿa* and *jihad*, Spanish authorities continued to insist on the originally Mālikī ritual practice of summoning to a superior religion. But by relabeling the practices, potential linguistic reminders of its Andalusi Islamic origins were erased.

The ability of individual Spaniards to declare war against indigenous people was also moderated in the renamed 1573 "Instrument of Obedience and Vassalage." If a Spanish leader decided that the natives had already received the faith and become obedient (through submission), he could attack the natives as "apostates and rebels." But if the peoples had never been subject before "and it was necessary to make open and

---

111 The Requirement was created in 1511 when there were only Spanish settlements on three islands in the Caribbean: Jamaica, Hispaniola, and Puerto Rico. Las Casas, *Historia de las Indias*, lib. 3, cap. 8, 2: 456.
112 Las Casas, *Aquí se contiene*, 217–459, esp. 229 (emphasis added).
113 This was reproduced in *Recop.*, lib. 4, tit. 1, ley 6.
114 Text of "Instrument of vassalage" in *CDI*, 16: 142–187. Examples of its use are *CDI*, 9: 30–45, 16: 88, 188–207.

orderly war against them, they were first to advise the Crown" before launching an attack.[115] The refusal to acknowledge Christian superiority and admit Christian preachers could still justify a military attack, but the responsibility for making the decision was removed from the hands of the individual soldiers or their leaders to the crown.

The crown continued to insist upon the political ritual of a summons:

[Spaniards] beforehand are to make to them [Indians] the requirements (summons) necessary, one, two and three times, and more if needed. [Spaniards were] not to war on the Indians of any province in order for them to receive the Holy Catholic Faith or give us obedience . . . [without] the necessary requirements.

As before, indigenous peoples were only offered submission. They were obligated to respond by "having received the Holy faith and given us obedience."[116]

As late as 1681, any new peoples the Spaniards encountered would have to be summoned to Catholicism:

Our captains and officials, discoverers, settlers and other people, arriving in those provinces [previously unreached by Spaniards must] try to make known . . . to the Indians and residents that they were sent to teach them good customs . . . instruct them in Our Catholic faith . . . and bring them to our lordship so that they would be treated, favored and defended as our subjects and vassals.[117]

Yet one major repercussion of the Requirement was far harsher than under Islam.

As innumerable commentators have pointed out, the Catholic Kings Ferdinand and Isabel began a period of religious intolerance on the Iberian peninsula. Members of religious minorities who had been tolerated there for centuries were expelled. Jews were exiled in 1492, Moslems in successive waves in the next century. Submission to Catholicism came to signify accepting of Spanish political authority.

This linking of obedience to religious authority with political obedience led to the Catholic Kings only important modification of the policy regarding treatment of defeated peoples. Breaking the surrender conditions granted to Granada in 1501, the Catholic kings severed the Islamic practice of protection (*jimma*) from one of its ideological moorings – the idea that it was offered in exchange for religious freedom. The Catholic Kings retained protection instead as a *technique* of rule – the right of defeated peoples of a different religion to self-

---

115 The idea that only those who had not previously heard of the religion needed to be summoned to it also characterized the Hanafī school. Noth, *Early Arabic Historical Tradition*, 163.

116 *Recop.*, lib. 3, tit. 4, ley 9.   117 Ibid., lib. 1, tit. 1, ley 2.

government and their own inheritance practices, while requiring them to pay head taxes, show deference, not ride horses, and exhibit all the other ritual forms of humiliation. When cultural borrowings occur, they are rarely incorporated in the identical forms by the borrowing society – or even less often are they given the absolutely identical rationalization. Eliminating the justification of religious freedom did not mean the Catholic Kings eliminated any other of the central political and economic dimensions of treatment of conquered peoples.

Following this precedent established in Granada, the Spanish crown also denied conquered peoples of the New World the right to practice their own religion even after payment of per capita tribute. Nor did they provide them with the choice of exile instead of conversion, as Moslems had sometimes granted during the Middle Ages. What became the option for evasion in the New World was cultural conversion. Only by shedding native dress, language, and/or residence, or by marrying non–tribute payers could Indians avoid the demands of Spanish tribute. The escape hatch of religious assimilation under Islam became the predominant escape hatch of cultural and linguistic assimilation in the New World.[118]

COMPARISONS

Resulting from an early struggle over creating Spain's legal authority over the New World, the ritual speech known as the Requirement became the principal means of enacting such authority. Every Spaniard encountering peoples who had never heard of Christianity was required to summon them to a new religion. Unlike the sometimes improvised quality of French speeches, the Spanish ritual speech was carefully and explicitly proscribed. Its content threatened with war those who failed to submit, and promised those who did submit "honors and advantages." These so-called honors and advantages were economic and political forms of subordination originally developed by Islamic rulers of the Iberian peninsula: payment of a tax (*jizya* or tribute) and the creation of quasi-independent self-governing communities, the so-called republics of Indians. They were honors and advantages only relative to slavery. But the conviction that religious and political obedience were equivalent was not part of France's historic tradition.

French officials were careful to secure the political consent or the appearance of consent by indigenous peoples. While the French sought a consensual "alliance" with the natives, the Spaniards sought

---

118 Flight was also an important mechanism, particularly in the New World. See Ann Wightman, *Indigenous Migration and Social Change: The Forasteros of Cuzco* (Durham, N.C., 1990).

submission. Even the most benevolent methods of enacting Spanish authority never sought consent from natives, merely offering honors and advantages as an incentive to submission.[119]

Spaniards created possession by lecturing the Indians, informing them that they were about to become subjects and vassals of the crown of Spain, and that they had little choice (short of war) except to submit. The Requirement demanded submission in a form that Bakhtin labeled "authoritative discourse" – not intended to be internally persuasive (as in a consensual relationship) – but only to obtain external compliance.

The distinctive Spanish equivalence of religious and political subservience failed to appear even in French ceremonies. Some (although not all) French ceremonies clearly separated the two – to the point of requiring separate ceremonies to institute religious and political authority (as in the Amazon). Late medieval and early modern French political writers often claimed that they separated church and state – one merely sanctified the other. In New World ceremonies, traditional religious objects – censers, candlesticks, crosses – visually dramatized God's blessing of French political activities. But for the Spanish conquest, religious and political obedience were one and the same.

The Requirement was thus the means by which Spanish political power would be extended over most of the Americas. When Pizarro attacked Atahualpa in the central square of Cajamarca simply because the Inca leader profaned a sacred Spanish text, political and religious leaders were horrified. Francisco Vitoria, the most influential political thinker of the sixteenth century, wrote that the actions of the men of Peru made "his blood run cold."[120] Atahualpa had not been carefully summoned to submission. But Cortés's carefully repeated statements that he had made the Requirement known to the natives solidified his position as the undisputed representative of Spanish authority in the New World.[121] For he had legitimated Spanish political authority the

119 "Con mucho cuidado se informen . . . que número de gentes y naciones las habitan . . . sin enviar gente de guerra . . . y habiéndose informado . . . toman asiento y capitulación, ofreciéndoles las honras y aprovechamientos, que . . . se les pudieren ofrecer." *Recop.*, lib. 4, tit. 3, ley 1 (ordenanzas of 1573). Las Casas, *The Only Way*, also idealizes this form.

120 "Cuanto al caso del Perú . . . no me espantan ni me embarazan las cosas que vienen a mis manos, excepto trampas de beneficios y cosas de Indias, que se me hiela la sangre en el cuerpo." P. Beltrán de Heredia, "Ideas del P. Vitoria sobre la colonización de América según documentos inéditos," *Anuario Associación Francisco Vitoria*, no. 2 (1931): 23–68, esp. 32. In general, the Requirement was infrequently read in Peru. However, it was read in Cuzco. Pedro Sahco, *Relación para S. M. de lo sucedido en la conquista y pacificación de estas provincias de la Nueva Castilla y de la calidad de la tierra*, trans. P. Means (New York, 1917), 173.

121 Hernán Cortés, *Letters from Mexico*, trans. and ed. Anthony Pagden (New Haven, 1986), 63, 146, 207, 346. There are countless additional examples.

way that it was supposed to be instituted – summoning natives to submission, the central political ritual of Andalusi Islamic warfare.

When the conquest of the New World began, many Spaniards had directly experienced a war aimed at eventual conversion of people of a different faith. Spanish forces had been battling Islamic ones until 1491, the year before Columbus reached America. By contrast, in Portugal by the start of colonization, such frequent encounters with Islamic military rituals belonged to a remote past. The last Moslems had been couquered by 1250, and the residual Islamic population was quiescent. Yet while Islamic military rituals were not as important for Portugal's overseas ventures as for Spain's, Portugal's Islamic heritage was equally significant. For it was in Portugal that Islamic sciences, elaborated through Jewish interpreters, provided first Portugal and then the rest of the world with the navigational expertise that made possible the expansion of Europe. That navigational expertise rested upon the heritage of medieval Islamic achievements in mathematics and astronomy. Not surprisingly, the rituals of Portuguese possession in the New World were initially astronomical.

4

"A NEW SKY AND NEW STARS"

ARABIC AND HEBREW SCIENCE, PORTUGUESE
SEAMANSHIP, AND THE DISCOVERY OF AMERICA

New islands, new lands, new seas, new peoples; *and what is more a new sky and new stars.*

Pedro Nunes, *Tratado em defensam da carta de marear* (1537)[1]

In 1537 Pedro Nunes, royal cosmographer to King João III declared that the Portuguese had discovered many new things. Sailing farther out into the South Atlantic than anyone had ever done before, the Portuguese discovered new seas, new currents, new winds. In traversing new seas they came across islands and lands – the Azores, Canary, and Cape Verde Islands, and navigated the coast of Brazil from the Amazon to Argentina, and the harbors and bays of western Africa from Guinea to the Cape of Good Hope. They came into contact with thousands of humans who lived in these regions, their trade goods, and their commercial structures. They were the first Europeans to trade directly with the peoples of sub-Saharan Africa and what is now Indonesia, the first to contact the peoples of Brazil who would inspire works as diverse as Montaigne's essay "On Cannibals" and Thomas More's *Utopia*. As the royal cosmographer put it in 1537, the Portuguese had discovered "new islands, new lands, new seas, new peoples."

But Nunes was not as impressed with those things as he was with yet another Portuguese discovery. More than the lands, waters, and people, he wrote, the Portuguese had found "a new sky and new stars." Uncovering heavens previously unknown to Europeans did not mean mere stargazing to Nunes. Rather it signified new astronomical knowledge, precise descriptions of skies that Europeans knew little or nothing about. It meant taking exact measurements of where stars were in the sky in order to locate a previously unknown landmass or eventually to situate a ship anywhere in the world. It was this astronomically based knowledge that the Portuguese master pilot John provided the

1 Pedro Nunes, *Tratado em defensa*, in *Obras*, 2 vols. (Lisbon, 1940; orig. pub. 1537), 1: 175.

king on the occasion of the first European landing on the coast of Brazil in April 1500:

> Yesterday, Monday [April 27, 1500] . . . I [Master John], the pilot of the Captain Major, and the pilot of Sancho Tovar [captain of another ship] set foot on land [at Porto Seguro, Brazil]. We took the height of the sun at midday and found it at 56 degrees and the shadow was to the north which according to the rules of the astrolabe [manual] we judge ourselves to be 17 degrees from the equinoctial [equator].[2]

Thus, the master pilot of the second Portuguese expedition to Asia reported the discovery of Brazil. He neither made a solemn speech nor led a ceremonial parade. He did not plant a garden or construct a fence or house. He described neither the land nor its people, but the heavens above. His carefully prescribed actions after landing on the coast of America constituted an exact accounting of how he determined the latitude of the New World using the position of the sun.

While obtaining latitudes is not customarily considered a ritual, Master John performed very precise gestures: lifting an object (the astrolabe used for measuring) in one hand, holding it out at the waist, performing these motions only at a specific time – midday – all operations as tightly regulated as ceremonial conduct.[3] Although he executed a technique rather than a conventional ritual, Master John's movements were as central to the Portuguese monarch's claims to the New World as were ceremonies for the French, speeches for the Spaniards, and fences and houses for the English. The Portuguese termed their methods of finding new lands *discovery*, the systematic process by which new lands and new peoples were found. And discovery constituted the core of their claims to authority overseas.

In 1562 the Portuguese ambassador asked Queen Elizabeth to acknowledge Portuguese sovereignty over "all the land *discovered* by the Crown of Portugal."[4] When the English queen replied that in "all

---

2 Abel Fontoura da Costa, "O Descobrimento do Brasil," in António Baião, Hernan Cidade, and Manuel Múrias, eds., *História da expansão portuguesa no mundo*, 3 vols. (Lisbon, 1937–1940), 2: 359–370. A slightly different English version of this appears in William Brooks Greenlee, ed. and trans., *The Voyage of Pedro Alvares Cabral to Brazil and India* (London, 1938), 34–40. Bensaude pointed out that the shadow would have been to the south. Joaquim Bensaude, *L'astronomie nautique au Portugal a l'époque des grandes découvertes* (Amsterdam, 1967; orig. pub. 1912), 22.

3 An engraving showing how to use the astrolabe in this fashion appears in Pedro de Medina, *Arte de navegar* (Valladolid, 1545), with the caption "Weighing the Sun."

4 Replication of the Portuguese ambassador, June 7, 1562, in Joseph Stevenson, ed., *Calendar of State Papers, Foreign Series, of the Reign of Elizabeth, 1562* . . . (London, 1867), 77 (emphasis added).

places *discovered* . . . he had no superiority at all," the irritated ambassador responded that "his master *has* absolute *dominion* . . . over all those lands already *discovered*."[5] Neither the English nor other European powers of the time officially regarded discovery as creating dominion.[6] Yet the Portuguese did so. While occasionally they planted objects such as stone pillars to indicate the extent of their discoveries, their ability to establish the latitude of a new place provided the central proof of their discovery.

Behind the concept of discovery lay Portugal's pioneering of the science of nautical astronomy.[7] Like modern technology or intellectual property rights, the Portuguese claimed a right to monopolize access to regions unattainable without the techniques they had pioneered.[8] This chapter will explore how this tiny nation perched on the edge of Europe came to create both modern nautical astronomy and the techniques of establishing global latitude, only to lose their technical superiority several decades later, never to have it return. Portugal's claim to overseas empire rested upon nautical knowledge based on accurate observations of the southern skies – Pedro Nunes's "new sky and new

5 Answer to the Portuguese ambassador, June 15, 1562, ibid., 95. Second replication of the Portuguese ambassador, June 19, 1562, ibid., 106 (emphasis added).

6 There are also two major contemporary misapprehensions about the term *discovery*. The first is the erroneous impression created by the U.S. Supreme Court's 1823 decision which misattributes "discovery" to founding sixteenth-century English claims to the New World. While some colonists argued for this, they did so either imitating or contesting Portuguese claims. Officially, England did not recognize Portuguese claims based upon discovery. The second misapprehension concerns the mid-twentieth century debate over "discovery." See note 7 for details.

7 There is a long history of misunderstanding this concept in English-language writing. "The absurdity of gaining possession of a continent by sailing along its coast line was so obvious that some writers (the Englishman Thomas Gage in 1648) facetiously suggested that Europe would have to be conceded to any Indian prince who happened to send a ship to "discover" it." Wilcomb Washburn, "Dispossessing the Indian," in James Morton Smith, ed., *Seventeenth-Century America* (Chapel Hill, N.C, 1959), 17. The trouble was that this was exactly why the Portuguese indeed considered themselves to have a right – since the technological achievement was theirs – and in fact no Indian was technologically capable of sending a ship to discover. Washburn also cites another contemporary U.S writer who describes the right of discovery as "the pre-eminent right of the first trespasser" (A. J. Liebling, *New Yorker* [Jan. 15, 1955], 36). The trouble with this second humorous observation is that the humor (and the critique) depend upon understanding historically English conceptions of the relationship between discovery and the law of trespass – a nonexistent connection in Portuguese law codes of the sixteenth century. The concept of trespass relies upon a wholly English conception of what discovery entailed – putting foot on land – which did not have anything to do with establishing possession in sixteenth-century Portuguese law, and still does not in either Portuguese or Brazilian law of the late twentieth century.

8 D. João III to Rui Fernandes (feitor of Flanders) May 2, 1534. "Os mares que todos devem e podem navegar são aquellas que sempre foram sabidos de todos e communs a todos, mas os outros, que nunca foram sabidos nem parecia que se podiam navegar e foram descobertos com tão grandes trabalhos por mim, esses não." Quoted in M. E. Carvalho, *D. João III e os francezes* (Lisbon, 1909), 64.

stars." The observations Master John made on the coast of Brazil in 1500 formed an important part of that knowledge. His trip itself began, however, as an expedition to India.

Because the wind and currents in the South Atlantic circle in a counterclockwise direction, Vasco da Gama's fleet, like other Portuguese voyages before it, sailed far west out into the Atlantic before turning eastward toward the Cape of Good Hope.

In April 1500, the Portuguese fleet bearing Master John was crossing the South Atlantic on its way to repeating Vasco da Gama's historic voyage around the Cape of Good Hope to India and first caught sight of signs that they were approaching land. On the evening of April 22, thousands of miles out into the South Atlantic, the fleet sighted land. The next morning, cautiously sounding the depth of the ocean floor (a usual Atlantic coast technique) the fleet, led by the smaller ships, headed for the mouth of a river.

The notary, Pedro Vaz Caminha, details how the fleet approached land, including the successively shallower anchorages and mouths of rivers:

> He (the expedition's leader, Pedro Alvarez Cabral) ordered the lead to be thrown. They found 25 fathoms; and at sunset some 6 leagues from the land, we cast anchor in 19 fathoms, a clean anchorage. There we remained all that night, and on Thursday morning we made sail and steered straight to the land, with the small ships going in front, 17, 16, 15, 13, 12, 10 and 9 fathoms, until half a league from the shore, where we all cast anchor in front of the mouth of a river.[9]

Once anchored, the commander ordered the senior most experienced captain to investigate the river. Putting ashore in a small boat on April 23, 1500, Nicolaú Coelho was met by about twenty natives, with whom he exchanged the characteristic red and blue hats of Mediterranean seafarers for the elaborate feathered headdresses of the Tupis. By the time the exchange was over at nightfall, Coelho returned to his ship.[10]

Thus ended the first recorded contact between the Portuguese and the people of what came to be known as Brazil on the mainland of South America. No symbols of European sovereignty were unfurled in the initial meeting, unlike Columbus's immediate planting of the

9 Gaspar Correa, *Lendas da India*, 4 vols. (Porto, 1975; orig. pub. 1858–1866), 1: liv. 2, cap. 2, writes of how another lost version of the event has similar information. Cabral ordered Andre Gonçalves "que fosse correndo a costa sempre em quanto podesse . . . e descobrio muyto della, que tinha muytos bons portos e rios, esecuendo tudo, e as sondas e sinaes; com que tornou a ElRey" (152). On the preoccupation with nautical precision at this time, see also Vitórino Magalhães Godinho, *Les découvertes XVᵉ–XVIᵉ: Une révolution des mentalités* (Paris, 1990), 42–43.

10 Correa, *Lendas*, 1: liv. 2, cap. 2, 15, has Coelho accompanied by his Moslem pilot.

royal banner and two flags. There were no ceremonies such as the French usually performed accompanying the landing on New World soil. There were no descriptions of places to plant houses and gardens as did the English. There was only a man in a boat attempting to investigate the mouth of the river and trading his headgear for that of others, the first hesitant steps at trading by a representative of a commercial seafaring power.

Sailing briefly northward after this exchange, the expedition spent the week resting and continuing to trade. Two masses were recited, on Sunday and then again just before the ships set forth for India, as was customary. A cross was planted as well. The expedition's notary, Pedro Vaz Caminha, concluded his account setting forth the potential economic benefits of the region, which he considered limited, suggesting that it would be best as a way station on the voyage to India. More importantly, Cabral, the commander, dispatched a second official account of the events of April 1500 composed by Master John, widely believed to have been a Jew who converted to Christianity in order to stay in Portugal.[11]

Master John reported the exact latitude of the discovery, relying not on the land below, but the heavens above: the position of the sun and the stars. But he made an additional contribution. On the coast of Brazil Master John made the first accurate European depiction of the most famous constellation in all the new skies, the Southern Cross.[12]

This constellation which lies close to the southern celestial pole, of course, was not, strictly speaking, new. The stars had been in the heavens for billions of years, perhaps since the beginning of time. And the navigators who had sailed the southern seas for hundreds of years be-

11 Greenlee, *Voyages*, 35. On the forced yet often nominal conversions to Christianity, see Meyer Kayserling, *História dos judeus em Portugal*, trans. Gabriele Borchardt Corrêa da Silva and Anita Novinsky (São Paulo, 1971), 105–134; on D. Manuel's protection of the *converso* community generally, see ibid., 122–134.

12 Abel Fontoura da Costa, *A Marinharia dos descobrimentos*, 3d ed. (Lisbon, 1960), 119–137. Earlier Portuguese voyages had noted the cross, but none had produced accurate representations of it. An earlier drawing thought by some to be the Southern Cross is the constellation drawn by Cadamosto in G. R. Crone, ed., *Voyages of Cadamosto and Other Documents on Western Africa in the Second Half of the Fifteenth Century* (London, 1937), chap. 39. The Portuguese version is José Manuel Garcia, ed., *As viagens dos descobrimentos* (Lisbon, 1983), 121. But Cadamosto's constellation (which he calls a "car") consists of six big bright stars lying on their side, supposedly due south (by the compass). Master John, whose drawing is known to be of the Southern Cross, describes five stars (none bright) described as somewhat hard to locate. All of these tally with subsequent descriptions of the constellation. Also see Vitórino Godinho, ed., *Documentos sobre a expansão portuguesa* (Lisbon, 1943–1956), 3: 174–175, 191n50. Other controversies relating to Cadamosto's observations are in Pierre Chaunu, *European Expansion in the Later Middle Ages*, trans. Katharine Burton (Amsterdam, 1979), 254–255. For some minor inaccuracies in Master John's drawing, see Luís de Albuquerque, *Historia de la navegación portuguesa* (Madrid, 1991), 102–104.

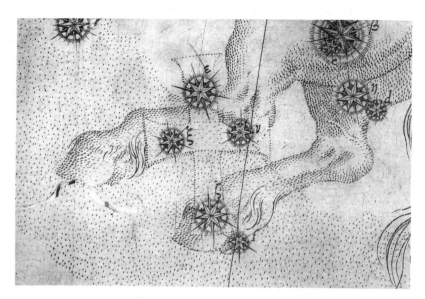

Figure 3. The Southern Cross. From Johannes Bayer, *Uranometria.*

fore the Europeans arrived both knew of these stars and had names for them. Arabs named the constellation after a geometric shape – the quadrilateral – and Polynesians (who also used it for navigation) called it "the net" or "sacred timber" (i.e., wood for ship masts).[13] But the Portuguese, the first Europeans to regularly observe these southern skies, were the first to mathematically track its apparent movement through the skies in order to use it for celestial navigation; their name is the one by which it is known today in most of the world – the Southern Cross.

Yet Master John apologized for his drawing, saying he was "only sending Your Highness (a drawing of) how the stars (the Southern Cross and Antarctic pole) are situated." He had hoped to measure the position of the stars above the horizon, but added by way of explanation, "At what degree each star is, one cannot tell rather it seems impossible to take the height of any star at sea." Master John had wanted to send the numbers which would have fixed the positions of the stars, not as places, but as points on an invisible grid in space.

While pilots from other nations in subsequent years would sometimes report steering directions and latitudes for reaching the New

13 The Polynesian names are those given by the Anutans in Richard Feinberg, *Polynesian Seafaring and Navigation: Ocean Travel in Anutan Culture and Society* (Kent, Ohio, 1988), 101. Another Polynesian name for the constellation is Newe. The Arabs called the pole star Gah. Abel Costa, *Marinharia*, 63.

World, none would provide astronomical descriptions as part of their official records of discovery.[14] Nor would other European leaders consider astronomical observations central to their legal claims to the New World. But their importance to Portuguese officials can be gauged in two different ways.

First, the commander diverted a ship from the all-important voyage to India – leaving the expedition short one potentially important vessel – all in order to send back the notary's and Master John's reports to Lisbon.

The second key to the importance of astronomical knowledge is contained in the letter of Master John himself. Unlike the formal and distant tone of the notary's narrative, which begs the king's indulgence for writing to him, Master John's writes as a man on familiar speaking terms with the monarch. He tells the king what to do – "Your Highness should order a mappa mundi to be brought which Pedro Vaz Bisagudo has" – and tells him to use it to determine the location. He apologizes for not having been able to do as much work as the king had requested. "Your Highness will know that I have done whatever work I could concerning the stars, but not much, because of a very bad leg . . . and also because this ship is very small." The closeness continues as Master John expresses how he thinks the king will respond to some of the news he is sending: "If Your Highness knew how they (the Maldivean sighting devices) all disagreed in the inches you would laugh at this." Even more than his being privy to the king's knowledge of scientific and navigational experiments, his understanding of the king's likely emotional response is revealing. This formerly Jewish astronomer understands that this monarch will be amused rather than annoyed by the ranges of the results. Only someone high in the king's regard would have the confidence to write such a letter. The king's evident familiarity with and concern for obtaining astronomical and scientific information demonstrate its importance. But Manuel's reaction was not unusual. Portugal's royal families had come to view astronomical observation as critical over the course of the fifteenth century, as ships began to sail farther and farther south of Lisbon into the South Atlantic. To achieve their military, strategic, and even economic objectives on these voyages, the royal family would sponsor the

---

14 The most detailed accounts were Jacques Cartier's logbook and John Winthrop's log, neither of which was ever sent as part of an official record to the crown. Neither contains any astronomical information. Jacques Cartier, *Voyages of Jacques Cartier* (Ottawa, 1924), and James K. Hosmer, ed., *Winthrop's Journal "History of New England," 1630–1649*, 2 vols. (New York, 1909). Nor would the Dutch have provided the kinds of information that Master João provided in the sixteenth century, since prior to the 1550s, the principal Dutch means of navigation were rutters, sounding lead, and compass. Gunther Schilder, "The Netherlands Nautical Cartography from 1550 to 1650," *Revista de Universidade de Coimbra*, 32 (1985): 97–119, esp. 100. Even the use of charts to sail by were not introduced in the Netherlands until the 1580s.

invention of celestial navigation by drawing heavily upon the Iberian peninsula's unique scientific heritage, the long-standing traditions of Islamic and Hebrew mathematics and astronomy.

During the Middle Ages, the Islamic world had developed astronomy to a level unknown in the West. As historian Owen Gingerich remarked, "Historians who track the development of astronomy . . . refer to the time from the eighth through the fourteenth centuries as the Islamic period. During that interval most astronomical activity took place in the Middle East, North Africa, and Moorish Spain."[15] While Islamic astronomers had virtually disappeared from Portugal by the fifteenth century, the tradition remained still vibrant in the hands of Jewish astronomers and mathematicians who had been their traditional collaborators and peers.[16] They in turn used their scientific knowledge of astronomy and trigonometry to solve the practical problems of navigation, an application never developed by its Islamic counterpart.[17]

THE UNFOLDING OF PORTUGUESE NAUTICAL SCIENCE

Before Portuguese voyages out into the South Atlantic, few Europeans had strayed far from coastal waters.[18] When traveling along the northwestern coast of Europe, they found their position by taking depth

15 Owen Gingerich, "Islamic Astronomy," *Scientific American*, 254 (1986): 74–83, esp. 74. Kedar notes that medieval writers on science were always careful to describe them as Arabs rather than Moslems. They used the derogatory term "Saracen" to mean Muslim. Benjamin Kedar, *Crusade and Mission: European Approaches Toward the Muslims* (Princeton, N. J., 1984), 91.

16 On the Jewish heritage see Costa, *Marinharia*, 13, 80–81, 85–95; Luís de Albuquerque, *Introducção à história dos descobrimentos portugueses*, 2d ed. (Lisbon, n.d.), 202–214, 218–220. More recent information on Iberian Jewish scientists is in Bernard Goldstein, "The Survival of Arabic Astronomy in Hebrew" and "The Hebrew Astronomical Tradition: New Sources," in his *Theory and Observation in Ancient and Medieval Astronomy* (London, 1985), sects. 21 and 22.

17 One reason may be that much of the navigational techniques of the Indian Ocean were originally developed by Persians rather than by Arabs. Much Arabic nautical terminology derives from Middle Persian. See André Wink, *Al-Hind: The Making of the Indo-Islamic World*, vol. 1 (Leiden, 1990). Arabic Indian Ocean nautical practice in 1497 is contained in Ahmad ibn al-Majid, *As-Sufaliyya "The Poem of Sofala,"* trans. and explained by Ibrahaim Khoury (Coimbra, 1983). An earlier flawed translation is idem, *Arab Navigation in the Indian Ocean Before the Coming of the Portuguese*, trans. Gerald R. Tibbetts (London, 1971). On the usual Arab uses of astronomy and trigonometry, see Gingerich "Islamic Astronomy," 74–83. Nor did the Arabs use their astronomical knowledge for geographical purposes. J. Spencer Trimingham, "The Arab Geographers and the East African Coast," in H. Neville Chittick and Robert I. Rotberg, eds., *East Africa and the Orient: Cultural Syntheses in Pre-Colonial Times* (New York, 1975), 137.

18 Even in the early sixteenth century, navigation in northern Europe was still coastal. David W. Waters, *The Rutters of the Sea* (New Haven, 1967); idem, *The Art of Navigation in England in Elizabethan and Early Stuart Times* (New Haven, 1958), 11; E. G. R. Taylor, *The Haven-Finding Art: A History of Navigation from Odysseus to Captain Cook*, 2d ed. (London, 1971). For Polynesian navigation and astronomy, the best guide is

soundings – a measurement of the continental shelf which extended even far out to sea. While Vikings had traveled for (at most) several days in the North Atlantic without sighting land, they followed currents, winds, and the path of sea birds, guided by the nearly always visible midnight sun and north polestar, and where possible, by the high continental shelf.[19] Within the narrow confines of the Mediterranean with its constantly nearby coasts, seafarers principally built upon knowledge of shorelines rather than of oceans.[20] Yet none of these was possible in the South Atlantic, an environment wholly unlike any in which Europeans or indeed any other seafaring power had sailed before. There was neither a continental shelf nor a coast to follow. Nor were there winds or ocean currents that would carry a ship easily southward and back again. Unlike the North Atlantic, Pacific, and Indian Oceans, which could be, and indeed had been, sailed using just such techniques for hundreds and in some cases thousands of years, the South Atlantic had never been successfully sailed before the fifteenth century. The Portuguese were the first to do so, but finding the solution to navigating the South Atlantic was neither simple nor easy.

In sailing around Africa, therefore, Portuguese sailors were also unable to draw on the classical techniques of land explorers – native guides, landmarks, or even the paths carved over a terrain by traditional trade routes. There was no indigenous tradition of coastal navigation from which they could profit. The South Atlantic was brand new sailing territory. As Pedro Nunes bragged, "The sea voyages of this kingdom over the last hundred years are greater and more marvelous . . . than those of any other people in the world. The Portuguese dared to venture fearlessly into the great ocean sea (the Atlantic)."[21] The South Atlantic presented significant challenges in terms of ship

Nicholas J. Goetzfridt, *Indigenous Navigation and Voyaging in the Pacific: A Reference Guide* (New York, 1992); for Micronesia, see K. G. Oatley, "Mental Maps for Navigation," *New Scientist*, 64 (1974): 863–866; W. H. Alkire, "Systems of Measurement on Woleai Atoll, Caroline Islands," *Anthropos*, 65 (1970): 1–73; T. Gladwin, *East is a Big Bird: Navigation and Logic on Pulwat Atoll* (Cambridge, Mass., 1970).

19 Geoffrey J. Marcus, *The Conquest of the North Atlantic* (Woodbridge, Eng., 1980), 105–118. Marcus suggests that the Vikings may have had "crude" methods for using the pole star and sun for navigation. Like the Polynesians the Vikings did not have a compass.

20 Medieval navigational charts, or portolans, are basically coastal guides. Boies Penrose, *Travel and Discovery in the Renaissance, 1420–1620* (Cambridge, Mass., 1960), 241–243; Avelino Teixeira da Mota, "A Evolução da Ciência Náutica durante os séculos XV–XVI na cartografia portuguesa da epoca," *Memorias da Academia das Ciências de Lisboa*, 7: 3–22. Arab navigation appears to have been principally coastal as well. André Miquel, *La géographie humaine du monde musulman jusqu'au milieu du 11ᵉ siècle* (Paris, 1988), 156–157.

21 "As navegações deste reyno de cem anos a esta parte: sam as mayores mais maravilhosas: de mais altas e mais secretas conjeyturas: que as de nehu a outra gente do mundo. Os portugueses ousaram cometer o o grande mar Oceano. Entrarã per elle sem nehũ reçeo." Nunes, *Tratado em defensa*, in *Obras*, 1: 175.

design, methods of sailing, ascertaining distance traveled, and fixing location at sea. Portuguese mariners needed to be able to describe a position unmarked on any map, nor described in any ancient chronicle or traveler's lore – a position that they reached not by a path known to others – but by sailing the open seas.[22]

Portuguese oceangoing knowledge developed gradually. Starting with voyages southward to the Azores in the 1420s, the Portuguese began to sail the open seas by relying upon traditional means: following ocean currents, winds, and the path of sea birds, as well as noting the presence of seaweed. Traveling for the first time without depth soundings or coastline to guide them,[23] they initially relied upon a compass, developed by the Chinese and brought to the West by Moslems and adopted widely during the twelfth and thirteenth centuries. The compass consisted of a magnetized needle suspended over a card showing wind directions.[24] They became highly proficient at following winds and currents, at noting exact directions on a more precise compass, and knowing exactly how long to travel on a given course (the art of dead reckoning).

The Portuguese were soon to encounter new obstacles to their southward voyages, however, principally at two junctures: crossing Cape Bojador (1434) and later the equator (1471). The first set of major hurdles appeared immediately after rounding the southern limit of European and Arab navigation in the Atlantic, Cape Bojador. While vessels had previously sailed as far south as this cape on the West African coast, no one had successfully rounded it and returned. Once having both crossed Cape Bojador and returned in 1434, Portuguese navigators began to journey through what were previously uncharted

22 The science of astronomy was originally created by Babylonians and then the Greeks. It was substantially altered during what Gingerich calls "the Islamic period." Pingree observes that Greek astronomy in the thirteenth and fourteenth centuries was completely reliant upon translations of Arabic and Persian astronomical works. David Pingree, "Gregory Chioniades and Palaeologan Astronomy," in *Dumbarton Oaks Papers*, 18 (1964): 135–140, 144–146. European historians have customarily ignored the Islamic heritage for reasons George Sarton explains: "As the history of the Renaissance has been written by scholars unfamiliar with the Arabic past, it has not yet been realized clearly enough that the Renaissance was a revolt not only against scholasticism but also against all the Arabic learning which had been the vehicle of Greek learning and had sometimes adulterated it or replaced it." In the case of astronomy, it had substantially improved it. George Sarton, "Arabic Science in the Fifteenth Century," in *Homenaje a Millás Vallicrosa* (Barcelona, 1956), 2: 317. One of the few U.S. writers to acknowledge this is Norman Thrower, "The Art and Science of Navigation Before 1900," in Herman Friis, ed., *The Pacific Basis: A History of Its Geographical Exploration* (New York, 1967), 18–39.
23 The Vikings had depth soundings; Arabs and eastern Mediterranean sailors had coastline. Teixeira da Mota, "Evolução," 6–7.
24 Ibid., 3. The Portuguese made the instrument capable of greater precision by increasing the number of divisions from twenty-four to thirty-two. Costa, *Marinharia*, 166.

areas of the South Atlantic. Wind directions and tides were to pose the first serious challenges to their existing technology.

South of Cape Bojador, winds and sailing conditions rendered traditional Mediterranean ship design useless. Mediterranean ships were designed to sail with the wind from behind; but off the bulge of Africa, ships endured a long period with the wind coming across the beam, subjecting them to long periods of little or no winds or those from a contrary direction. In the 1440s the Portuguese began to pioneer a new kind of ship design, the caravel.[25] Built to navigate in shallow coastal waters as well as to sail into the wind, the caravel combined a long shallow hull that enabled it to sail longer distances swiftly with the greater flexibility of triangular (lateen) sails.[26] The latter was the key to navigating with contrary winds. Lateen sails enable vessels to sail toward the wind in a zig-zag pattern – commonly called tacking – with the wind blowing at an angle toward the ship rather than from behind.[27]

Prevailing winds during the long return journey made it necessary to tack for long periods far out of sight of land on the return voyage from West Africa. Beginning in the 1440s, Portuguese sailors began to spend an unprecedented three weeks on the open sea.[28] Having to tack so long meant that more precise methods of calculating distance had to evolve. Keeping track of the distance traveled in a single direction involved only simple addition, but when the distance was traveled in a zig-zag manner, calculating distance was more complicated. To travel a hundred leagues north, in a zig-zag pattern, a pilot might sail

25 Henrique Quirino da Fonseca, *A caravela portuguesa e a prioridade técnica das navegações henriquinas*, 2 vols. (Lisbon, 1978), 2: 166–173; Dieter Messner, *História do lexico português* (Heidelberg, 1990), 42, argues that *caravela* is a Genoese word and is so named in a Latin document of 1230. His lexical argument would bear out the contention by Freitas Riberio, Vizconde de Lagoa, *Grandes viagens portuguesas de descobrimento e expansão* (Lisbon, 1951), 78 that Genoese shipbuilders may have played an important role in the design of the caravel. French scholars such as Jean Favier, *Les grandes découvertes d'Alexandre à Magellan* (Paris, 1991), argue that the word is French in origin.

26 Roger C. Smith, *Vanguard of Empire: Ships of Exploration in the Age of Columbus* (New York, 1993), 36–41. For a brief account of how such ships differed from other European vessels, see ibid., 27–34. Jaime Cortesão, *A política de sigilo nos descobrimentos* (Lisbon, 1960), 34, dates the caravel from 1442. The earliest treatise on Portuguese ships is Manuel Fernandes, *Livro de traças de carpinteria*, facsimile ed. (Lisbon, 1989; orig. pub. 1616).

27 Comandante Henrique Quirino da Fonseca (1868–1939) first argued for the originality of long-distance tacking (*arte de bolinar*) and the Latin caravel (with the triangular sail) in Portuguese voyages. *A caravela portuguesa*, 1: 166–182, 2: 71–74.

28 The method was so familiar to pilots by this time that even a sixteen-year-old boy with little experience could pilot a ship back across the open ocean when the pilots were killed in a shore skirmish in 1446. Albuquerque, *Introducção à história dos descobrimentos*, 196–198; idem, *História da Náutica*, 42–43. To see how, for example, even highly experienced French sailors were unable to do this even by the start of the sixteenth century, see the account of Paulmier de Gonneville, *Campagne du navire l'Espoir de Honfleur, 1503–1505*.

seventy-five leagues northwest. Having sailed that leg, he needed to know how far to travel in a northeasterly direction in order to sail a hundred leagues north. But to calculate that he had to know how to find the value of a side of a triangle, using the two sides or one side and two angles. The first solution required simple geometry, the second plane trigonometry.[29] Portuguese pilots (who were probably unfamiliar with the mathematics involved) needed access to a table in which the calculations had already been made. By 1436 they were readily using such a table called a *toleta* with ready-made indications of distances to tack.[30] Thus, when beginning to tack back and forth on the high seas, Portuguese mariners relied upon an abstractly derived set of numbers. The confidence that mere numbers could accurately tell a pilot how far to sail miles from land, for days, even weeks, at a time began to encourage a habit of relying upon calculation to provide solutions to the navigational challenges of the South Atlantic.

After the winds, there was a second difficulty sailors soon encountered: the existence of powerful tides first encountered in the vicinity of Cape Bojador. These tides could recede quickly, beaching even a large ship quickly or else splintering it to pieces against rocky shores.[31] Far more powerful than those in the Mediterranean, these tides presented a formidable new obstacle. Since tides were determined by lunar cycles, precise knowledge of lunar movements became imperative in order to enter or leave a South Atlantic harbor safely.

At the end of the fourteenth century, a Portuguese monarch invited Jacob ben Abraham Cresques, son of the famous Jewish cartographer of Barcelona, to develop Portuguese nautical charts. Cresques had been working with other Jewish cartographers at Mallorca under royal (Aragonese) patronage and had turned the region into a celebrated center of nautical mapmaking.[32] Lured away from Aragon by the Por-

---

29 Albuquerque, *Historia de la navegación portuguesa*, 243–244, shows how the calculations were made, along with the Portuguese nautical terminology for each of the different tacks. It is not known which of these methods was used for calculating the Portuguese tables.

30 Costa, *Marinharia*, 356–363; Luís de Albuquerque, *Curso de História da Náutica* (Coimbra, 1972), 21–23. While possibly Venetian, scholars have argued that it was originally Arabic because its first known appearance is the work of an avid translator of Arabic texts, Ramon Lull. Tony Bell, "Portolan Charts from the Late Thirteenth Century to 1500," in J. B. Harley and David Woodward, eds., *The History of Cartography*, vol. 1 (Chicago, 1987), and Albuquerque, *Historia de navegación*, 238–247. In either case, the Italian use of it for tacking was only for limited periods and not far from sight of land. Alfredo Pinheiro Marques, *Origem e desenvolvimento da cartografia portuguesea na época dos descobrimentos* (Lisbon, 1987), 40–41. In Portuguese it was called the *toleta de marteleio*, coming from *tela do mar* or *teia maritima*.

31 "Grandes inundações do mar, a que os Portugueses chamam correntes." Diogo Gomes, "Primeiro descobrimento da Guiné," in Garcia, ed., *Viagens*, 29–30.

32 Martín Fernández Navarrete, *Disertación sobre la historia de la Nautica* (Madrid, 1846), 92–95; see also Duarte Pacheo Pereira, *Esmeraldo situ orbis*, 3d ed., (Lisbon, 1955); also trans. and ed. George H. Kimble, (London, 1937); Armando Cortesão, *History*

tuguese, not long after anti-Jewish riots in the Castilian- and Catalan-speaking regions of the peninsula which had killed a prominent astronomer, Cresques departed for the unscathed kingdom of Portugal, accompanied by several of his fellow Jewish cartographers. Portugal, as it turned out, had far greater need for Cresques's skills since one of his contributions was an accurate method of determining the tides by lunar cycles, knowledge that was relatively unimportant for sailing in the Mediterranean where Catalan efforts had been directed. By the final years of the fourteenth century, Portuguese nautical charts incorporated the senior Cresques's method of determining the tides.[33]

In order to anchor safely in South Atlantic ports, it was also necessary to keep track of time accurately on board ship. Abraham Cresques's Catalan atlas also contained a very useful method of keeping track of time using the constellations. While nocturnal timekeeping via the stars had been known to the ancient Egyptians, the method employed by Cresques was in use in Portugal by the end of the fourteenth century, and shortly thereafter the Portuguese began to experiment with this method for timekeeping at sea.[34] Knowing the time with greater accuracy made it possible to know exactly when to safely approach or leave from a South Atlantic port.

A third problem the Portuguese faced after rounding Cape Bojador was the absence of any charts. The cape was the limit of European and Arab mapmakers' knowledge of the coast.[35] The Portuguese needed to create new charts in order to keep track of the new regions they en-

of Cartography, 2 vols. (Coimbra, 1971), 2: 93–97, argues that there was an indigenous Portuguese tradition before the arrival of Catalan information on making nautical charts and instruments. Verlinden argues from the other side that the Portuguese tradition of nautical charts did not develop until the 1440s. Charles Verlinden, Quand commença la cartographie portugaise? (Lisbon, 1986). Verlinden's comments, however, presuppose that only Prince Henry would have been interested in navigation. For a recent perspective on the controversy, see Albuquerque, Navegación portuguesa, 242–254.

33 The best medieval account of the relation between tides and lunar cycles was by Albumassar. Edgar S. Laird, "Robert Grosseteste, Albumasar, and Medieval Tide Theory," Isis, 81 (1990): 684–694; Teixeira da Mota, "A Evolução," 3–22; Costa, Marinharia, 10, 290; John F. Guilmartin, Gunpowder and Galleys: Changing Technology and Mediterranean Warfare at Sea in the Sixteenth Century (Cambridge, 1974), 64; Millás, Don Pedro el Ceremonioso, 77, 82–83; Cresques's method was still being used by the end of the fifteenth century. Bensaude, L'astronomie nautique, 156–157. On the killing of the Aragonese king's astronomer in the 1391 riots, see Millás, Don Pedro, 82. Pinheiro Marques notes that there is some controversy about whether the Mallorcan cartographer at Henry's court was actually the son of Abraham Cresques. But it is clear that there was a Mallorcan and Jewish tradition of cartography that passed to Henry's court. Pinheiro Marques, Origem e desenvolvimento, 72–76.

34 The method used by the 1375 Catalan letter is the same used in the Regimento. King Duarte was personally familiar with these calculations. Bensaude, L'astronomie nautique, 155–156; Costa, Marinharia, 42–47; Teixiera da Mota, "A Evolução," 15; Gingrich, "Islamic Astronomy," 76–77. Catalan Raymond Llull in 1272 was the first Christian to note the practice of using stars to establish time at night.

35 The Genoese portolan by Albini de Canepa (1489) covers the Mediterranean region as far as Cape Bojador. It has the thirty-two-point rose showing navigational in-

countered. But in so doing they came up against some crucial limitations in the existing practices of chartmaking.

Nautical charts called portolans were first developed for the Mediterranean at the end of the thirteenth and start of the fourteenth century. Originally designed for coastal navigation and employing directions of a compass to establish directions in which to sail, portolans rarely recorded the distance between ports, crucial information for sailing the previously uncharted waters of the South Atlantic. Furthermore, portolans often erred considerably in fixing the location of ports.[36] While trivial in Mediterranean waters where coasts were never far away, this inaccuracy was potentially lethal in the South Atlantic. An error of 6 degrees was a significant but rectifiable error when sailing in waters where landfalls could be quickly made, but a similar or larger mistake on the open ocean was unthinkably disastrous.[37]

Portolans were unreliable basically because they relied upon the compass.[38] The directions shown by a compass are not true north and south directions because they are affected by variations in the earth's magnetism. While useful as an approximation, a compass actually only points to the magnetic north, a variable point on the globe, sometimes five hundred miles from real north. (On land magnetic north additionally varies in relation to the presence of iron and is affected by daily, monthly, and even weekly variations, as well as by occasional shifts caused by magnetic storms.) Because of the unreliability of compass directions due to the variance of magnetic north, Portuguese pilots in the 1440s turned to astronomical observation.[39] They began to

structions but nothing out into the Atlantic. The portolan is in the James Ford Bell Library in Minnesota.

36 Pinheiro Marques, *Origem e desenvolvimento*, 40–47; Bell, "Portolan Charts," 380–385. On the inaccuracy of port location, see Costa, *Marinharia*, 290; Albuquerque, *História da náutica*, 11–12; also Pinheiro Marques, *Origem e desenvolvimento*, 40–47.

37 Albuquerque, *História da náutica*, 39.

38 While Bell in "Portolan Charts," 384–385, is cautious about attributing the problems to magnetic variation, Portuguese scholars, beginning with Pedro Nunes, *Tratado em defensa* (1537), declared without hestitation that the errors in Mediterranean portolans were due to variations in terrestrial magnetism.

39 Before 1508 Portuguese navigators were measuring the difference between magnetic and true north in India, indicating that they had been aware of the difference long before then. By the 1530s there were three Portuguese scientific treatises on deviations caused by terrestial magnetism. See Luís Albuquerque, "A contribução portuguesa para o conhecemiento do magnetismo terrestre no século XVI," in *As navegações e sua projeção na ciência e na cultura* (Lisbon, 1987), 81–100; Albuquerque, "O magnetismo terrestre no século XVI" *Crónicas de história de Portugal* (Lisbon, 1987), 112–116. By 1514 there were also Portuguese methods for correcting for the magnetic deviation of the compass at sea in João de Castro, *Tratado da agulha de marear* (1514). Other methods appeared in Pedro Nunes, *Tratado*, and Francisco Faleiro, *Tratado del esphera y del arte del marear* (Seville, 1535); Albuquerque, *Navegación*, 220–238. No other European writings mention such a device until the final quarter of the sixteenth century. Ernst Crone, "Navigation, Introduction," in *The Principal Works of Simon Stevin*; vol. 3, *Navigation* (Amsterdam, 1961), 382–391.

use the stars to check on direction they were sailing at sea, as well as to establish where they were upon arriving in ports of the South Atlantic.

Arriving in ports where no one had sailed before, for which there were no maps and no guides, Portuguese navigators identified these places by turning to the most stable and predictable objects they knew, namely, the sun and stars. Beginning in the 1450s, pilots began to measure the highest point (meridian transit) of the pole star above the horizon to fix the latitude of the place where they had arrived. By subtracting this height taken at their destination from the known height of the pole star at Lisbon (at approximately the same time) and multiplying by the number of miles (or leagues) in a degree, they would know how far south of Lisbon they had sailed.[40] By 1462 pilots on successive voyages were writing these observations down in a table. As each pilot's numbers were incorporated, the tables gradually came to contain a series of locations, found by the height of the pole star.[41] Thus, Portuguese navigators began to describe places they had reached based not upon terrestrial descriptions, but upon heavenly ones, fixing new locations by the use of numbers.

To know how many miles or leagues were in a degree required a fairly accurate idea of the size of the earth.[42] Since Babylonian times the earth had been divided into 360 degrees. Knowing the size of the earth and dividing that by 360 established the distance in a degree. Using the calculations made by Moslem astronomers to establish the size of the earth, by 1483 the Portuguese had approximately the correct size of the earth and were able to calculate the distances traveled accurately using degrees.[43]

---

40 Albuquerque, *História da náutica,* 48–49. The height of the pole star varies not daily but more slowly than that. Originally, the calculations were made upon the return to Lisbon, where the numbers taken abroad were compared with observations made in Lisbon at approximately the same time. For the calculations of the size of a degree, see note 41.

41 Albuquerque, *História da náutica,* 44–45, 50–51. The navigators later used a device called a Polaris wheel to account for the variation in the position of the pole star (polar radius).

42 Albert Van Helden, *Measuring the Universe* (Chicago, 1985), studies these calculations principally from the sixteenth century forward.

43 Raymond P. Mercier, "Geodesy," in *Cartography in the Traditional Islamic and South Asian Societies,* 175–179, notes that the Ptolemaic calculations were useless in the Islamic world because no one knew what distance was represented by the Ptolemaic terminology of *stade.* Therefore, all the calculations of the Islamic period were based upon their own observation. After originally erring on the small size (16.67 leagues per degree), by 1483 or 1484 the Portuguese had the right size, 17.5 leagues per degree. At that time the *regimento de leguas* (subtracting the difference in degrees latitude) began to replace the *toleta* to establish distance traveled. The first extant manuscript with the calculations laid out dates from 1505. Costa, *Marinharia,* 365; Joaquín Bensaude, *Guía náutica de Munich,* fascimile edition (Munich 1913). One reason the Portuguese monarchs dismissed Columbus's project is that they, unlike him, had an accurate idea of the size of the earth. On Columbus's mistakes, see J. Brian Harley, *Maps and the Columbian Encounter* (Milwaukee, Wis., 1990), 39.

In solving the problems of navigating the South Atlantic, Portuguese mariners were not borrowing local or indigenous knowledge; nor were they relying upon folk wisdom or experience. Rather, their knowledge depended upon their experience, the instruments they carried with them, and knowledge of the patterns of the skies. They depended upon information we would now call scientific.

Just as the Portuguese began to use the height of the pole star to fix the locations of places they had reached, they also began to call what they were doing "discovery."[44] These were discoveries in two senses. First, the Portuguese were traveling to regions that neither Arabs nor Europeans had reached before and were discovering peoples previously unknown to Arab or European societies.[45] But it was also discovery in a second sense. They were creating an objective, scientific knowledge of locations along the West African coast, knowledge that consisted of numbers. The process of establishing latitudes thus became the principal technique the Portuguese would observe when encountering previously unknown territories and peoples. It was this act of claiming (but using a brand-new technology) that Master John performed on the coast of Brazil in April 1500.

By the 1470s the Portuguese sailed south of the equator and could no longer use the height of the pole star to establish their location. But the habit and reliability of astronomical solutions had already been established: the Portuguese were successfully observing stars for timekeeping, lunar cycles for tides, and height of the polestar for locating position.[46] It was to astronomy that the Portuguese would again turn once south of the equator. In the process they would create the principal instrument of high-seas navigation for the next hundred years – the mariner's astrolabe – and would also first establish the globe in its modern form – as a set of uniform imaginary lines called latitudes.[47]

---

44 Donation of Infante D. Henrique, Dec. 16, 1457, in João Martins da Silva Marques, *Descobrimentos portugueses: documentos para sua história publicados e prefaciados*, 3 vols. (Lisbon, 1944), 1: 544–545. See also Armando Cortesão, " 'Descobrimento' e descobrimentos," in *Junta de investigações do ultramar* (Lisbon, 1972).

45 *Achar* implies a sustained effort to find something. It derives from hunting – sniffing out the game until finding it – "farejar a caça até enontrá-la." Serafim da Silva Neto, *História da língua portuguêsa* (Rio de Janeiro, 1952), 450. For *achar* as a synonym for *descobrir*, see Serapim de Freitas, *De iusto império Luistanorum asiatico* (Valladolid, 1925), chap. 3, ¶ 14, 126. See also Franco Machado, "O conhecimento dos arquipélagos atlânticos no século XIV," in Baião et al. eds., *Expansão portuguesa*, 1: 269–274.

46 They also began to use the position of the guard stars around the pole in order to pinpoint the direction (southwest, northeast) in which to travel, or to describe the direction of the place relative to Lisbon. Albuquerque, *História da náutica*, 63–91.

47 The idea of latitude came from Alexandrian Greeks, but the Portuguese were the first to use latitudes to describe the entire globe, not merely a fraction of it. Furthermore, they were the first to appropriate latitude for navigation.

SOUTH OF THE EQUATOR

Beginning with the voyages of the shadowy Lopo Gonçalves in 1473–1474[48] the Portuguese approached a territory unremarked by classical Greek scholarship, unknown even to the legendary Arab travelers and geographers of the Middle Ages. They had reached a territory that few in Europe had ever even imagined existed and had no models charts or strategies to fall back on. Previously all of their sailing, and indeed that of all Europeans before them, had been done primarily in latitudes north of the equator. The Mediterranean, the Red Sea, even the northern reaches of the Indian Ocean all lie north of the equator. Nor had Europeans often ventured by land south of the equator. Europe's overland trade with Arabia, Persia, and China had traversed terrain north of the equator. Consequently, navigational computations all revolved around using the north polestar, which became invisible south of the equator. During voyages south of the equator, the verb *descobrir* (to discover) appeared increasingly in Portuguese charters.[49] Not only were the Portuguese placing locations upon numbers, they were literally "uncovering" a globe whose dimensions Europeans had never even suspected.

Propelled by these ever-southward voyages, the Portuguese embarked upon the most intense period of navigational experimentation and investigation in their history.[50] For it was not simply enough to have arrived there once. The Portuguese needed to know exactly where they were, how to return securely home, and how to return safely and efficiently to those same locations over and over again. They needed a science whose results could be reproduced exactly. For this they would turn to the unique scientific heritage of the Iberian peninsula – the mathematics and astronomy of the Islamic period – to which Portugal had become the principal heir.

By the middle of the thirteenth century, the Portuguese reconquered their section of the Iberian peninsula from the Moslems. While a substantial number of Moslems remained – their numbers even increasing in Lisbon during the fourteenth century – the elite members of the Moslem community (including scientists) appear to have migrated east to the Moslem kingdom of Granada or south to

48 "Junta das missoões geográficas e de investigações coloniais," *Atlas de Portugal ultramarino* (Lisbon, 1949), map 2.
49 A. Cortesão, " 'Descobrimento.' "
50 J. Spencer Trimingham, "The Arab Geographers and the East African Coast," and "Notes on Arabic Sources of Information on East Africa," in Chittick and Rotberg, eds., *East Africa*; Costa Brochado, *Historiógrafos dos descobrimentos* (Lisbon, 1960), 51.

Morocco, thus leaving most of the scientific knowledge still in Portugal's significant Jewish population.[51]

Unlike most medieval Christian science, Islamic science openly allowed people of other religious faiths to participate in scientific discussions and dialogue. Hence, Jewish scholarship in astronomy existed from the start of astronomical work in the Islamic period.[52] On the Iberian peninsula, beginning in the twelfth century, Jewish astronomers translated numerous Arabic scientific texts into Hebrew and other languages. Yet these Jewish scholars were not simply transparent vehicles for Islamic astronomy; they commented upon and interpreted this tradition, and their commentaries and writings became accepted into the Islamic tradition.[53] Iberian Jewish astronomers composed at least fifteen known original treatises on instruments of observation and created the first scientific literature written in Hebrew.[54] They also created a distinctive astrolabe with Hebrew characters.[55]

51 Antonio Henrique de Oliveira Marques, *Novos ensaios de história medieval portuguesa* (Lisbon, 1988), 89, 96–107, esp. 102. On the decline of Islamic science, see George Sarton, "Arabic Science," in *Homenaje a Millás Villacrosa*, 2: 316.

52 The earliest treatise on the astrolabe was written by a Jewish scholar named Masha'allah. However, the Latin version of his treatise attributed to "Mesahalla," was actually the work of an eleventh-century Moslem astronomer of Cordoba named Ibn Ṣaffār. Kunitzsch, "On the Authenticity of the Treatise on the Composition and Use of the Astrolabe Ascribed to Messahalla," in his *Arabs and the Stars: Texts and Traditions on the Fixed Stars* (Northhampton, 1989); José Maria Millás Vallicrosa, *Las tablas astrónomicas del rey Don Pedro el Cermonioso* (Barcelona, 1962), 16, 70, cites two Hebrew treatises on the astrolabe composed in Aragon by Abraham ibn Ezra and Jacobo Corsini. The Catalan tables were composed by two Jewish scientists. See George F. Hourani, "The Early Growth of the Secular Sciences in Andalucia," *Studia Islamica*, 32 (1970): 143–156, esp. 152.

53 Jews translated three-quarters of the *Libro del saber de astrología* for Spain's Alfonso X. Francisco Vera, "A Study and Edition of the Royal Scriptorum of *El libro del saber de astrologia* by Alfonso X, el Sabio," 4 vols. (Ph.d. dissertation, University of Wisconsin, 1974), 1: xxvi, quoted in Norman Roth, "Jewish Collaborators in Alfonso's Scientific Work," in Robert I. Burns, S.J., ed., *Emperor of Culture: Alfonso X the Learned of Castile and His Learned Thirteenth-Century Renaissance* (Princeton, N.J., 1985), 228n18. For the names of the Jewish translators and the sections translated, see Roth, "Jewish Collaborators," 65–71. Goldstein, "The Survival of Arabic Astronomy in Hebrew," and "The Hebrew Astronomical Tradition," in his *Theory and Observation*, secs. 21 and 22.

54 Bensaude, *L'astronomie nautique*, 33–34, 51–59; Goldstein, "The Hebrew Astronomical Tradition: New Sources," sec. 22, and "The Role of Science in the Jewish Community in Fourteenth-Century France," sec. 20, 39–42, both in his *Theory and Observation*; see Millás, *Pedro el Ceremonioso*, 16, 70, 76–83, for Hebrew treatises in Catalonia. Watt says that Moorish Spain played an important part in mathematical and astronomical studies. There were two important astronomers in Seville. Jabir ibn Aflah, or Geber, who did work on spherical trigonometry, a discipline in which the Arabs in general made great advances. Early in the twelfth century a Jewish mathematician in Barcelona, Abraham bar-Hiyya ha-Nasi, known as Savasorda, began translating Arab scientific works into Hebrew and writing orignal treatises in Hebrew. W. Montgomery Watt, *The Influence of Islam on Medieval Europe* (Edinburgh, 1972), 35.

55 See Gingrich, "Islamic Astronomy," 79, for Jewish treatises and Hispano-Arab manufacture; Goldstein, "A Hispano-Arabic Astrolabe with Hebrew Starnames," and "The Hebrew Astrolabe in the Adler Plantetarium," secs. 18 and 19 in his *Theory and Observation*.

Hence, on the Iberian peninsula there were lengthy scientific treatises on astrolabes by Jewish scientists and even a craft of Hebrew astrolabes.

Elsewhere in Christian Europe, meetings between Christian and Jewish scientists were secretive and hidden from public view;[56] in recently reconquered areas of Iberia, Christian monarchs continued the policies of toleration permitting and even welcoming non-Christian scholars to participate in scientific discussions. Christian rulers of newly conquered Moslem lands were eager to learn about Islamic science, particularly the advances in astronomy. Since most Moslem scientists fled into Moslem-held territories at the conquest, Christian monarchs turned to Jewish scientists, a well-established custom on the Iberian peninsula. Alfonso X of Castile had convened Jewish and (one) Moslem astronomers in the thirteenth century to create the first set of astronomical tables in a vernacular European language; Pedro the Ceremonious of Catalonia did likewise in the fourteenth.

It was to these and other Jewish scientists on the Iberian peninsula that the Portuguese royal family turned for assistance in solving the navigational obstacles of the South Atlantic. First Prince Henry, who was nicknamed "the Navigator" for his patronage of the emerging science of navigation, and later kings D. Duarte, D. João II, and D. Manuel, relied upon Jewish astronomers such as Jacob ben Abraham Cresques, the brothers Moises and José Vizinho, and Abraham Zacuto (Zakkut) to create astronomically based solutions.[57] Portuguese monarchs had an additional reason for preferring Jewish astronomers. Envisioning their project as an ideological war (crusade) against Islam, Jewish scholars were probably politically far more acceptable to Portuguese royalty than were Islamic ones.[58]

Portugal's efforts to recruit Jewish scientists received an unexpected boost from political events elsewhere on the Iberian peninsula. In Catalonia the royal family had an intense interest in navigational affairs in the Mediterranean, involving frequent use of Jewish astronomers and cartographers. In 1391 waves of armed Christians attacked Jewish communities in Castile, Andalucia, Aragon, and Valencia, killing many Jews, including prominent Jewish scientists. Such attacks, followed by the issuance and implementation in 1412 of repressive measures

---

56 Levi-ben Gerson's connections with the Provençal community are an example of this.
57 See João de Barros, *Asia*, 6th ed. (Lisbon, 1944), dec. 1, liv. 4, cap. 2, for the Vizinho brothers; on the absence of Christian expertise in Portugal in the fifteenth century, see Albuquerque, *Crónicas*, 143–144.
58 "Epistola serenissmi regis Portugalie ad Julium papam secundum de victoria contra infideles, Sept. 25, 1507," in *Monumenta Henricina*, 15 vols. (Coimbra, 1960–), vol. 5; Luis de Camões, *Os Lusiadas* (Lisbon, 1579), canto 1. The mixture of commercial *and* crusading motives is pointed out by Gomes Eannes de Azurara, *The Chronicle of the Discovery and Conquest of Guinea, 1453*, trans. Charles R. Beazley and Edgar Prestage (London, 1896), 31; and Carl Erdmann, *A ideia da Cruzada em Portugal* (Coimbra, 1940).

against the remaining Jews in Aragon, a major center of Jewish scientific knowledge in the preceding century, led to a massive migration of Jewish residents.[59] One of the beneficiaries of this emigration was Portugal, where no such attacks had occurred.[60] The son of the Jewish cartographer Abraham Cresques migrated to Portugal not long after the pogroms, as did the financially prominent Abravanel family.[61] In offering protection for Jewish scientists (perhaps including his royal residence [Sagres]), Prince Henry ensured that their personal safety, at risk elsewhere on the Iberian peninsula, would remain secure.[62] Combined with its relative peace, fifteenth-century Portugal also offered Jewish scientists a chance to participate in an exciting new scientific project. Able to draw upon a historically unique reservoir of scientists familiar with both astronomical instruments and the relevant mathematics, Portuguese leaders were able to encourage Jewish scientists to turn their knowledge and abilities toward solving the technological problems of high-seas navigation.

The mathematical solutions to the navigational problems posed by the South Atlantic came from trigonometry, which had been perfected by Moslems.[63] To establish the direction toward Mecca, which all mosques had to face, Moslem astronomers by the ninth century had created five of the six basic trigonometric functions, having

59 Luis Suárez Fernández, *Judíos españoles en la Edad Media* (Madrid, 1988; orig. pub. 1980), 207–218, 224–226; Antonio Pons, *Los Judíos del reino de Mallorca durante los siglos XIII y XIV*, 2 vols. (Palma de Mallorca, 1984), 2: 157–201; Jaume Rivera Sans, "Los tumultos contra las juderías de la corona de Aragon en 1391," *Cuadernos de Historia: Añejos de la Revista Hispania*, 8 (1977): 213–225. While the Aragonese laws were rescinded in 1419, the Jewish communities remained in their reduced numbers (233–237). Yitzhak Baer, *A History of the Jews in Christian Spain*, trans. Louis Schoffman, 2 vols. (Philadelphia, 1961), 2: 95–99; Philippe Wolff, "The 1391 Pogrom in Spain, Social Crisis or Not?" *Past and Present*, 50 (1971): 4–18; Miguel Angel Motis Dolader, "La expulsion de los judios aragoneses," in *Destierros Aragoneses: Judios y Moriscos* (Zaragosa, 1988), 71–72. On the presence of Catalan materials in Portugal, see Albuquerque, *Introducção*, 215–217.

60 On the absence of such anti-Semitic riots in Portugal, see Albuquerque, *Introducção*, 214; Kayserling, *História dos judeus*, 25–36.

61 Suárez Fernández, *Judíos epañoles*, 234; Colette Sirat, *La philosophie juive medievale en pays de Chretienté* (Paris, 1988), 164, 169–170.

62 The mistaken idea that this was a school appears in Daniel Boorstin, *The Discoverers* (New York, 1983), 161–164. For critiques, see Bailey W. Diffie and George D. Winius, *Foundations of the Portuguese Empire* (Minneapolis, Minn., 1977), 115–116; Luís de Albuquerque, *Introducção a história dos descobrimentos portugueses* (Mem Martins, n.d.), 193–194. For an early critique of the idea of Sagres as a "school," see Marquis of Souza Holstein, "A Escola de Sagres e as tradições do Infante D. Henrique," in *Conferencias celebradas na Academia Real das Ciências de Lisboa acerca dos descobrimentos e colonisacoes do Portuguezes na Africa (1877–1880)* (Lisbon, 1892), 76–77; David C. Lindberg, *The Beginnings of Western Science: The European Scientific Tradition in Philosophical, Religious and Institutional Context, 600 B.C. to A.D. 1450* (Chicago, 1992), 263–267.

63 Trigonometry is the branch of mathematics dealing with angles. Greek attempts at solving the problems of angles were clumsy and awkward.

adopted one (the sine function) from India.[64] By the fifteenth century, trigonometry had been a standard component of mathematical knowledge on the Iberian peninsula for six hundred years.[65] Moslem and Jewish astronomers also developed a set of sophisticated instruments to measure and observe astronomical phenomena. These mathematics and astronomical instruments turned out to be the keys to establishing location along the previously uncharted coasts of the South Atlantic. But the process was not a straightforward application of already known information.

Furthermore, before the fifteenth century, even on the Iberian peninsula, only a tiny scholarly elite was familiar with either trigonometry or astronomy and its instruments. How to render the sophisticated astronomical instruments or trigonometric functions useful for navigational purposes was something neither Islamic nor Jewish scholars on the Iberian peninsula or elsewhere had ever successfully explored.[66] Such efforts had begun in Catalonia, but these had been halted in 1391.[67] After experimenting with a number of different devices over the course of a decade, the Portuguese settled on the best-known and best-regarded instrument of astronomical observation on the Iberian peninsula, the astrolabe.

THE ASTROLABE

An instrument of nighttime observation probably of Greek origin dating from the second or third century,[68] the astrolabe was a circular disk made of brass with a needle-like indicator attached at the center and a series of numbers engraved on the side. In what Gingerich calls "the Islamic era" – the eighth through fourteenth centuries – the astrolabe

---

64 E. S. Kennedy, "The Arabic Heritage in the Exact Sciences," *Al-Abhath*, 23 (1970): 327–344; idem, "The History of Trigonometry," in *Studies in the Islamic Exact Sciences* (Beirut, 1983), 3–29; David King, "On the Astronomical Tables of the Islamic Middle Ages," "Astronomical Timekeeping in Ottoman Turkey," and "Al-Khalili's Qibla Table," all in *Islamic Mathematical Astronomy* (London, 1986); a critique of the trigonometric solution to the *qibla* problem is Evert M. Bruins, "Ptolemaic and Islamic Trigonometry: The Problem of the Qibla," *Journal for the History of Arabic Science* 9 (1991): 45–68.

65 The first Christian treatise on trigonometry was not even composed until the fifteenth century.

66 Why Arab astronomy never developed the navigational application is a question that has been asked by numerous Arab scholars. Some argue that Arab navigation came from the Persians, since many Arabic nautical terms derive from Middle Persian (the Sassanian period). Trimingham, "Notes on Arabic Sources of Information on East Africa," in Chittick and Rotberg, eds., *East Africa and the Orient*, 281. Even in the sixteenth century there was an important center of Islamic astronomy at the court of Uleg Beg, but it too also failed to develop the practical applications to navigational astronomy.

67 Catalan scholars might have developed the technology to navigate using the astrolabe since they had much of the mathematics necessary. Millás, *Pedro el Ceremonioso*, 61–63, 71–73. But while there is some evidence they attempted to use it, there is no evidence that they actually succeeded.

68 Costa, *Marinharia*, 19. See also note 69.

was transformed into a superb instrument of astronomical observation, equipped with sophisticated calculating devices that facilitated keeping track of the constellations in the sky and the hours of the night.[69] By the fifteenth century, astrolabes were more popular on the Iberian peninsula than elsewhere in the Islamic world.[70] Their manufacture and use was a sophisticated science.[71]

While a few treatises on the astrolabe had been translated and disseminated elsewhere in Europe, they remained buried in monasteries, inaccessible to those interested in navigation.[72] Nor did those possessing the treatises have anything like the extensive practical experience of Iberian Jewish scientists in using the astrolabe. Furthermore, many of the Iberian scientists were also craftsmen capable of producing quantities of highly accurate devices.

While a popular instrument of astronomical observation on the Iberian peninsula, the astrolabe was also a device which Moslem astronomers in Islamic Spain had substantially modified. Astrolabes originally required a change of plates for use in different latitudes. But in the eleventh century, two Islamic astronomers in Andalusi independently created the first universal astrolabes that could be used at any degree of latitude.[73]

To orient themselves south of the equator without the familiar night skies of the northern hemisphere, the Portuguese opted to build a navigational system based upon the single constant of both hemispheres, namely, the sun.[74] But having selected the Iberian astrolabe

69 An excellent description of the complexity of Islamic astrolabes is Emile Savage-Smith, "Celestial Mapping," in J. Brian Harley and David Woodward, eds., *History of Cartography;* vol. 2, pt. 1, *Cartography in the Traditional Islamic and South Asian Societies* (Chicago, 1992), 12–70. See also Bensaude, *l'Astronomie nautique,* 79, for the weight and size of Arab astrolabes.

70 Sundials and quadrants were more common in the eastern Islamic world. David King, "Three Sundials from Islamic Andalucia," *Journal for the History of Arabic Science,* 2 (1978): 358–392; Richard Lorch, "A Note on the Horary Quadrant," *Journal for the History of Arabic Science,* 5 (1981): 115–120; King, "Astronomical Timekeeping in Ottoman Turkey," in his *Islamic Mathematical Astronomy,* describes how the quadrant was favored over the astrolabe in sixteenth-century Turkey.

71 George Saliba, "Islamic Astrology/Astronomy," *Dictionary of the Middle Ages,* 1: 616–624; Paul Kunitzsch, "Remarks Regarding the Terminology of the Astrolabe," in *The Arabs and the Stars;* David King, "The Origins of the Astrolabe According to Medieval Islamic Sources," *Journal for the History of Arabic Science,* 4 (1980): 43–62; Julio Samso, "Morlama al-Miajriti and the Alfonsine Book on the Construction of the Astrolabe," ibid., 3–8.

72 Albuquerque, *Introducção,* 210–211. The Latin translations were often riddled with errors. See Henri Michel, "Une traité de l'astrolabe du XV siècle," in *Homenaje a Millás Vallicrosa,* 2: 41–71.

73 The two astronomers were 'Ali ibn Khalaf and al-Zarqēllo (Azarquiel). Both dedicated their works to the penultimate Moslem ruler of Toledo before the Christian conquest. Savage-Smith, "Celestial Mapping," 28–31. Andalusi is the correct name for the medieval Islamic area.

74 João de Barros dates the decision to use the sun from the period after the discovery of Guinea. "Verdade de caminho a altura [do sol] e muy certa mostrador." Barros, *Asia,* dec. 1, liv. 3, cap. 2, 127. See also Albuquerque, *Introducção,* 201.

to do that, they needed first to transform the nocturnal astrolabe into an instrument of daytime observation.

Following the suggestion of Ibn Assafar, a twelfth-century Moslem astronomer from Cordoba, the Portuguese altered the design of the astrolabe so that when held by an outstretched arm at the waist, the needle pointing to the sun, the sun passed through two small holes in small squares attached to the top and bottom of the needle. This produced a small circle of light (against the shadow of the squares) which fell upon numbers providing the height of the sun above the horizon (solar altitude).[75] The technique, called "weighing the sun," avoided the problem of having to stare directly at the sun as would have been necessary using the traditional nighttime astrolabe.[76] Ten years after they first crossed the equator, Portuguese explorers began regularly using the astrolabe on land to measure the height of the midday sun.[77]

For the next sixteen years, the daytime astrolabe was used only on firm ground.[78] The procedures that pilots followed upon reaching a new southern point on the west coast of Africa were identical to those Master John later performed on the coast of Brazil. Reaching a new latitude south of the equator, the pilot of the ship or the scientific emissary of the crown disembarked and, taking the astrolabe carefully, noted the height of the midday sun above the horizon and observed the direction in which the sun's shadow fell. Knowing whether he was north or south of the equator, he then calculated the location in degrees latitude. These carefully observed steps marked the Portuguese "discovery" of the region, with the information it produced relayed

75 Albuquerque, *Introducção*, 235. A different procedure for using the astrolabe for the sun had appeared in the Iberian Islamic scientist Arzquiel's treatise and was translated in the *Libros de saber de astronomia*, in ibid., 237. But this method was not adopted for navigation.

76 José Vizinho in 1485 in Guinea and Bartholomeu Dias in 1487 calculated latitudes on land by the height of the sun. Bensaude, *L'astronomie nautique*, 111; David Waters, "The Sea or Mariner's Astrolabe," *Revista da Faculdade de Ciências*, 39: 5–36. An early-sixteenth-century description of how the Portuguese used this instrument is in the letter of Alessandro Zorzi reproduced in *Portugal–Brazil: The Age of Atlantic Discoveries* (New York, 1990), 56–57. An early drawing illustrating how to use this astrolabe is in Pedro Nunes, *Tratado*.

77 The earliest record of an astrolabe's navigational use occurred during Diogo d'Azambuja's West Africa voyage of 1481. David Waters, "The Sea or Mariner's Astrolabe," 8. See also, Albuquerque, "The Art of Astronomical Navigation" in *Portugal–Brazil*, 49.

78 João de Barros admits that sailors had been using the height of the sun for navigational purposes only for a short while before Vasco da Gama's voyage in 1497, and admits that the pilots were unfamiliar with the device at sea. Bensaude, *L'astronomie nautique*, 111; Barros, *Asia*, dec. 1, liv. 3, cap. 2, 126. Master John was clearly still testing it at sea in 1500. While it was unreliable for obtaining the heights of stars at sea, it would prove useful for "shooting the sun." By 1502, Da Gama's second voyage, it had clearly been added to the navigational equipment. For a description of Da Gama's use of the astrolabe on land, see Camões, *Os Luisadas*, canto V, stanzas 25–26.

promptly back to the crown in Portugal, where it was incorporated into the navigational guides for the next overseas voyage, just as had been done when using the pole star.

While modifying an instrument to measure accurately the height of the midday sun above the horizon in a repeatable and scientific fashion overcame the first major navigational obstacle the Portuguese encountered south of the equator, the second problem was translating these measurements into an exact expression of where they were.[79] Just as traversing the equator had led the Portuguese to create a system based upon the single constant of the sun, the selection of a system of noting where a place was also had to be uniform.

The numerical expression of position, long known in astronomical circles, were latitude and longitude. Using their knowledge of the coasts of Africa, calculating the time since the last lunar eclipse, and later magnetic declination at sea, the Portuguese were able to approximate longitude in ways that would prove adequate for navigational purposes for the next two centuries. But they would invent a simplified yet accurate technique that would enable any pilot or mariner to fix the latitude of any landmass correctly, and later any position on the globe. To do so, astronomers drew upon the science and mathematics of the Islamic era.

In the eleventh century, an Islamic astronomer produced the first tables relating latitude to the height of the midday sun above the horizon, but only for use north of the tropic of Capricorn.[80] Subsequent astronomers, almost all Islamic, developed a series of rules hypothetically useful further south,[81] which Portuguese navigators began to use after having crossed the equator.

These earlier tables, however, had failed to settle three important issues. The first was the situation the Portuguese encountered close to the equator, that of being in one hemisphere while measuring the sun in the other. In 1485, the king of Portugal sent two Jewish scientists,

---

79 The most important Portuguese contribution was adapting the table of solar declination to determine latitude. Use of the midday sun's height to calculate position at sea appears to date from the voyages of Diogo Cão (1471). Teixeira da Mota, "Evolução," 9, 16–17.

80 See note 57. Albuquerque, "Astronomical Navigation," in *Portugal–Brazil,* 53, perpetuates the mistaken idea that the tables originated in the ninth century. Kunitzsch, "On the Authenticity of the Treatise;" Gingerich, "Islamic Astronomy," 78.

81 Albuquerque, *História da náutica,* 94–95. Boorstin denigrates the achievements of Portuguese latitude calculations in *The Discoverers,* 48, by erroneously claiming far greater accuracy for "medieval nautical manuals." Not only did the effort require application of a trigonometric formula to predict solar declination, it also required an accurate calendar. An additional barrier to the creation of latitude measures became apparent in the southern hemisphere where such calculations involved negative numbers which were not commonly accepted in mathematics until the seventeenth century.

along with a German invited for the occasion, to decide which of the existing measures produced the best results near the equator.[82]

The second problem centered on describing the apparent movement of the sun throughout the year. The solution was not going to come from observation, since the Portuguese were seeking a means that could be used where the sun's height had never been measured before. The answer would come from a trigonometric equation, which could be used to predict the sun's movement.

The earth's axis of rotation inclines it toward or away from the sun providing us with the experience of seasons. This tilting can be described as the angle of the sun's height above or below the equator. Each day the sun reaches a maximum height in the sky relative to the equator which is called its zenithal latitude, or solar declination.[83] Using a trigonometric equation, Zacuto predicted the sun's declination for each day of the four-year period.[84] (Because the solar year is 365¼ days long and the fraction is made up by adding a day every fourth year, the sun reached a different midday height relative to the equator on nearly every day of a four-year period.) Zacuto created his tables in 1473, shortly after the first crossing of the equator.[85] Latitude could then be calculated by subtracting the noon sun's height above the horizon from 90 degrees, and then subtracting that figure from the solar zenithal latitude reached on that day.

However, there was a final problem. Being able to calculate latitude required that the sun's declination (position with respect to the equator) and noonday height above the horizon be linked to an accurate calendar of the solar year.[86] Fifteenth-century Christian calendars were substantially out of step with the solar year, and only reestablished coordination late in the sixteenth century (and in North America in the middle of the eighteenth). By the eleventh century, however, Jew-

82 Albuquerque, *História da náutica*, 104-106. The German was Martin Behaim.
83 Declination is the angular distance of a celestial object north or south of the celestial equator in a plane perpendicular to the equator.
84 Zacuto's equation relied upon the sine function; a subsequent solution by Nunes used the cosine. For the two equations, see Albuquerque, *História da náutica*, 122. The Europeans most experienced in applying trigonometry to astronomy were Jewish scientists residing in lands formerly under Islamic rule. Not until Regiomontanus (a German astronomer familiar with Portuguese advances) was there a single systematic treatise in a European language. Arab treatises had been in existence for six hundred years.
85 Albuquerque, "Astronomical Navigation," in *Portugal–Brazil*, 26, 58–59, has the date as 1472, but Bernard Goldstein's exhaustive survey of the Hebrew, Arabic, Latin, Spanish, and Ladino versions of the manuscript date it to 1473. Goldstein, "The Hebrew Astronomical Tradition," in his *Theory and Observation*, sec. 22, esp. 246–247.
86 The sun's meridian height remained constant for several periods of successive days, called the "curso do sol." Albuquerque, *História da náutica*, 119. Calculations for subsequent four-year periods required only the addition of a constant (1°46') as Zacuto noted. Ibid., 115. The pole star had been easier to use because its position did not vary daily (as did the sun's).

ish and Islamic astronomers had established the length of a solar year to a high degree of accuracy and had translated these observations into accurate calendars.[87] Beginning in the fourteenth century, the first efforts were made in Portugal to establish tables linking height of the midday sun above the horizon (solar altitude) to the days of a solar year.[88]

Zacuto's final contribution was a means of translating the correct days of the solar year into the days of the Julian calendar. To indicate the correct times of the solar year, he used the nonreligious signs of the zodiac. Giving the location of the sun in the zodiac in degrees and minutes on one side of the table, along with the date of the Julian calendar, enabled pilots to have a means of checking their calculation of the day to be sure that they were picking the correct figures for solar declination.

While Zacuto's first tables linked the apparent movement of the sun relative to the equator (solar declination) to the day, a second table linked solar declinations and solar altitudes, thus requiring a pilot to consult two separate tables.[89] Zacuto next combined and simplified the two tables into one so that an ordinary pilot, knowing the date and measuring the height of the midday sun above the horizon, could determine his latitude exactly in either the southern or northern hemispheres.[90] This handbook, probably created around 1484, was known as the *Rules for the Astrolabe* (*Regimento do astrolabio*). Once developed, the *Rules* made it possible to establish accurate latitudes any day of the year on any landmass on the globe – regardless of whether anyone had ever traveled there before.[91] It was Zacuto's *Rules* that Master John con-

87 According to Ṣāʿid al-Andalusī (1029–1070 A.D.), the eleventh-century Andalucian Jewish solar calendar had 365.25 days; the eleventh-century Persian Islamic astronomer ʿUmar al-Khayyam calculated 365.2424 days. The Jewish calendar was off by only 0.00739 days, al-Khayyam by only 0.00021. Ṣāʿid al-Andalusī, *Science in the Medieval World*, trans. Semʿan I. Salem and Alok Kumar (Austin, Tex., 1991), 79, 89. See also Charles O. Frake, "Lessons of the Mayan Sky: A Perspective from Medieval Europe," in Anthony F. Aveni, ed., *The Sky in Mayan Literature* (New York, 1992), 274–291. These calendars generally used the signs of the zodiac rather than the divisions of the conventional Christian/Roman calendar.
88 Almanachs, the forerunner of the rules used for navigation, were being developed on the Iberian peninsula early in the fourteenth century. There is a 1306 Almanach translated from Arabic into Latin in 1306 and into Portuguese in 1321. Millás, *Pedro el Ceremonioso*, 57; Albuquerque, *História da náutica*, 116. A reproduction of one in *Portugal–Brazil*, 26–27, appears to indicate maximum solar heights for a single year and single location.
89 Albuquerque, *Introducção*, 212n68.
90 Brochado, *Historiógrafos*, 51, dates the creation of the *Regimento do astrolabio* from ca. 1484. The exact date is uncertain, with estimates ranging from the early 1480s to the early 1490s. Bensaude, *L'astronomie nautique*, 22. As Cotter notes finding latitude using the height of sun is more complex than using a system referencing the north pole. Charles C. Cotter, *A History of Nautical Astronomy* (New York, 1968), 137–138.
91 Costa, *Marinharia*, 109. Portuguese also replaced the *toleta* with a method of calculating the distance traveled by measuring the distances between two latitude read-

sulted after measuring the height of the midday sun above the horizon in April 1500.

Fixing the latitude of this new landmass, Master John performed the central act of "discovery" of a new territory. Establishing the latitude, as in all science, constituted a repeatable result that could be verified by anyone using accurate instruments. Pedro Nunes would write in 1537, "It is evident that the discoveries of coasts, islands, continents, has not occurred by chance, but to the contrary, our sailors have departed very well informed, provided with instruments and rules of astronomy and geometry."[92]

Portuguese mariners could initially determine only the latitude of a landmass, because they could use the astrolabe to measure the sun's height above the horizon only while standing still. However, within two years of the discovery of Brazil, Portuguese sailors were using the astrolabe at sea to measure the height of the noonday sun.[93] Thus, they were able to fix latitude at any place on the globe, not just on land. Finally, fifty years after Zacuto's original *Rules*, Pedro Nunes devised a means for calculating latitude whenever the sun shone, not just at noon.[94]

The *Rules for the Astrolabe* became the basis of Portuguese navigation of the South Atlantic. Its principles were later applied in the Red Sea and the Indian Ocean as well.[95] The *Rules* were subsequently copied by other European powers including the English and the Dutch, laying the foundation for those nations' navigational expertise.[96]

In the process of creating a system of locating any landmass on the globe, and eventually locating the latitude of any place in the world, the Portuguese were breaking new ground. For the first time positions throughout the globe were being described by a set of numbers. Latitude previously had been only considered a series of purely imaginary circles in the skies, knowledge of which was limited to a small number

ings (*regimento de leguas*). Costa believes the first such calculation dates from 1483 or 1484. The first extant manuscript with the calculations laid out dates from 1505. Costa, *Marinharia*, 365.

92 "Manifesto e que estes descobrimentos de costas, ilhas e terras firmes não se fizeram indo a acertar, mas partiam os nossos mareantes muito ensinados em regras de astrologia e geometria," Pedro Nunes, introduction to his *Tratado em defensam da carta de marear* (1537), in *Obras*, 1: 175. *Astrologia* in this instance signified astronomy. "In astronomy there is reason, because it expresses itself in depth." João de Barros, *Ropica pnefma* (1532), quoted in Godhino, *Les découvertes*, 56.

93 See note 78.   94 Costa, *Marinharia*, 109.

95 Bensaude, *L'astronomie nautique*, 66–67, 181. Zacuto had provided a means of keeping his solar calendar accurate for future years, by observing that precession required the addition of 1°46′ for all future tables. His advice was not always followed since the amount of error was initially small.

96 There was sometimes a Spanish intermediary between the Dutch and the Portuguese. See David Waters, *Navigation in the Renaissance,* 15–16, 23–25.

of elite scientists. But no one had created an accessible yet accurate science for fixing the latitude of any city or place in the world.[97]

Creating a numerical system capable of fixing equidistant positions north and south of the equator, however, did not mean that these numbers could be automatically transferred to maps. Latitudes are actually imaginary circles around the earth, each parallel to the imaginary line at the equator.[98] In 1504 following the two Corte–Real expeditions exploring the coastline of the continents of North and South America, Portuguese cartographer Pedro Reinel created the first flat map with accurate latitudes for both the northern and southern hemispheres of the Americas.[99] To compensate for the pattern of magnetic deviation in the northern hemisphere, Reinel included a second latitude scale (called oblique latitude) accurately setting the latitudes as they were to be found sailing north from Lisbon.[100] Two years later the first accurate single-scale latitude markings were drawn. This Portuguese nautical chart, lost after the Second World War, shows a single scale of latitudes for the North and South Atlantic.[101]

While navigators were not able to determine longitude accurately all over the world until the eighteenth century, fifteen years after the first accurate latitude map, Pedro Reinel's son, Jorge, produced the first map of the globe with both latitudinal and longitudinal markings, many of the latter accurate. The map covered South America, the Pacific, and much of present-day Indonesia, with both latitude and longitude measured on the same scale. While Jorge Reinel's map was

97 The idea of preserving scale may have also come from Ptolemy's second model, introduced into the Latin West in the fifteenth century. According to Woodward, it "was constructed to preserve scale along certain parallels and meridians." David Woodward, "Maps and the Rationalization of Geographic Space," in Jay Levenson, ed., *Circa 1492: Art in the Age of Exploration* (New Haven, 1991), 83–87. Actual realization of scale would be achieved first by the Portuguese.

98 On the Reinel map of 1500 the scale of latitudes is too small. But the longitudinal extension of the Mediterranean is roughly correct at 44.8 degrees (only slightly less than it actually is). A. Cortesão, *Portugaliae*, 1: 28.

99 Albuquerque, *História da náutica*, 212–213; Hans Wolff, "The Munich Portolan Charts: Past and Present," in Wolff, ed., *America: Early Maps of the New World* (Munich, 1992), 130–132.

100 For the adjustment as corresponding to magnetic deviation, see Armando Cortesão and Avelino Teixeira da Mota, *Portugaliae monumenta cartographica*, 6 vols. (Lisbon, 1960–1962), vol. 1, fig. 6, which is a 1506 Portuguese chart showing a latitude grid with West Africa and both North America (Newfoundland, Labrador, and the Gulf of the St. Lawrence) and South America (Brazil from Cabo São Roque to Rio Cananea) (136). The data is from a Corte–Real expedition, probably the one on which Amerigo Vespucci traveled. Hans-Joaquin König, "Newly Discovered Islands, Regions, and Peoples," in Wolff, ed., *America*, 106. See also Avelino Teixeira da Mota, "Evolução dos roteiros portugueses durante o século XVI," *Revista da Universidade de Coimbra*, 24 (1969): 1–32, esp. 31; Luís de Albuquerque, *Historia de la navegación portuguesa* (Madrid, 1992), 225–226.

101 The map also has the compass rose with the lily pointing north (introduced by Reinel), which later became international. Cortesão, *Portugaliae*, 1: 15. It has Iceland at its correct latitudes.

flawed for many nautical purposes (because of a number of errors of longitude), it was sufficiently useful to allow Magellan to circumnavigate the globe and to settle the Maluku (present-day Indonesia) boundary dispute between Spain and Portugal over zones fixed by the treaty of Tordesillas.[102] Not until the start of the second phase of colonialism in the eighteenth century would it be necessary to address the problem of determining longitude.[103]

CONTESTING POSSESSION

But having discovered new stars and a new sky, how did one possibly own or "take possession" of the heavens above and the seas below? The answer, of course, was that there was no way to own the seas and the stars, only ways to own the knowledge of how to sail across them, how to note the passage of time on the night seas by the movement of constellations, and how to keep track of position on the open seas by techniques of navigation.

In the twentieth century, we do not own outer space, the stars, the planets, the moon. What we have is the knowledge and the science to travel there – the rocket designs and spaceships, just as the Portuguese had the ship designs and the caravels, ocean-going vessels invented to sail the South Atlantic. Likewise in our century we have created the techniques of navigation in outer space using mathematics and scientific instruments, just as the Portuguese developed the mathematics and instruments of high-seas navigation. In their disputes with other European powers, Portuguese officials claimed a right to exercise a commercial monopoly over regions inaccessible without their techniques. While the moon has no apparent commercial advantages, if it did, it would not be surprising that the United States would claim a right to a monopoly on grounds that they had pioneered the means of navigating to its surface.

D. João III of Portugal claimed in a letter to his trade representative in Flanders in 1537 that

the seas that can and should be navigated by all are those which were always known and always known by all and common to all. But those others [such as the South Atlantic] which were never

102 Teixeira da Mota, "A evolução da ciência," 14; Marcel Destobes, *L'hemisphere austral en 1524: Une carte de Pedor Reinel a Istanbul* (Leiden, 1938), 180, says that this map was probably drawn up for Magellan in 1519 and retouched in 1522.

103 David. S. Landes, "Finding the Point at Sea," (*Proceedings of the 1994 Harrison Longitude Symposium,* Harvard University,) forthcoming. Landes argues increased competition between maritime powers and the vulnerability of conventional routes to ever more numerous predators also contributed to the increased urgency for precisely determining longitude. The greater numbers of ships also increased the scale of nautical disasters.

known before (*sabidos*), and never even appeared navigable, these seas (that) were discovered by such great efforts on my part [i.e., the Portuguese crown] may not [be navigated by all].[104]

The Portuguese did not claim exclusive rights to all the seas, only to those for which they had pioneered the means of sailing. Furthermore, the king called the process of ascertaining the characteristics and means of sailing these seas "discovery."[105]

The term *discovery* (*descobrimento*) in its contemporary scientific sense, means to obtain knowledge for the first time of something previously unknown. The waters of the South Atlantic had not been navigated previously, making the Portuguese indisputably the first to learn of these seas and, furthermore, the first to provide precise nautical descriptions of them. The process of discovery signified a deliberate effort involving the expenditure of considerable energy and funds.[106] In the earliest surviving navigational itinerary for sailing to the Indies, the author, Duarte Pacheco Pereira, described how the kings of Portugal "ordered discovered" the West African coast by sailing the South Atlantic:[107]

> Due to the intelligence of our princes . . . and the courage of their hearts, they spent their treasure in the discovery of these lands . . . . The discovery of these Ethiopias (Africa) cost . . . the deaths of many men and much expense . . . . It is with no small effort that we have written of the laborious way and greater difficulty of discovery than might appear. Our princes who undertook this did not spend their (country's) lives and treasures in vain.[108]

104 D. João III to Rui Fernandes (*feitor* of Flanders) May 2, 1534, quoted in Carvalho, *D. João III*, 64.

105 The twentieth-century debate about discovery (from 1940 to the early 1960s) used the phenomenological criterion of the intention of the sovereign individual *actor* to "discover," rather than on imperial or official intentions. Samuel Eliot Morison, *Portuguese Voyages to America in the Fifteenth Century* (Cambridge, Mass., 1940), 5–10; Edmundo O'Gorman, *La idea del descubrimiento de América* (México, 1951); Marcel Bataillon and Edmundo O'Gorman, *Dos concepciones de la tarea histórica: Con motivo de la idea del descubrimiento de América* (México, D.F., 1955), trans. as *The Invention of America: An Inquiry into the Historical Nature of the New World and the Meaning of Its History* (Bloomington, Ind., 1961); Marcel Bataillon, "L'idée de la découverte de l'Amérique," *Bulletin Hispanique*, 55 (1953): 23–55; Wilcomb Washburn, "The Meaning of 'Discovery' in the Fifteenth and Sixteenth Centuries," *American Historical Review*, 68 (1962): 1–21.

106 "Discover" and "Discovery," *OED*; Silva Neto, *História da língua portuguêsa*, 450. Before the Portuguese voyages, the word *discover* in English merely meant reconnoiter or divulge a secret (§ 4, 5) rather than "bring to fuller knowledge" (§ 8, 9).

107 Pacheco Perbira, *Esmeraldo*, 2–4, 100–101, 105. Identical language in Gaspar Correa's prologue to his *Lendas da India* describing Dom Manuel as having ordered "the discovery of India," and in chap. 1 as "endeavor[ing] to discover and conquer."

108 Pacheco Perbira, *Esmeraldo*, 141, 146, 152. Similar sentiments were expressed by D. João III in Jan. 16, 1530, letter to his French ambassador, João da Silveira, in Carvalho, *D. João III*, 182, 184. In these, as in many Portuguese writings of the time, the discovery was attributed not to the private citizen who had actually

The concept of a right to what they had discovered stemmed from the "laborious" nature of the effort the Portuguese had undertaken, and the "greater difficulty of discovery." It stemmed from the cost in human lives, and in financial terms as well – "their (country's) lives and treasures."

The argument is a familiar contemporary one. The person (or corporation) who pays the salary, provides the equipment, and organizes the scientific project owns the right to a patent on the ideas that are discovered. The individual scientist – who created the idea – is not the owner of the right to exploit it; rather it is the company that provided the money for the laboratory and laid out the tools and equipment that has a right to receive an income from the discoveries. The Portuguese claims, repeatedly voiced in international conflicts, that they had right to a commercial monopoly on the seaborne trade with the new lands was an explicit claim that because of their vast expenditures on developing the science and technology of high-seas navigation, they had a just right to compensation.

Other competing powers were unwilling to accept Portuguese claims for a monopoly on sea routes in exchange for their discoveries. Grotius exaggerated the Portuguese claim, stating that they claimed to rule the entire ocean, rather than simply the regions to which they had discovered the navigational means of access.[109] He also added that the Portuguese had no boundaries save "an imaginary line."[110] Since all mathematical lines are imaginary, Grotius thereby rejected the entire mathematical and scientific basis of Portugal's claims to discovery.

A different set of objections emerged from English competitors. In 1562, Queen Elizabeth had stated that Portugal had no dominion over "places *discovered*," to which an irritated Portuguese ambassador had replied that "his master *has* absolute dominion . . . over all those lands already discovered."[111] In a scientific sense, discovery created rights of dominion for the Portuguese, but did not do so for the English.

embarked upon the voyage, but to the royal official who subsidized and sanctioned the voyages of discovery. Thus, Prince Henry is characterized as the discoverer of the regions of West Africa even though he never traveled on any of these voyages. João de Barros, *Ropica pnefma* (1532), writes, "With the importance of the worlds the enlightened kings of Portugal have discovered." Quoted in Godhino, *Les découvertes*, 56.

109 Hugo Grotius, *De iure praedae commentarius,* trans. Gwladys L. Williams (Oxford, 1950). Chap. 12 is the slightly revised treatise *De mare liberum.* He argued that the Portuguese did not "discover" these routes but rather that they "pointed them out" (242). He objects to the size of the ocean claimed by the Portuguese as "immoderate power" (239).

110 Ibid., 240.

111 Answer to the Portuguese ambassador, June 15, 1562, *Calendar of State Papers,* 95. Second replication of the Portuguese ambassador, June 19, 1562, ibid., 106 (emphasis added).

Some Frenchmen were unsympathetic, while others had a certain amount of respect for the Portuguese position. On the one hand, the Dieppe captain Jacques Parmentier declared, like Grotius, that the Portuguese possessed an "excessive ambition" and "it seems that God only made the seas and the land for them, and that other nations are not worthy of sailing."[112] André Thevet, on the other hand, wrote that the Portuguese do not easily tolerate the French in Brazil "because they assess and attribute ownership of things [to themselves] as first possessors, which considering that they have made the discovery, is true."[113]

Because Portuguese claims to the New World and to West Africa were founded upon the creation of knowledge, they left few physical markers as signs of discovery, since it was the knowledge of means – not the ends – that they claimed to possess. While the Portuguese primarily marked their discovery of regions by latitude numbers, recorded in logs and transferred to maps, they sometimes noted their discoveries by an object on land – a stone pillar or a cross.

Crosses were the traditional objects Europeans planted during their travels to new regions, but their actual cultural and political significance varied widely. For the English they were mere markers of presence, signs that Englishmen had once passed that way, while for the French, Spanish, and Portuguese alike, they were political indicators of a claim upon a region.[114] For the Frenchmen taking possession of the Amazon, they were the symbol of a political alliance between the natives and the French king; for the Spanish they had been a physical manifestation of the idea that the area was now under Christian (i.e., Spanish) command. But for the Portuguese, their meaning was and had been historically distinctive.

Beginning with Gil Eannes's first rounding of the navigationally treacherous Cape Bojador in 1434, Portuguese explorers had often erected crosses on the land they had attained, indicating the southernmost reach of their voyage.[115] Sailing southward down the west

---

112 Gaffarel, *Histoire du Brésil français*, 84–112.
113 André Thevet, *Les singularitez de la France Antarctique* (Paris, 1878; orig. pub. 1558), 308.
114 The 1580 English expedition searching for a northeast passage through Europe to Asia described a cross upon which "Master Pet did grave his name with the date of our Lourde . . . to the end that if the William did chaunce to come thither, they [*sic*] might have knowledge that wee had beene there." "The Discoverie Made by M. Arthur Pet and M. Charles Jackman of the Northeast Parts," in Richard Hakluyt, *Principal Navigations, Voyages, Traffiques, and Discoveries of the English Nation* (Glasgow, 1904), 3: 288. For other examples, see Seed, "Taking Possession and Reading Texts," 193–194.
115 When west winds blow, the waves can reach fifty feet, and from October to April thick fogs are usual. Antonio de Oliveira Marques, *History of Portugal*, 2 vols. (New York, 1972), 1: 149. When "Gil Yanez attempting what none durst before him passed beyond Cape Bojador, and there planted a Crosse." Manuel Faria y Sousa, *The History of Portugal* (to 1640), trans. John Stevens (London, 1698), bk. 4,

coast of Africa, Portuguese explorers continued the custom of placing crosses. But after crossing the equator, the Portuguese began a distinctive practice of recording the southernmost limit of their navigational discoveries, by planting tall stone pillars.[116] These pillars were six- to eight-foot-tall columns each topped by a square stone on which were carved in Latin and Portuguese the year and the names of the king and expedition leader. Perched on top of the square was a cross, slightly taller than the square.

Such pillars had been prevalent in medieval Portugal.[117] Planted on tall hilltops on the African, Indian, and, later, American continents, such pillars were directed at other passing European seaborne observers rather than natives. In placing these giant stone markers on African shores, the Portuguese were principally noting their discoveries of regions previously unknown to Europeans. The inscriptions on the stone were quite specific. They were records of discovery. "In the year 6685 of the creation of the earth and 1485 after the birth of Christ," reads one, "the most excellent and serene King Dom João II of Portugal ordered this land to be discovered and this padrão to be placed by Diogo Cão, nobleman of this house."[118] More than simply an indication of having passed through, the stone pillar proclaimed the Portuguese technological achievement. Thus, the Portuguese began recording the discovery (literally "uncovering") of lands hitherto unknown to Europeans on the African continent. The prominent Portuguese legal scholar Seraphim de Freitas argued that "the Portuguese were the first to investigate and open the new navigational path to the Indies, which is why they acquired the right to it."[119] He continued that "Vasco Da Gama communicated this understanding by placing stone columns in some ports, as testimony of Portuguese lordship."[120]

chap. 3, 274. Upon reaching Cape Branco, Diego Affonso "caused to be erected on land a great cross of wood that his partners might know he was going on before them." Azurara, *Discovery and Conquest of Guinea*, 103.

116 The voyages of Diogo de Cão in approximately 1471 were the first during which the massive stone pillars were planted. This was approximately one decade after the first Portuguese voyage south of the equator. Paulo Merêa, *Novos estudos de história de direito* (Barcelos, 1937), 27n27.

117 Placed on the boundaries of property they signified the boundaries, but also had historically signified that the land was not subject to taxation by the king. Hence, the markers (and in some cases crosses) signaled royal revenue agents to keep off the property. Revenue agents of other European powers were thereby presumably put on notice of Portuguese economic intentions, if not their actual accomplishments. Alexandre Herculano, *História de Portugal*, ed. José Mattoso, 4 vols. (Amador, 1980–1981), 2: 245, 386. This commercial dimension entered into Portuguese use of the pillars in the sixteenth century. See the next chapter.

118 Translation given in *Portugal–Brazil*, 67.

119 "Portugueses . . . foram os primeiros a investigar e a abrir o caminho da navegação da India . . . quer porque adquiriram o direito da predita navegação." Freitas, *Do justo império asiático*, chap. 3, ¶ 14, 1: 127.

120 "Conforme Gama o deu a entender, colocando, em alguns portos, colunas de pedra que fossem testemunhos do domínio lusitano." Freitas, ibid., chap. 8, ¶ 5,

The Portuguese notations of discovery were visibly fixed upon tall stone monuments and occasional crosses. But in so marking their progress across the oceans to new lands, the Portuguese were also mapping a grid – an imaginary network of numbers – latitudes noted by astronomers and pilots, recorded both in the subsequent guides and fixed upon the land by the visible symbols of stone pillars and occasional crosses. For the stone pillar did not occupy a place or a territory the way a house or a fort did; rather most importantly it marked a point, a location. The actual fixing of the point was done by numbers – degrees and minutes – which were calculated on the basis of the height of the polestar and later the sun, written down, forwarded to the crown, and then incorporated into the pilots' guides. The coordinates of the pillar, carefully recorded in subsequent guides, could be used by sailors at sea to check their location. The *padrão*, like a giant pin stuck into the earth, was the visible and prominent fixing of a position, which could be then used by pilots to check their onboard records against the known coordinates of the giant pillar. By fixing large landmarks atop promontories visible from the ocean, they also noted the exact extent of their previous achievement and provided a potential benchmark for future expeditions. The Portuguese discoveries mapped space with a network of numbers, rather than describing or occupying a place.

Alone among Western Europeans, the Portuguese carried out an astronomical ritual upon arrival that bore political significance. Unlike the elaborate ceremonies of the French, the construction of house sites and gardens by the English, and declarations to native people by Spaniards, the Portuguese established their claim to dominion through discovering numbers that fixed the place on earth by the position of the sun in the sky.

Before the fleet bearing Master John departed from Brazil, back across the South Atlantic to India, a small ceremony was arranged to accompany the planting of a cross which had been cut from some local wood. After a discussion about "where it seemed to us that it would be better to plant the cross, *so that it might better be seen* . . . the cross was planted with the arms and devise of Your Highness which we first nailed to it" (emphasis added). Then just as they departed, Nicolau Coelho placed tin crucifixes around the necks of all the natives present. Like the wooden cross, placed where it was most visible from the ocean, the tin crosses around the natives' necks also served as visible reminders to the Portuguese presence. Individuals wearing or owning those crosses could be identified as having prior contact with the Portuguese (or the natives they had met). These were not the only crosses used in the first Portuguese contact. There was also the cross in the sky above, de-

1: 293. The identical understanding also appears in João de Barros, *Asia*, dec. 1. liv. 3, cap. 2, 79–80. See also Gaspar Correa, *Lendas da India*, prologue.

scribed in the only other lengthy account of the discovery known to have reached King Manuel,[121] the first description of the Southern Cross, the astronomical discovery of a "new sky and new stars."

While subsequent history has tried to make the first Mass celebrated into the founding moment of Brazil, it was not so regarded at the time.[122] King Manuel sought information not about a religious ceremony, but about the stars and the skies. Indeed, the clergy (and their actions) were relegated to a minor role in the course of the discoveries.

Clergy played no role in the first thirty-five years of the Portuguese presence in Brazil – nor were there any early efforts to claim or Christianize indigenous peoples.[123] The first settlement plans for Brazil contained no mention of any role for clerics. The first time that clerics became involved in a political role in Brazil was in the middle of the sixteenth century, when the first governor-general, Tomé de Sousa, was sent with a contingent of Jesuits.

Clerics traditionally played a far more constrained role in Portuguese political affairs than anywhere else in Western Europe. Alone in Western Europe, medieval Portuguese coronation ceremonies had no role for clergymen. In 1438 the Papacy tried to force Portuguese monarchs to establish such a ceremony, but to no avail. Eventually the pope backed down and the clergy remained without a role in legitimating Portuguese royal power.[124] In the absence of a legitimate political role for the clergy, anti-Semitic sentiments were not mobilized into violent action until well into the sixteenth century. In fourteenth- and fifteenth-century Spain and Aragon, clerical leadership legitimated violence against religious minorities.[125] The attacks on Seville's

121 There is another account reportedly written by Ayres Correa, but to date no copy of this has been found in the Portuguese archives. Abel Foutoura da Costa, *Os sete únicos documentos de 1500, conservados em Lisboa, referentes à viagem de Pedro Alvares Cabral* (Lisbon, 1940).

122 The association was probably created later because in Portuguese the word *ceremonia* most usually refers to a religious occasion. The Mass was celebrated as the founding of Brazil most memorably in the nineteenth-century painting "A Primeira Misa no Brasil" by Vitor Meireles at the Museu Nacional de Bellas Artes in Rio de Janeiro. But celebrating Mass was part of the customary Sunday activities on long ocean voyages; masses were also customarily said prior to departure. See *Voyage of Vasco da Gama*, 96. Neither the words *possession* nor *taking possession* were mentioned in connection with the cross-planting, whereas they were frequently invoked in connection with the padrões.

123 Religious issues were not given a priority anywhere in the Portuguese empire until 1532 when João III (el Rey Piadoso) created the Mesa da Consciência. Baiao et al., eds., *Expansão portuguesa*, 2: 74. Freitas subsequently rewrote this history in order to justify Portuguese dominion on the basis of the papal bull. Freitas, *De justo imperio*, 156.

124 The Portuguese monarchs constituted themselves by proclamation and oaths of loyalty. Marcelo Caetano, *Lições de história do direito português* (Coimbra, 1962), 225.

125 Thomas Glick sees this process as beginning in the eleventh century. *Islamic and Christian Spain*, 160.

Jewish communities which began the pogroms of 1391 were led by powerful clerics, including the acting archbishop of the city. The equally anti-Semitic Portuguese clergy historically had little influence on politics.[126] Elsewhere on the Iberian peninsula during the fourteenth and fifteenth centuries, clerics successfully enacted legislation banning Jews from positions of political power or influence. Portuguese clerics alone failed to secure such legislation.[127]

Excluding the clergy from political power also permitted Portuguese monarchs to practice the religious toleration that permitted them to pursue mathematical and scientific goals. When Catholic clergymen played a role in the technical advances, they did so because of their mathematical skills rather than their traditional clerical ones. João II, for example, is reported to have selected priests for voyages to southern Africa on the basis of their mathematical rather than their religious skills.[128] Unlike Isabel of Castile, who soon founded Spanish dominion upon the imposition of a foreign religion, Portuguese rulers initiated their claims to the New World through science, which had been created for them by Jewish astronomers based upon the heritage of the Islamic era.

Portuguese leadership in scientific navigation began to grind to a disastrous halt at end of the fifteenth century. The fanatically intolerant Catholic Kings of Spain demanded that Manuel expel the Jews before being allowed to marry their daughter. In this way the Catholic monarchs not only ended the centuries-old tradition of Moslem and Christian tolerance in Spain, they in effect forced Portugal to do so as well.

Between December 1496 and April 1497, Jews were given the Almohad option of conversion or exile. But then the pressure was increased. In April 1497, all children under fourteen were to be forbidden to leave the kingdom, so many parents converted so as not to lose their children. They were known as New Christians, or *conversos*. Thus, Jewish scientists such as Abraham Zacuto departed for North Africa and eventually Israel, while Master João was forcibly converted, as was Pedro Nunes, the man whom even the chronicler of D. João III's reign described as "the great Portuguese mathematician, who in his time had no equal" – the man who had characterized Portugal's contribution as the "new sky and new stars."[129]

---

126 For anti-Semitism among clergy, see Herculano, *História de Portugal*, 2: 164.
127 Albert A. Sicroff, *Les controverses des statuts de 'pureté du sang' en Espagne du XVᵉ au XVIIᵉ siècle* (Paris, 1960).
128 Bensaude, *L'astronomie nautique*, 196–197. For sixteenth-century critiques of the role played by clergymen in the expansion, see Camões, *Lusiadas*, canto 10, stanzas 85, 108–119, 150.
129 For Nunes, see Bensaude, *L'astronomie nautique*, 63; António Baião, *Episódios dramáticos da Inquisição portuguesa*, 2 vols. (Lisbon, 1936), 1: 163–165; "Grande

Dom Manuel had high regard for his converted Jewish scientists, including Master John who established the latitude of Brazil and the first accurate drawing of the Southern Cross. But Manuel's expulsion and forcible conversion decrees effectively sanctioned outpourings of anti-Semitic violence among his subjects. In 1506 the first pogrom erupted in Lisbon, causing the death of 2,000 converted Jews.[130] The peace and toleration of Portugal began to disappear. Dom Manuel's offspring followed the example of their fanatically intolerant Spanish grandparents rather than their more tolerant father, bringing the clergy into politics, establishing the Inquisition, and in 1543 burning the first Portuguese at the stake.[131] While personally protected by powerful patrons, even the grandchildren of the famous cosmographer Pedro Nunes were harassed by the Inquisition.[132]

The expulsion of the Jews was widely lamented at the time and seen by many of Portugal's elites as a catastrophic mistake. By 1513 there was a shortage of astronomers in Portugal. By the 1520s the scientific and technological edge that Portugal had enjoyed was eroding, the claim to making new discoveries coming to an end.[133] The exiling of its mathematical and scientific talent effectively put an end to the scientific experimentation that had rendered Portugal the pioneer in the science and mathematics of modern navigation.

The technologies that they had developed through the 1530s came to be widely shared by sailors throughout the world. When Master John landed on the coast of Brazil, only the Portuguese could accurately describe a place using latitudes. Soon all Europeans were able to do so. The mariner's astrolabe, first created by Abraham Zacuto for

matemático português Pêro Nunes, que em seu tempo não teve igual." Frei Luís de Sousa, *Anais de D. João III*, ed. M. Rodriges Lapa, 2 vols., 2d ed. (Lisbon, 1954), 2: 193, parte 2, liv. 1, cap. 15.

130 Oliveira Marques, *History*, 1: 213; Kayserling, *História dos judeus*, 127–132.

131 Oliveira Marques, *History*, 1: 207; Kayserling, *História dos judeus*, 145–207.

132 Nunes managed to escape the persecution, but not through royal protection. As Luís de Albuquerque has shown, Nunes was the teacher of the Inquisitor General Cardinal D. Henrique and was protected in that way. Albuquerque, *As Navegações*, 61. Nunes's grandchildren, however, were scrutinized by the Inquisition. Baião, *Episódios*, 1: 163–165.

133 M. Gonçalves Cerejeira, *O Renascimento em Portugal*, 4th ed. (Coimbra, 1974), 333; Baião, *Episódios*, 305; I. S. Révah, *La censure inquisitoriale portugauise au XVIᵉ siècle* (Lisbon, 1960), 8, 33; Rodolpho Guimarāres, *Les mathematiques en Portugal*, 2d ed. (Coimbra, 1909), 26; Jaime Cortesão, *Os descobrimentos portugueses*, 2 vols. (Lisbon, 1959–1961), 2: 362, chap. 12; M. Gonçalves Cerejeira, *O Renascimento em Portugal* (Coimbra, 1918), 132; Reijer Hooykaas, *Humanism and the Voyages of Discovery in Sixteenth Century Portuguese Science and Letters* (Amsterdam, 1979), 58; Bensaude, *L'astronomie nautique*, 214–215. On Portuguese efforts to create a Christian astronomical and mathematical tradition (and the persecution that good astronomers faced on suspicion of being Jewish), see Albuquerque, *Crónicas*, 144–148.

Vasco da Gama on his first voyage to India in 1497,[134] soon was widely adopted in Western Europe. Spanish sailors adopted it by the 1550s; twenty years later English mariners acquired it, and by the 1580s Dutch sailors were using it on their voyages to the East, having learned how while sailing on Portuguese vessels. Once this knowledge became widely known, as it inevitably did, Portugal no longer exclusively held the instruments or the technologies needed to sail the high seas. Nor was it continuing to innovate in these areas.

By the 1560s scientific leadership in navigation passed to the hands of the Dutch. Superior astrolabes began to be made in Louvain.[135] Many of the most educated Portuguese Jews fled to Antwerp, and then after its fall to Amsterdam, bringing their knowledge with them.[136] Dutch sailors traveling regularly on Portuguese ships became familiar with Portuguese nautical and oceanograhic guides (called *itineraries*). Jan Linschoten modified the Portuguese guides and published them as *Itineraries*.[137] Portuguese navigators' observations of variations in terrestrial magnetism came into the hands of Simon Stevin, who wrote a well-known treatise on the subject.[138] Even the solutions to mapping nautical routes were inspired by Portuguese science.

Upon returning from Brazil in 1532, Martim Afonso da Souza observed to Pedro Nunes that when sailing east or west along the same latitude his boat appeared to be heading to the equator but in fact, never reached it. Nunes responded that using a compass to sail east or west along an identical latitude was different than following a great circle course. The compass-driven course, Nunes remarked, was actually a sequence of separate great circle courses. Nunes then drew a picture

134 Bensaude, *L'astronomie nautique*, 40, 79; Barros, *Asia*, dec. 1, liv. 3, cap. 2, 1: 126–127, describes it as "3 palmos" in diameter but does not mention that Zacuto was its creator. Modern equivalents of these dimensions are from Smith, *Vanguard*, 56. Fourteenth-century astrolabes were usually more than double this size, 7 palmos. Millás, *Pedro el Ceremonioso*, 67–69. Besaude calculated the Arabic astrolabe of 95 to 125 mm in diameter, weighing 1 kilo; and that of 1632 being 184 mm in diameter and weighing 3.84 kilos. The Arabic ones are 360 degrees, the nautical ones go four times from 0 to 90 degrees. Bensaude, *L'astronomie nautique*, 79. The "new astrolabe" described by Camões as a "sage and wise invention" is thought to refer to Zacuto. Camões, *Os Luisadas*, canto V, stanza 25.

135 By the mid-sixteenth century, the Louvain had become the center for the manufacture of scientific instruments, including astrolabes. Astrolabe manufacturers trained at the Louvain school dispersed throughout northern Europe. A. S. Osley, *Mercator: A Monograph on the Letter of Maps, etc. in the Sixteenth Century Netherlands* (New York, 1969), 91–97.

136 Kayserling, *História dos judeus*, 233–236.

137 Jan Huygen van Linschoten, *Itinerario, voyage ofts schipvaert*, 3 vols. (Amsterdam, 1596).

138 Albuquerque, *História da naútica*, 214–215; idem, *Navegación*, 238; Stevin, *Principal Works*; vol. 3, *Navigation*. The English editor of Stevin's treatise mentions only two of the three Portuguese treatises on measuring magnetic variation.

of the compass-driven course, the first depiction of the loxodromic curve,[139] and subsequently mathematically described these curves.[140]

To eliminate the problem of the loxodromic curve on a navigator's map was the problem that Gerardus Mercator (1512–1594) later solved. Latitude lines lie parallel to each other, with the distance between lines virtually identical at the equator as at the poles.[141] Lines of longitude, however, resemble cuts in the rind of an orange, farther apart in the center, but converging at the ends.[142] In 1569 Mercator increased the spacing between latitude lines the further they were from the equator, thus making all loxodromes appear as straight lines.[143] While there are inevitable distortions of sizes of landmasses closer to the poles,[144] Mercator's map allowed pilots to draw a constant compass course in a straight line – solving the problem originally identified by a converted Portuguese mathematician and first observed on a voyage to Brazil.

Many of the Portuguese scientific and technological achievements remain to this day. Trigonometry is still widely used in both mapping and navigation, applications discovered by the Portuguese. But perhaps Portugal's most important legacy is how its mariners and cartographers changed the way in which the world is seen. Where medieval European maps had envisioned a world with Jerusalem at its center, the Portuguese reinvented the world as a uniform set of latitude co-

139 *Loxodrome* derives from the Latin translation of the Dutch word for curved line (*kromstrijk*), which appeared in Stevin's analysis of Nunes's description. W. G. L. Randles, "Pedro Nunes and the Discovery of the Loxodromic Curve," *Revista da Universidade de Coimbra*, 25 (1989): 123, 129. "Tratado que ho doutor Pero Nunez fez sobre certas duvidas da navegação" (1537), in Nunes, *Obras*, 1: 166; Costa, *Marinharia*, 225–249. To change from a compass-driven to a great circle course Nunes drew upon Jabir ibn Aflah's theorem that the sines of the angles of a spherical triangle are in inverse proportion to the sines of the arcs opposite them. Nunes, "Tratado em defensam," in *Obras*, I, 176–178; Randles, "Nunes," 125.

140 Idem, in *Opera* (1566) bk. 2 chap. 23 cited in Randles, "Nunes," 129. Mercator never provided a mathematical explanation of this projection. See note 143.

141 At the equator a degree of latitude is 68.7 miles, while near the poles it is 69.1 miles, a discrepancy of 0.4 miles or 1.1 kilometers.

142 Technically called meridians, they are arcs of a great circle connected at the poles. The distance between meridians is zero miles at the poles, but 69.2 miles (111.3 km) at the equator.

143 "Text and Translation of the Legends of the Original Chart of the World by Gerhard Mercator, issued in 1569," in *Hydrographic Review*, 9 (1932): 7–45, esp. 11. Mercator's solution was visual, although Nunes's description of the solution for sailing was mathematical. J. A. Bennett, The *Divided Circle: A History of Instruments for Astronomy, Navigation, and Surveying* (Oxford, 1987), 61, attributes the mathematical explanation to Edward Wright in 1599.

144 Distances are distorted at higher latitudes, but the direction remains a straight line. Costa, *Marinharia*, 225–249. See also Boorstin, *Discoverers*, 273. Most European sailing in the age of expansion took place between 45° north and 45° south. The unequal landmass critique is frequently made. See Marshall Hodgson, "The Interrelations of Societies in History," *Comparative Studies in Society and History*, 5 (1963): 227–250.

ordinates, the form in which we know it today. They reimagined the globe as a single object where any place could be described and located by a number. The uniform latitude scale may be marked on globes but it is not visible anywhere. Latitudes are a set of imaginary lines that people the world over recognize and treat as real. They form the continuing legacies of Portugal's adapting its Islamic and Jewish scientific heritage to solve the problems of high-seas navigation.

Over the course of centuries, millions of other peoples in the southern hemisphere had seen the stars near the celestial pole; two large groups had even chosen it for navigation. Navigating Arabs called it a geometric shape – the quadrilateral; some of their Polynesian counterparts called it "the net," others the "sacred timber."[145] Aborigines trekking through the vast spaces of the Australian outback named the guard stars "the two brothers" and the cross "the lance"; nomadic peoples of the Sahara called one of the guards "the weight." Naming involves selecting an object the stars resembled from one's own cultural catalog – a Polynesian fishing net, a timber crucial to the construction of ocean-going canoes, an aboriginal hunting lance, a trading nomad's commercial weighing device.[146] But the Portuguese picked a different symbol from their catalog – a cross.

Like other Europeans, Portuguese represented their particular political ambitions and interests in the southern hemisphere as the expression of a global Christianity. In sailing over the oceans they were establishing dominion for a Christian power – not converting the people – but by dominating the seas and using the stars above to achieve that goal.

Naming the sky above by the cross in a sense takes possession of it. The stars oversee the ocean itself, the movement of ships as they sail from point to point. The rotation of stars across the heavens marks the time of watches on board ship; their position guides the navigators checking the course through the nighttime sky. Naming the constellation the Southern Cross expresses an imperial ambition, but the cross above, like those planted on land, designated not a place but a point in space.

Because other Europeans learned their navigational astronomy from the Portuguese, they borrowed their nomenclature as well.[147] The Portuguese named the Southern Cross; a Portuguese pilot first

145 The Polynesian names are those given by the Anutans in Feinberg, *Polynesian Seafaring and Navigation*, 101. Another Polynesian name for the constellation is Newe. The Arabs called the pole star Gah. Costa, *Marinharia*, 63.

146 Guiseppe Maria Seta, *The Glorious Constellations*, trans. Karin H. Ford (New York, 1992), 299.

147 Henri Lancelot-Voisin, sieur de La Popellinière, in *Les trois mondes* (Paris, 1582), describes "that we call the Star of the South, and the others of midday, around which there are some others in a Cross that is called the Southern Cross." He then also describes finding the height of the sun at midday with the astrolabe (6–6v).

drew it for the European world. Thus, in the nighttime skies above the southern hemisphere, lies the principal legacy of Portuguese claims of possession – the Southern Cross – as Pedro Nunes said nearly five centuries ago, a new sky and new stars.

Ships that glide silently over the seas leave no traces, no permanent marks on the face of the earth; even their remains, buried at thousands of fathoms beneath the surface of the sea, are erased from visibility, from permanency. The measurements of the height of the sun and other stars left no visible traces; the mathematical lines which divide our world exist nowhere except in our minds and imaginations. The luffing of the sails, the creaking of the wood, the rush of the wind, the sounds of men's voices all are gone. The legacies of the once vast Portuguese empire are in the names of the stars above and, occasionally, in the sounds of ships navigating below.

APPENDIX: PORTUGUESE AND ENGLISH APPROACHES TO BOUNDARIES AND THEIR LEGACIES

Just as they claimed dominion over Brazil by describing it with a number (latitude), the Portuguese crown also distinctively employed numerical and mathematical descriptions in founding Brazil. Using mathematical descriptions to fix the limits of political divisions, Portuguese monarchs differed sharply from their English counterparts, who preferred to describe the boundaries of their New World colonies using landscape features. This appendix will briefly contrast the two methods of establishing the original political boundaries of New World colonies, and illustrate how these two preferences continue to operate in contemporary survey law in the Portuguese-American and Anglo-American legal systems.

Initially Brazil was merely a way station on the voyage to the East Indies,[1] where Portuguese traders purchased brazilwood from natives. Unable to keep the French out, in the 1530s, King João III decided to order the establishment of permanent settlements called donatary captaincies.[2] He demarcated the boundaries of these captaincies (roughly equivalent to early North American colonies) with numbers, using mathematical expressions – sixty leagues, fifty leagues.[3] "At

1 J. Lucio de Azevedo, *Épocas de Portugal económico* (Lisbon, 1929), 247.
2 "Considering what great effort was needed to expel people who populated it, after being established there," Carta de El-Rei a Martim Affonso de Sousa, Sept. 28, 1532, in Pero Lopes de Souza, *Diario da navegação* (Lisbon, 1839), 81–83, esp. 82.
3 Francisco Pereira Coutinho's grant extended from the Rio São Francisco south to Bahia do Santos. Martim Afonso de Sousa's second grant began at the Rio São Vicente. For Francisco Pereira Coutino's grant, see August 26, 1534, *Documentos históricos*, 13: 216; for Sousa's grant, ibid., 137; for donation of two islands to D. Antonio de Athaide, Mar. 12, 1558, ibid., 192.

times," Portuguese legal historian Paulo Merêa writes, "not even a beginning point was indicated from which the captaincy started: It was determined just by the number of leagues counted from the limits of the prior concession."[4] The grant to Pero do Campo "began where the fifty leagues that I [the king] have given to Jorge Figueiredo Correa comes to an end." That to Vasco Fernandes Coutinho was "fifty leagues beginning where the fifty leagues that I [the king] have given to Pedro de Campo Tourinho end." The donation to Jose Figueredo Correa began at Bahia and went 50 leagues south. When physical landscape features were mentioned, they rarely actually fixed the boundary. For example, Martim Affonso de Sousa's grant included the well-known landmark Cape Rio Frio, but his grant actually began "thirteen leagues north of the cape;" his second began at the Rio São Vicente and ended "twelve leagues to the south of the Isle of Cananea."[5]

How far the grants extended into the interior of Brazil were also not fixed by physical place, or even natural objects such as mountains or ravines, but by mathematical coordinates usually describing a geometric shape, such as a square. Pero do Campo received a square, "fifty leagues of land . . . along the coast, and the same distance going inland to the back country," as did Jorge Figueredo Correa.[6] Some grants such as Martim Affonso de Sousa's (the largest) did not have the geometric shape but was simply "entering into the back country and mainland, as far as possible."[7] Physical or natural objects were not assumed to have any obvious connection to property boundaries. Rather, creating boundaries resembled the way in which a course might be plotted at sea; sailing so many leagues south by southwest, then so many leagues due south. Traversing the boundaries of the captaincies resembled changing course on the high seas: no physical points determined when you turned to head off in a different direction, only a mathematical calculation.[8]

When marking the limits of seaborne discoveries, the crown sometimes ordered captains to establish the location of their journey by fixing a *padrão*, and these were used occasionally in the New World. The

4 Malheiro Dias, ed., *Historia da colonização portuguesa*, 3: 170.
5 Ibid., 13: 92; Vasco Fernandes Coutinho, ibid., 122; "traslado do donação à Jorge Figueredo Correa, July 26, 1534," ibid., 158; Sousa, ibid., 137.
6 "Cinqüenta leguas de terra . . . e serão de largo ao longo da costa, e entrarão na mesma largura pelo sertão a dentro," Campo, *Documentos históricos*, 13: 92; "Traslado do donação à Jorge Figueredo Correa, July 26, 1534," ibid., 157.
7 Ibid., Jan. 20, 1535, 138.
8 The astrolabe used for high-seas navigation had also been developed by Iberian Islamic scientists beginning in the tenth century in order to survey property – using principles of triangulation. While land surveys on the Iberian peninsula continued to be carried out using older, less accurate Roman measures, information on using the astrolabe to calculate boundaries did indeed exist. Thomas Glick, *Islamic and Christian Spain* (Princeton, N.J., 1979), 228–229.

largest grant (Martim Affonso de Souza's) involved placing several *padrões*. Souza's first stone pillar was to be placed

> traveling 13 leagues along the coast north of Cape Rio Frio, and at the end of these [leagues] a padrão will be placed with my [royal] arms and a line drawn to the northwest up to 21 degrees [latitude] and from this point a line will be drawn running directly to the west. Another padrão will be placed on the north of said Rio Curpare from which a line will be drawn to the northwest up to 23 degrees.[9]

Martim Affonso was a seasoned naval commander, but leaders of other expeditions, not sufficiently familiar with latitude calculations, had to be given extensive written instructions, instead of precise mathematical coordinates. Duarte Coelho, for example, was told to place his pillar fifty steps from the fortress-warehouse on the south side of the Iguarassú River and "from this padrão will draw a line cutting westward inland, and the land from that line to the south will be Duarte Coehlo's."[10] The imaginary line (not the course of the river) determined the northern boundary of Coelho's grant, just as latitudes fixed Martim Affson de Souza's.

Like a giant pin stuck into the Brazilian coast, the padrão did not occupy a place or a territory; rather it pinpointed a location. Radiating from this single point were a series of imaginary lines – a mathematical grid which fixed the outline of the territory which Portuguese captains were to govern. The actual size of the grant was a set of numbers – the leagues in each direction, north, south, east, and west.

While the original political boundaries of Brazil were a series of lines – "a line drawn to the northwest up to 21 degrees [latitude]," "a line . . . drawn running directly to the west" – English descriptions of original political boundaries largely followed the natural phenomena of rivers, mountains, and forests.[11] The first patent to the Virginia Company claimed a colony between 34° and 45° north.[12] But only three years later, the colony's charter described physical boundaries, "all those lands . . . from the point of land called Cape or Point Comfort, all along the sea coast, to the northward two hundred miles, and . . . southward two hundred miles."[13] Physical boundaries were of-

9 Ibid., 137.
10 Ibid., 70; Malheiro Dias, ed., *Historia da colonição portuguesa,* 3: 309.
11 Occasionally geometric forms were followed, but as boundaries for particular plots. Furthermore the forms were inconsistent – sometimes circles, squares, rectangular or five-sided figures. David Thomas Konig, "Community Custom and the Common Law: Social Change and the Development of Land Law in Seventeenth-Century Massachusetts," *American Journal of Legal History,* 18 (1974): 142.
12 First Virginia charter, Apr. 10 1606, Lucas, *Charters,* 1; third charter, Mar. 12, 1612, ibid., 20–28; changes to within 41 and 34 degree northerly latitude, ibid., 21.
13 Second charter, ibid., 12.

ten explicitly preferred to numerical ones. In William Penn's grant for his colony a latitude boundary was given, but if he found the Delaware River to extend there, then the river was to be the boundary.[14] The Massachusetts Bay Charter mentions latitudes as rough guidlines, but primarily describes the area between two natural landmarks, the Merrimack and Charles Rivers.[15] By contrast, Duarte Coelho's grant mentioned a natural feature, the Iguarassú River, but the boundary was drawn by an imaginary line cutting westward from a stone pillar. Portuguese monarchs showed a distinctive preference for mathematical descriptions of boundaries, while their English counterparts preferred actual physical landmarks.

This latter preference appeared even more striking in the description of the boundaries of the colony granted to Lord Baltimore in 1632. The grant covered

> all that part of a peninsula lying . . . between the ocean on the east
> and the bay of Chesapeak on the west . . . from the promontory
> or cape of land called Watkin's point . . . [to] the first fountain of
> the river Potowmack and from thence tending toward the south
> unto the further bank of the aforesaid river, and following the
> west and southside thereof unto a certain place called Cinquack,
> situated near the mouth of said river, where it falls into the bay of
> Chesapeak, and from thence by a straight line unto the aforesaid
> promontory and place called Watkins' Point.[16]

The boundary rehearsed what a person actually walking would observe by way of natural landmarks. Such descriptions originated with seventh-century Anglo-Saxon charters called "perambulations." A tenth-century example begins: "Start from Twyford along the road to Bracken Ridge, from there along the road to Carrion Barrow, then in a straight line to the pear tree, then along the road to Cedric's Barrow . . . along the hedge to the old maple tree . . . then . . . along the bank back to Twford."[17] The 840 earliest English land charters mention no fewer than 14,432 natural objects. By contrast, medieval Portuguese property boundaries mention far fewer such objects. Writes

14 "All that tract of part of land in America . . . bounded on the east by the Delaware river from twelve miles distance northwards of Newcastle Town, unto the three and fortieth degree of northern latitude, if the said river doth extend so far northwards; but if the said river shall not extend so far northwards, then by the said river so far as it doth extend," Grant to William Penn, Feb. 28, 1681, ibid., 100–108.

15 Massachusetts Bay Charter extends from 40° to 48° north, provided the limits do not impinge on grants to the south, March 4, 1628, in ibid., 32–35.

16 Ibid., 88–89. Latitude measurements are interspersed with the perambulation, but the descriptions of the latitudes are interwoven with physical descriptions of boundaries, almost as though the latitude line was used only when the knowledge of physical signs was exhausted.

17 There are 840 extant Anglo-Saxon perambulations between 600 and 1080 A.D.. Oliver Rackham, *Trees and Woodland*, 44, 184–186.

Alexandre Herculano, "a tree, a gully, a river current, a mountain ridge mark the limits of the terrain." Only the limits of salt or metal mines were described in great physical detail.[18]

While the mathematical precision of the early political boundaries along the coast failed to continue as Portuguese settlers moved into the interior, this did not mean that the Portuguese adopted anything like the English approach to boundaries. Instead, descriptions of boundaries remained imprecise: a single stone for an entire property or "a large crossbow shot" wide.[19]

"I have . . . in the Captaincy of Ilheos . . . two and a half leagues of earth. . . . [and] I have in the Captaincy of Bahia do Salvador three and a half leagues of the coast and four towards the hills (*sertão*) with two islands in Sergipe,"[20] wrote one of Brazil's wealthiest men in his will. The dimensions of his private landholdings were simple numerical indications: "two and a half leagues" in one place, "three and a half leagues" along the coast, and "four" leagues to the interior. No landmarks or boundary objects – either natural or placed by man – indicated the territorial limits of one of Brazil's wealthiest landholders.

The estate inventory of the most profitable agricultural enterprise in sixteenth-century Brazil catalogued everything from military weapons to vats used in sugar-making in painstaking detail, but made no mention of the boundaries of the land. Nor did maps or diagrams accompany the will or any subsequent register.[21]

By contrast, estate inventories in colonial New England recited the physical boundaries of land at length, no matter how small or poverty-striken the plot.[22] Furthermore, town council records in the English colonies are filled with disputes over property boundaries. Yet similar records for Brazil have little or no evidence of such disputes. The town council records for São Paulo, for example, from 1562–1622 have not a single case of dispute over property boundaries.[23] Fixing the boundaries of plots carried far greater symbolic and cultural weight for settlers in the English colonies.

18 For medieval Portuguese salt mines (personal communication, Francis Dutra of the University of California-Santa Barbara); *Actas da câmara da vila de São Paulo, 1596–1622* (São Paulo, 1915), 2: 172–173.

19 Affonso d'Escragnolle Taunay, *S. Paulo nos primeiros annos (1554–1601)* (Tours, 1920), 100; Daisy Bizzocchi de Lacerda Abreu, *A Terra e a lei: Estudo de comportamentos sócio-economicos em Sao Paul nos séculos XVI et XVII* (São Paulo, 1983), 34; Alcântara Machado, *Vida e morte do bandeirante*, 2d. ed. (São Paulo, 1978), 26–27, 32.

20 Testamento de Mem de Sá (1569), *Documentos para a história do açúcar*, 3 vols. (Rio de Janeiro, 1954–1963), 3: 6.

21 "Inventário do engenho de Sergipe" (1572), ibid., 3: 37–68; "Inventário do engenho de Sant'Ana" (1572–1574), ibid., 3: 83–105. According to Machado, *Vida e morte*, 26–27, this was generally true of wills in the capitania de São Vicente.

22 Darrett B. Rutman, *Husbandmen of Plymouth: Farms and Villages in the Old Colony, 1620–1692* (Boston, 1967), 60.

23 *Actas da câmara da Vila de São Paulo*, vol. 1 (1562–1596), vol. 2 (1596–1622) (São Paulo, 1914–1915).

In the sixteenth century, surveying became the preferred means to resolve conflicts by definitively fixing the boundaries of private property.[24] Because surveys established legally valid boundaries, the English crown itself ordered surveys; the 1609 charter for the Virgina company mentions that land was to be surveyed and distributed.[25] Whether land was "surveyed first . . . and peopled second" as in New England, or settled first and surveyed second, as in Virginia,[26] land surveys were crucial to creating legal possession for the English.

English surveyors at home and abroad were normally guided by physical objects. They first looked at the land by climbing to a high place to find things that could be used to define borders.[27] Where there were none, they often placed a stick in the ground or marked a tree. Less often a chain was used to measure the length of the sides of the property or a compass used to determine the perimeter.[28] But even these means were far from accurate. Seventeenth-century English surveyors in the New World were often unaware of the differences in geomagnetism (which had led the fifteenth-century Portuguese navigators to turn to astronomical calculations and latitude measurements).[29] By 1508, and probably well before then, Portuguese sailors were measuring the degree of magnetic declination at sea.[30]

Terrestrial magnetism presented an even greater obstacle to the use of the compass on land. Compass readings vary if iron is nearby or during magnetic shifts beneath the earth's crust. Readings also shift (although less dramatically) over time, during a day, a year, or even decades. Such variations could and did result in large discrepancies

---

24 A. W. Richeson, *English Land Measuring to 1800: Instruments and Practices* (Cambridge, Mass., 1966), 29.

25 Lucas, *Charters,* 12; Susan Kingsbury, ed., *Records of the Virginia Company,* 4 vols. (Washington, D.C., 1906–1935), 1: 458, 474.

26 Roger Kain and Elizabeth Baigent, *The Cadastral Map in the Service of the State: A History of Property Mapping,* (Chicago, 1992), 265, 285. In New England the process of actually surveying individual plots was often ineffectively carried out in the 1630s. Konig, "Community Custom," 143–144. For Virginia see Kingsbury, *Virginia Company,* 3: 485–487; Nell Marion Nugent, *Cavaliers and Pioneers: Abstracts of Virginia Land Patents and Grants, 1623–1800,* 5 vols. (Richmond, Va., 1934–1979).

27 Richeson, *English Land Measuring,* 34–35, 37, 76.

28 Raleigh A. Skelton, *Saxton's Survey of England and Wales with a Facsimile of Saxton's Wall-Map of 1583* (Amsterdam, 1974), 8; Kain and Baigent, *Cadastral Map,* 265. Placing a stick is the method called metes and bounds; the chain method is described on page 275. The chain method was common in the sixteenth and seventeenth centuries. Richeson, *English Land Measuring,* 35–42, 108–109. The two compass-based instruments were the theodolite and circumfentor. An excellent history with splendid illustrations is J. A. Bennett, *The Divided Circle: A History of Instruments of Astronomy, Navigation and Surveying* (Oxford, 1987), 40–48, figs. 33 and 37. For the popularity of the compass in the New World even in the eighteenth century, see ibid., 149.

29 Albuquerque, *Introducção,* 242.   30 Albuquerque, *Navegações,* 84.

over longer intervals.[31] Even by the end of the eighteenth century, English maps in the New World remained highly inaccurate. George Washington's campaign maps, for example, have the Delaware River in the wrong place.[32] Oral knowledge communicated by local guides was more likely to have gotten him across the Delaware than his maps.

Despite what contemporary cartographers Roger Kain and Elizabeth Baigent have called the "technically deficient" and "slipshod" techniques of surveying in the American colonies,[33] as well as the inability of surveryors to reproduce the same results exactly (the central characteristic of a science), surveying was carried our far more extensively and more often in the English-speaking colonies. Surveys fulfilled centrally significant political functions; they established the extent of English private property ownership of the New World.

Furthermore, natural objects – sticks, hedges, or fences – frequently symbolized the boundaries. Using such materials contributed to the impression that such objects were "natural" rather than culturally constructed.[34] By contrast in colonial Brazil, borders were noted at most by the purposeful movement of a ceremonial march around the edges rather than by setting up objects.[35] Even when objects were used they signified entirely different things.

Take boundary stones, for example. In England, small agricultural plots in open fields sometimes used such stones, placed upon a ditch

31 Even English latitude readings were not particularly accurate. In Saxton's 1583 map of England, Land's End is at 50°20′ instead of 50°3′ and the southernmost point of England is off by 11 minutes. Skelton, *Saxton's Map*, 11. Examples of massive New World mistakes are found in Sarah S. Hughes, *Surveyors and Statesmen: Land Measuring in Colonial Virginia* (Richmond, 1979).

32 J. Brian Harley, Barbara B. Petchenik, and Lawrence W. Towner, *Mapping the American Revolution* (Chicago, 1975); Douglass W. Marshall and Howard H. Peckham, *Campaigns of the American Revolution: An Atlas of Manuscript Maps* (Ann Arbor, Mich., 1976).

33 Kain and Baigent, *Cadastral Map*, describe both in Virginia, and "in Maryland early seventeenth century surveying of tidewater land grants was similarly slipshod. . . . Field measurements of distance, direction, and area were also very approximate"(269). "Seventeenth-century surveying was technically deficient"(288).

34 In conventional historical accounts these actions are characteristically rationalized as "practical," i.e., keeping the cattle fenced in or out of agricultural fields. But while all European colonists fenced land for these reasons, none placed the ideological weight upon fencing that the English did.

35 Stuart Schwartz, *Sugar Plantations in the Formation of Brazilian Society: Bahia, 1550–1835* (Cambridge, 1985), 290, describes a single such ceremony from 1662, details, 548n96. The other elements of this single ceremony were placing a green branch in the hand of the last bidder, walking around the boundaries, and opening and closing the doors of the building. It would be useful to know how widespread such ceremonies were, when they were used or not used. Seventeenth-century indigenous communities in highland Mexico also performed a ceremonial march around the border of community lands, stopping overnight, greeting and/or fighting with neighbors. Sometimes they placed stones as well, but carved (indigenous fashion) with faces or stone serpents. Serge Gruzinski: *The Conquest of Mexico*, trans. Eileen Corrigan (Cambridge, 1993), 120.

or a furrow, to indicate a plot's edge. The stone, which was sometimes engraved with the initial of the plot's owner, signified that the ditch or furrow on either side of the stone constituted his property's limit.[36] Thus, the stone signaled that the physical object (the ditch) constituted a boundary. In Brazil, however, a boundary stone signified something quite different. It marked a point from which the actual boundary lines radiated in a geometrical pattern, just as they had from the *padrões*.

Physical markers or natural objects themselves created neither possession nor a presumption of possession in Portuguese law. A written description of the plot's geometric shape or its measurements delimited the extent of ownership.[37]

This distinctive difference between the Portuguese and English preferences continues to characterize the legal systems of both postcolonial states. Latitudes and a regular polygon were preferred to eighteenth-century descriptions of natural landmarks when the boundaries of the states of Pará and Amazonas were settled.[38] Even today, numerical and geometrical indicators legally define Brazilian property boundaries. "The boundary is a *geometric figure corresponding to a succession of points*," writes the author of one of contemporary Brazil's most popular legal guides.[39] To illustrate such limits visually, Brazilian television programs flash an image of the landscape across the screen, and then using a giant laser marker draw the geometric shape of the property (e.g., a triangle) on the television screen. Indigenous peoples of the Amazon also understand that property boundaries are imaginary lines. In the recent demarcation of their territorial possessions in the Amazon, the Yanomami utilized the word "dry line" (as opposed to a wet line or river) to describe the mathematical boundary line of their property.[40]

Yet the preference for natural objects remains in contemporary U.S. law. The authors of a recent treatise observe, "An original monument (physical object such as a tree, stone, or stake) is considered as more certain in fixing the location of a line or a corner, [and] it is given preference over distance, direction, or area."[41] In the comparable

---

36 Eric Kerridge, *The Farmers of Old England* (London, 1973), 49–50. Plate 11 shows a picture of such a marker.

37 Everyone who had land grants (*chãos e quintaes*) in the lands of the council was to bring their letters or titles before the council within fifteen days from Jan. 19, 1620. Failing to do so would result in the loss of the lands. They would be given to those who asked for them. Those who live along the waterways of the council had a month to bring their titles. *Actas da câmara da vila de São Paulo*, 2: 423.

38 Epitácio Pessoa, *Obras completas*, tomo 1, *Questões forenses* (Rio de Janeiro, 1958), 256–257, 337, 348, 356.

39 Humberto Theodor Júnior, *Terras particulares: Demaracação, divisão, tapumes* (São Paulo, 1992), 284 (emphasis added).

40 Alcida Ramos, personal communication.

41 Curtis M Brown, Walter G. Robillard, and Donald A. Wilson, *Boundary Control and Legal Principles*, 3d ed. (New York, 1986), 87–88. Such objects must have been placed prior to the written deed.

Brazilian treatise, "The mere existence of fences, walls and buildings does *not* correspond to the existence of boundaries. . . . Even the act of placing definitive [physical] landmarks cannot eliminate controversy . . . since by fraud or blunder, a boundary marker may be in a place that does not correspond to it."[42] Physical markers of boundaries continue to be regarded skeptically in contemporary Brazilian laws, yet are preferred in their U.S. counterparts. Mathematical lines – the succession of points describing a geometrical figure – rather than physical objects continue to fix property boundaries in contemporary Brazil, the legacy of a mathematical "discovery" of the New World. And the fence and the hedge still constitute the central means of establishing boundaries in the formerly English New World.

42 Theodoro Júnior, *Terras particulares,* 187 (emphasis added).

5

SAILING IN THE WAKE
OF THE PORTUGUESE

That quarter of the West Indies (I say) named by us "New Netherland" was first precisely discovered at the cost of our own Netherlanders [and] due to our own efforts. . . . [We were] the first to discover . . . and to navigate.[1]

From Southeast Asia to the New World, Dutch ships sailed in the wake of the Portuguese, trailing over shipping lanes the Portuguese had pioneered, buying and selling at distant Asian and Brazilian ports where once the only Europeans to trade directly were the Portuguese. From the design of their ships to the details of their sailing routes, Dutch mariners initially borrowed all their means to overseas empire from the Portuguese. Nautical guidebooks and maps which the Dutch printed were taken from the Portuguese, many Dutch sailors and pilots on India-bound ships learned their craft on Portuguese vessels, including their techniques of high-seas navigation and naval warfare.[2] The most famous Dutch treatise on navigation, Simon Stevin's *De Havenvinding* (Haven-Finding) (1599), describes techniques for nearing Portuguese-controlled coasts of America, Africa, and Asia.[3] Considerable amounts of early Dutch capital originated with the Portuguese themselves or

1 Joannes De Laet, *Nieuwe Wereldt* (Leiden, 1630), 109; idem, *L'histoire du Noveau Monde* (Leiden 1640), 75.
2 Gunther Schilder, "The Netherlands Nautical Cartography from 1550 to 1650," *Revista da Universidade de Coimbra*, 32 (1985): 97–119. Jan Huygen Van Linschoten, whose legendary *Itinerario, voyage ofts schipvaert*, 3 vols. (Amsterdam, 1596), became the model of Dutch navigational accounts, was originally the secretary of the bishop of Goa, where he collected Portuguese itineraries (*roteiros*). Dutch mapmaker Mercator's projections were based on Pedro Nunes's graphic description of the trajectory of rhumb (compass) lines when mapped on a flat surface. David Waters, *Science and the Techniques of Navigation in the Renaissance,* 2d ed. (London, 1980), 22–25. Cornelius Hotman's two-year spying in Lisbon preceded the first major Dutch assault on the East India trade. J. S. Furnivall, *Netherlands India: A Study of Plural Economy* (Cambridge, 1967), 21. Even Waghaenaer's general chart of northwest Europe (in Lucas Janszoon Waghenaer, *Spieghel der zeevaerdt,* [1584], facsimile edition [Amsterdam, 1964]) derived from Portuguese models. Skelton, "Map Compilation," 50.
3 *The Principal Words of Simon Stevin;* vol. 3, *The Haven-Finding Art* (*De Havenvinding*) (Amsterdam, 1961; orig. pub. 1599). On the subsequent importance of Stevin for Dutch science, see K. Van Berkel, *In het voetspoor van Stevin: Geschiedenis van de Natuurwetenschap in Nederland, 1580–1940* (Amsterdam, 1985).

their traditional business partners.[4] In the Indian Ocean the Dutch adopted the Portuguese safe-conduct (*cartaz*) system and copied their construction of fortified trading posts.[5] The law enforcement official at Dutch forts was called by the Portuguese term *fiscal* (*fiscaal*); Portuguese accounting practices for seized vessels were adopted.[6] But the Dutch borrowed more than navigational expertise, naval tactics, commercial strategies, accounting practices, and capital from the Portuguese; they also derived their right to rule as founded upon discovery and related claims to commercial monopolies.

Sailing in the wake of the Portuguese meant that the Dutch rarely made the initial nautical approach to a region, rarely uncovering regions whose existence no European had ever dreamed of before. Rather, the Dutch more often found places whose details or exact contours were imprecisely understood. Hence, Dutch discoveries occurred most notably in nautically accessible areas of the world that were relatively unknown in the early years of the seventeenth century, namely, Australia and the northeastern coast of what is presently the United States.

While Portuguese claims rested confidently upon the assumption that no Europeans had been able to sail to the regions they attained, Dutch claims over a century later were more cautious. Sailors looked for what one writer later termed "sure and undoubtable signs" that Christians had been there before: crosses planted or marked anywhere, coats of arms, shipwrecks, ruins of houses, or European goods of any kind.[7] Finding no such evidence in the region now called the Hudson River valley, Dutchmen argued that they had discovered the area.[8] Johannes de Laet, director of the West India Company wrote, "In walking all around they [the Dutch] found and judged that in former times no ships or Christians had yet been in that quarter so that they were *the first to discover* this river *and to navigate* to these latitudes."[9]

4 Meyer Kayserling, *História dos judeus em Portugal* trans. Gabriele Borchardt Corrêa da Silva and Anita Novinsky (São Paulo, 1971), 233–237.

5 George Winius and Marcus Vink, *The Merchant-Warrior Pacified: The VOC and Its Changing Political Economy in India* (Delhi: 1991), 78.

6 Ibid., 12–13, 21–22.

7 The French (1640 edition) *Noveau Monde* reads, "Ils virent bien par signes certains & indubitables qu'auparavant il n'estoit entre aucun Chrestien dan la rivière."

8 De Laet, *Nieuwe Wereldt*, 100; idem, *Nouveau Monde*, 71; *Documents relative to the colonial history of the State of New York* (hereafter cited as *New York Colonial Documents*, 15 vols. (Albany, 1853–1887), 1: 94. Verrazzano had sailed rapidly through the region in 1524, but the voyage left no credible marine chart records. The text of voyage is in Lawrence C. Wroth, *The Voyages of Giovanni da Verrazzano* (New Haven, 1970), 131–143, esp. 137. While Wroth claims that the names appear on subsequent maps, most of the maps to which he refers are political rather than nautical charts, many of them Italian. For the latitude errors in maps which rendered them useless for navigational purposes, see ibid. 172–173, 189–191.

9 De Laet, *Nieuwe Wereldt*, 100 (emphasis added). The statement was repeated in *Beschrijvinge van Virginia* (Amsterdam, 1651 ed.), 15. The States General made an identical claim on Oct. 25, 1634. "The said river and adjacent countries had been dis-

Other directors of the West India Company repeatedly argued that "the first discovery by your [Dutch] subjects in 1609" created their rights to the locale.[10]

As with the Portuguese, discovering was not linked to the first landing in a region, but the *first sailing* there. De Laet's and other West India Company directors' expression – "the first to discover . . . and to navigate" – was identical to the phrase appearing consistently in Portuguese accounts since late in the fifteenth century.[11] Dutch law also supported the contention that the first nautical voyage to an undiscovered region created a valid legal claim. The eminent Dutch jurist Hugo Grotius wrote, "Under this heading (property which can be rightfully acquired) comes unknown land that is *discovered at sea*,[12] a proposition Dutch officials asserted on countless other occasions.[13]

Since voyages of discovery created legal rights, both Portuguese and Dutch states insisted upon formally authorizing such expeditions. Beginning with journeys along the west coast of Africa, the Portuguese crown commissioned all subsequent voyages of discovery. Prince Henry "ordered the island of Madeira to be discovered . . . and after his death the excellent king Afonso V ordered the discovery to be continued from Serra Leon. . . . King João II . . . ordered the discovery of the islands of S. Tomé and S. Antonio."[14] Official backing for Dutch voyages likewise began with Hudson's initial expedition. De Laet wrote, "The first *discovery* of consequence in the year 1609 [was] dispatched by the ministers of the chartered East India Company."[15]

Dutchmen described their discoveries with a precision matched only by the Portuguese.[16] Findings of New Netherland were registered as the discovery of latitudes, squarely set in degrees. "This coast, stretching forward (*als voren*) with one Island and two large rivers,

covered in the year 1609, at the cost of the East India Company, before any Christians had ever been up said river, as Hudson testified." *New York Colonial Documents,* 1: 94.

10 West India Company to the States General, May 5, 1632, in *New York Colonial Documents,* 1: 50–52.

11 De Laet, *Nieuwe Wereldt,* 109; *Beschrijvinge van Virginia,* 14; *New York Colonial Documents,* 1: 94. The introduction to Pacheco Pereira, *Esmeraldo situ orbis,* also uses the phrases "descoubriu e navegou" and "decoberta e nouamente achado," (7).

12 Hugo Grotius, *Inleidinge tot de Hollandsche rechts-geleerdheid,* ed. S. J. Fockema Andreae and R. Fruin, 2 vols. (Arnheim, 1895), bk. 2, deel 4, § 33, 1: 37 (emphasis added).

13 Verrazzano's earlier rapid passage along the coast of the United States to discover a sea route to Asia had not provided accurate information on either latitudes or coastlines – the core of Dutch ideas about discovery. For comments on the debates over Verrazzano's voyages, see Wroth, *Verrazzano,* 71–90.

14 Pacheco Pereira, *Esmeraldo,* 2–4. Pacheco Dereira said, "Mandou descoubrir . . . em muitos lugares e rios da costa da Guinee." "At your command [he addresses King Manuel] a great portion of the sea was discovered." Ibid., 5, repeated 100–101, 105.

15 *Beschrijvinge van Virginia,* 14.

16 Neither the Spanish, French, nor English explained the details of the regions claimed save in exceptionally broad terms of latitude.

whose southern latitude lies at 38° 50′ and in the north at 40° and 30′ . . . was first precisely discovered by our Netherlanders."[17] De Laet wrote that the 1609 Dutch-backed expedition was "the first to discover this river and to navigate to these latitudes." The United Company of Merchants in 1614 reported they had "discovered and found New Netherland . . . the sea coasts whereof lie in the latitude of forty to forty-five degrees."[18] On August 16, 1616, Cornelius Henricxson declared to the States General that he "had discovered a new land between the 38 and 40 degrees [latitude]."[19] In disputing other Europeans, principally the English, Dutch representatives consistently referred to precise latitudes to assert the boundaries of their claim. In complaining to the Maryland colony, Peter Stuyvesant's representatives declared, "The English established and seated their Colony of Virginia . . . from the degree 34 to about 38. The Dutch the Manhattans from 38 to 42, and New England from the degree 42 to 45, the French . . . ."[20] Not having invented the techniques of high-seas navigation, the Dutch claimed discovery upon having revealed, scrutinized, or precisely described previously unknown coastlines, harbors, rivers, and channels.

Like the Portuguese crown, the Dutch overseas companies regarded much of the information about overseas navigation as proprietary. The Portuguese king prohibited dissemination of navigational routes south of the equator. Dutch officials also established strict controls over sailing guides and charts (particularly to southeast Asia).[21] In the North Atlantic where navigational routes had been well-known for decades, the Dutch company tried to keep secret its information on the trade goods most often sought after by indigenous peoples. "No foreigners in addition to those from outside the company or those coming under its factors . . . [are to be] made familiar with the profits, wants, and opportunities of the place," Dutchmen were instructed.[22]

17 De Laet, *Nieuwe Wereldt*, 109.
18 Resolution of the States General on the Report of the Discovery of New Netherland, in *New York Colonial Documents*, 1: 10 (Oct. 11, 1614).
19 *Resolutionen der Staten Generaal*, ed. A. Th. Van Duersen (Hague, 1984), 2: 680. A slightly different version dated Aug. 18, 1616, appears in *New York Colonial Documents*, 1: 12.
20 Declaration by Augustine Herman and Resolvert Waldron to the Governor and Council of Maryland, Oct. 6, 1659, in *Collections of the New York Historical Society* (New York, 1811–1859), 3: 374–375.
21 Schilder, "The Netherlands Nautical Cartography," 109.
22 *Documents Relating to New Netherland 1624–1626 in the Henry E. Huntington Library*, trans. and ed. A. J. F. Van Laer (San Marino, Calif., 1924), 14. All translations are mine based on Van Laer's Dutch transcriptions, unless otherwise noted. On the importance of learning what the natives wanted, see Van Laer, *Documents*, 67 (instructions to Verhulst, Jan. 1625). Company trading and management were also to be kept secret (under oath).

Portuguese proprietary rights originated with royal patronage, organization, and partial financing of overseas expeditions. Netherlanders also widely held that information from a discovery belonged to those who had authorized, arranged, and underwritten the expedition. When English officials detained the pilot Henry Hudson following his 1609 discovery of the river which bears his name, Dutchmen on board his ship expressed amazement. "Many thought it strange [alien] that sailors not be allowed to make accounts and statements before their employers," wrote Emanuel van Meteren in his *History of the Netherlanders* (1614). The Amsterdam chamber of the East India Company had authorized and organized the voyage of discovery and paid the pilot.[23] Portuguese princes and kings had hired pilots of many nationalities (including the infamous Amerigo Vespucci), but the knowledge they had uncovered belonged to those who initiated and either funded or arranged for funding of the expedition.[24]

Also like the Portuguese, nautical discovery was represented as a substantial effort of labor and capital which created ownership rights. A general charter for discovery granted by the States General in 1614 described the "diligence, labor, danger, and expense" of discovery, as well as the "outlays, trouble, and risk." A more specific charter granted several months later referred to "great expenses and damages by loss of ships and other dangers."[25] The labor and expense of discovery were often invoked as "due to our own efforts" and "at the cost of our own Netherlanders."[26]

23 Emanuel Van Meteren, *Historie der Nederlanden,* in G. M. Asher, *Henry Hudson the Navigator* (London, 1860), 147–153. A somewhat different translation appears in J. Franklin Jameson, ed., *Narratives of New Netherland, 1609–1664* (New York, 1909), 8. David de Vries recounted how an anonymous Englishman on Apr. 18, 1633, argued to him that the river was English because Hudson was English. Vries replied "Hy (Hudson) was by de Oost-Indische Companie van Amsterdam uyt gemaeckt op haer kosten." *Korte Historiael ende jornaels aenteyckeninge van verscheyden voyagiens in de vier deelen des wereldts-ronde, als Europa, Africa, Asia, ende Amerika gedaen* (Hague, 1911), 175.

24 See Luís de Albuquerque, *Historia de la navegación* (Madrid, 1992), 16–25, on the participation of multiple "nationalities" in the Portuguese ventures.

25 General Charter, March 27, 1614, in *New York Colonial Documents,* 1: 5–6; Grant of Exclusive Trade, Oct. 11, 1614, in ibid., 1: 11.

26 *Beschrijvinge van Virginia,* 14; Representation of the Assembly of the XIX to the States General, Oct. 25, 1634, in *New York Colonial Documents,* 1: 94. Even dissident colonists used the same language. "The country . . . was first discovered in the year of Our Lord 1609 . . . at the expense of the chartered East India Company. . . . (I)t was first discovered . . . by Netherlanders, and at their cost." Adriaen Van Der Donck, Jacob Van Couwenhoven, and Jan Everts Bout, *Vertoogh van Nieuw Neder-land, Weghens de Ghelegentheydt, Vruchtbaer heydt, en Soberen Staat desselfs* (Representation of New Netherland, concerning its location, productiveness, and poor condition) (The Hague, 1650), trans. in Jameson, *Narratives of New Netherlands,* 293–354, esp. 293.

Similar sentiments had been expressed over a century before by Portuguese navigator Duarte Pacheco Pereira. Pereira declared that "our princes . . . spent their treasure in the discovery of these lands [which] cost . . . the deaths of many men and much expense."[27] Portuguese legal scholar Seraphim de Freitas argued that "he who makes the preparations or publicly known expenditures . . . is held as the owner."[28] In Portugal kings (rather than private citizens) had made the scientific preparations necessary for the voyages and spent funds from their treasury; hence, they had a right to control the maritime approaches to regions they had discovered.[29]

COMMERCE: MAINTAINING POSSESSION

While discovery (by sailing to new latitudes) originated Dutch title to the New World, both Dutch and Portuguese merchants, navigators, and officials argued that they had maintained their possession of the New World by controlling commerce. The principal object of overseas possession for the Portuguese was not land, as it was for the English, or people, as it was for the Spanish, but trade and commerce.[30]

27 Pacheco Pereira, *Esmeraldo*, 141, 146, 152; D. João III in Jan. 16, 1530, letter to his French ambassador João da Silveiro, in M. E. Carvalho in *D. João III e os francezes* (Lisbon, 1909), 182, 184. In these as in many Portuguese writings of the time, the discovery was attributed not to the private citizen who had actually embarked upon the voyage, but to the royal official who subsidized and sanctioned the voyages of discovery. Thus, Prince Henry is characterized as the discoverer of the regions of West Africa even though he never traveled on any of these voyages. João de Barros, *Ropica pnefma* (1532) writes, "With the importance of the worlds the enlightened *kings of Portugal have discovered*" (emphasis added), quoted in Vitórino Magalhães Godinho, *Les découvertes XVᵉ–XVIᵉ: Une révolution des mentalités*, (Paris, 1990), 56. The Dutch attributed the discovery to the person making the voyage.

28 "Que este faça para esse efeito (occupação) preparativos ou despesas públicamente conhecidas . . . e tido como ocupante . . . conforme responde Ulpiano . . . Bártolo n. 10 citado por Ripa no n. 49 à lei Quominus do tít. de fluminibus do *Digesto*." Serapim de Freitas, *De iusto império Luistanorum asiatico* (Valladolid, 1925), chap. 8, ¶ 13, 1: 227.

29 When privately funded – as the two Corte–Real expeditions were – the language of discovery was identical, ("com navyos e homes de buscar e descobrir e achar com muyto seu trabalho o e despesa de sua fazenda e peryguo de sua pesoa"). *Les Corte–Real et leurs voyages au Noveau Monde*, ed. Henry Harrisse (Paris, 1883), 196–197. Grotius objected principally to the Portuguese demand for public or political ownership of sea lanes – but accepted the Dutch practice of private merchants' rights.

30 Contrast the different versions of the Portuguese ambassador's remarks in Manuel Francisco de Barros, vizconde de Santarém, ed., *Quadro elementar das relações políticas e diplomáticas de Portugal com as diversas potencias do mundo*, 18 vols. (Paris, 1842–1876) 15: 128–134, 136–45, with Cecil's translations in Joseph Stevenson, ed., *Calendar State Papers, Foreign Series, 1562*, (London, 1867) pp. 41–42, 54–55, 75–79, 106–107. Tupinambá Miguel Castro do Nascimento, *Posse e propriedade (Rio de Janeiro*, 1986), 130–131. See also Patricia Seed, "Taking Possession and Reading Texts: Establishing the Authority of Overseas Empire," *William and Mary Quarterly*, 49 (1992): 183–209.

Portuguese imperial authority over "important transactions, commerce and trade" in newly reached regions was usually asserted either by a formal agreement, such as a treaty with the native inhabitants, or by informal agreements that João de Barros termed "introducing and maintaining the rules of prudence" (what we now call the market).[31] Portuguese authorities claimed to be bringing prudence and market discipline into communities they described as previously operating solely on individual greed.[32] No permanent physical presence or fixed dwellings were necessary for the Portuguese to assert dominion, only a set of contractual agreements or customary practices relating to trade. The Portuguese exercised dominion over a market economy.

While Netherlanders rarely argued that they were introducing the rules of the market, they did maintain that their dominion over the New Netherland colony was linked to their trade. Dissident colonist Adriaen Van Der Donck began his chapter "On the right that the Netherlanders have to all New Netherland" by asserting that "our Netherlanders have themselves *possessed* the places from that time forward *in sailing and trading.*" Possession was not sustained by landing or settling but by sailing and trading. Donck further says that the Netherlanders' right was "sufficient in the long and peaceful trade that grew [there]."[33]

Dutch West India Company members frequently argued that repeated voyages to the region demonstrated their "long and peaceful" possession. Following this "first [authorized] discovery of consequence," wrote Director De Laet of the West India Company, a second Dutch exploratory mission was sent, this time organized by merchants. "Accordingly in the year 1610 some merchants again dispatched a ship there to learn of this second river."[34] Merchants began "to frequent this river [the Hudson] and other nearby regions in order to

31 For examples of the conditions of trade established in the treaties with India, see Júlio Firmino Júdice Biker, *Collecção de tratados e concertos des pazes que o estado da India portuguesa fez com os reis e senhores . . . da Asia e Africa e oriental . . .* (Lisbon, 1881), vol. 1. These conditions were sometimes acceded to under duress.

32 "Gentes sem ley nem regras de prudencia, sômente se governava & regia pelo impeto da cobiça que cada huũ tinha; nos o reduzimos & possemos em arte (do commerço) com regras universaes & particulares como tem todalas sciencias." João de Barros, *Asia, primeira decada* (1539), rev. António Baião 4th ed. (Coimbra, 1932), Dec. 1, liv. 1, cap. 1, 10.

33 Adriaen Van Der Donck, *Beschrijvinge van Nieuw-Nederlant* (Amsterdam, 1655), 3 (emphasis added). Ignoring Hudson's description of a contentious early trading encounter, De Laet writes, "Là deux sauvages vestus de peaux d'estans les furent voir & les receverent assez humainement." *Nouveau Monde*, 71; Hudson, *Voyages*, 90. The right to long and peaceful trade was asserted in the dispute with England over the detention of the *Eendracht* in 1632 with the phrase "where your High Mightinesses's subjects have long peaceably traded." *New York Colonial Documents, 1: 48–50.*

34 ". . . Which they gave the name of Manhattes for the nation of wild men that live at the mouth of the river." *Beschrijvinge van Virginia,* 15.

trade."[35] "In the years following this [official authorization] they began to trade with the natives, and our people wintered there."[36] De Laet wrote that "our saints [i.e., our Dutch] yearly continued the conclusion [end] of this shipping and our people usually remaining in place in order to carry out the trade with the wild men [Indians]." He concluded "through which [trade] this quarter has been rightfully vested with the name New Netherland."[37] It is important to note that title to the place – and the right to name it "New Netherland" – was considered to belong rightfully to the Dutch on account of their *regular trade* with the natives. Thus, an activity carried out largely by private citizens – commerce – was essential to sustaining Dutch dominion over the New World, as it had been for the Portuguese.

In both empires, seafaring discoverers were customarily compensated for their risks and expenditures by a temporary commercial monopoly to regions they uncovered. In March 1614 the States General resolved that "whosoever . . . shall . . . discover shall alone resort to the same . . . for four voyages without any other person directly or indirectly sailing . . . to the said newly discovered and found passages . . . until the first discoverer shall have made . . . the said four voyages."[38] In requesting the grant, the merchants of Holland argued for the right "as a compensation for their outlays, trouble, and risk . . . [as] first discoverers and finders."[39] Any person who "shall . . . discover such new lands and places, shall alone be privileged to make four voyages . . . exclusive of every other person." Director De Laet wrote that "their High Mightinesses of the States General granted these merchants a charter allowing *only them* to navigate and to carry on trade all around this

---

35 Anon., "Journal of New Netherland" (1647), in Jameson, ed., *Narratives*, 271. "The subjects of the Lords States General had for a considerable time frequented this country solely for the purpose of trade." De Laet, *Noveau Monde*, 71. Nicolas Wassenaer describes ten voyages by Hendrick Christiaensz in *Historisch verhael*, trans. in Jameson, ed., *Narratives*, 78. Other details are in Nellis M. Crouse, "The White Man's Discoveries and Explorations," in Alexander C. Flick, ed., *History of the State of New York;* vol. 1, *Wigwam and Bouwerie* (New York, 1933), 133–175, esp. 162–163.

36 De Laet, *Noveau Monde*, 71. The traders on the "Mackreel" traded all winter near Albany in 1623–1624; Van Laer, ed., *Documents*, xiii.

37 *Beschrijvinge van Virginia*, 15. Interestingly enough the phrase is changed somewhat for the French edition, emphasizing instead the continuity with the present. "Ende door-gaens van ons volk daer blijven legghen om den handel met de Wilden te drijen; waer door dit quartier ten rechten den naem van Niew-Nederlandt heeft verkreghen." De Laet, *Nieuwe Wereldt*, 101. "Par ces commencemens on donna le nom de Noveaux Païs-bas à cette partie de la Continente Septentrionale, le qual lui continuë encore pour le iourd'hui." De Laet, *Noveau Monde*, 75.

38 Originally proposed in a resolution of the States of Holland and Westvriesland, Mar. 20, 1614, it was reaffirmed in a resolution of the States General on Mar. 27, 1614, as well as in a charter that same day. *New York Colonial Documents*, 1: 4, 5.

39 Ibid., 5. Since the original resolution was from Holland and Westvriesland, it is likely that these two were the origin of the merchants. Merchants requested an additional monopoly after having discovered in 1616 the bay and three rivers between 38° and 40° north latitude. Ibid., 1: 12–15.

river,"[40] thereby providing commercial advantage for individual investors in voyages of discovery.

These States General's grants directly continued a Portuguese practice dating from the 1460s. First in Africa and later in Asia, Portuguese monarchs granted time-limited monopolies to successive merchants or merchant partners.[41] In 1502 the Portuguese king granted the first such time-limited commercial monopoly for the New World. In exchange for a three-year monopoly on trade with Brazil, Fernão de Loronha was to discover an additional three hundred leagues of the coast.[42]

Virtually identical terms were extended by Dutch authorities to the merchant trading partners Hendrik and Adriaen Block in 1612. In return for a three-year grant of exclusive trading rights in the New York region, they were to continue to explore it.[43] Like the Portuguese commercial contracts, Dutch ones were also time limited and renewals were often denied.[44] When the first monopoly partnership dissolved, one of its members received a nearly identical individual privilege from the States General. Upon the expiration of that privilege, a group of merchants calling themselves the New Netherland Company received the trade monopoly for a period of four voyages, but their request for a renewal failed.[45] Even the Dutch East and West India Companies were given renewable contracts, the former initially only for ten years, the latter for twenty-four years.

As in the Portuguese New World possessions, the policies of monopoly grants were punctuated by periods during which no monopoly held – although official consent for trading was still required.[46] When

---

40 *Beschrijvinge van Virginia*, 15 (emphasis added).
41 Gastão Sousa Dias, "Diogo Cão," in Antonio Baião et al., *História da expansão portuguesa no mundo*, 1: 363–374, esp. 363; Antonio de Oliveira Marques, *History of Portugal*, 2 vols. (New York, 1972), 1: 343–344. In 1474, when there were still five years to run on a contract between the crown and one of its subjects, Afonso V transferred the rights to this trade directly to his son João II. Ibid., 2: 7.
42 Carlos Malheiro Dias, ed., *História da colonização portuguesa do Brasil*, 3 vols. (Porto, 1924) (hereafter cited as *HCP*), 2: 325.
43 Nicolas Wassenaer, *Historisch verhael* (Dec. 1624) (Amsterdam, 1625), 65–113; trans. in Jameson, ed., *Narratives*, 78.
44 The Loronha contract was not renewed; it was apparently followed by a period of free trade. *HCP*, 2: 326; ibid., 73. Monopoly contracts for African and Asian trading were also rarely renewed.
45 New Netherland Company's contract (forerunner of the West India Company's contract) excluded all other Dutch merchants and granted a monopoly to Dutch merchants to trade Jan. 1, 1615, to Jan. 1, 1618. This text is in James Grant Wilson, *The Memorial History of the City of New York* (New York, 1892), 1: 128–130. Grants for a determined number of voyages also characterized some Portuguese grants as well.
46 For Brazil see note 44. Free trade was in effect in the Portuguese Asian empire from 1570–1576 (except for pepper, which remained a royal monopoly). That was followed by a monopoly to private companies, a system like that experimented with by the Dutch. After 1581 free trade was reinstituted for five years (except for silk and cinnamon, which belonged to the crown, and pepper, which was rented out). The

the New Netherland Company monopoly expired in 1618 and it was refused another monopoly contract, a ship owned by an independent merchant was licensed to travel. And in 1621 when the newly sanctioned company was unable to fund its own voyages, fifteen private merchant ships were designated to sail to and trade in the New World for periods not longer than a year – the expected delay before the company could mount its own trading organization.[47] Since the Dutch claim to empire was, as Donck expressed it, based upon the "long and peaceful possession of the trade," maintaining the continuity of that trade was essential, even if any group of merchants was unable to fulfill its obligations. In April 1624 Wassenaer defended the company, saying that it was "chartered to navigate these river, [and] did not neglect to do so."[48] Forts were created "for the security of the said trade."[49]

Furthermore Dutchmen carefully specified the range of latitudes in which trade could be carried out.[50] The States General charter of 1621, for instance, explicitly authorized trading between 40° and 45° north along the coast, and along the rivers betweeen 38° and 40° north latitudes (the Hudson and Delaware Rivers).[51]

Since commerce performed an economic and a political function (maintaining possession) in both Portuguese and Dutch empires, both required official authorization for trading journeys. Laws by João II and Afonso V forbade anyone – native or foreigner – from "trading, bartering, or fighting without our [royal] license and authority."[52] The Dutch also insisted that all trade – not just discovery voyages – be accredited by the States General "under special charter and other authority . . . of the United Provinces."[53]

old monopoly system was reinstituted from 1598 to 1642, when free trade was established with the exception of cinnamon, which was in royal hands. Marques, *History of Portugal*, 2 vols. (New York, 1972), 1: 343–344. In the Dutch New World, monopoly contracts were in effect for six years, 1612–1618, suspended for the next three, and then officially reasserted in 1621 but suspended in fact until 1624. After 1638 New Amsterdam was opened for free trade. Jameson, ed., *Narratives*, 199. For the shift between free trade and monopoly contracts between 1614 and 1620, see Barnouw, *History of New York*, 1: 219–224. On the Portuguese history of monopoly contracts in Brazil, see Antonio Baião, "O Comerço do pau brasil," *HCP*, 2: 324–330.

47   *New York Colonial Documents*, 1: 26–27; Van Laer, *Documents*, xii–xiii.
48   Wassenaer, *Historisch verhael*, trans. in Jameson, ed. *Narratives*, 74–75.
49   Assembly of XIX to States General, Oct. 25, 1634, in *New York Colonial Documents*, 1: 94.
50   *New York Colonial Documents*, 1: 10–13 (Oct. 11, 1614, and Aug. 18 and 19, 1616).
51   Resolution of the States General, Sept. 25, 1621, in *New York Colonial Documents*, 1: 27.
52   *Ordenaçoes manuelinas*, (Lisbon, 1984, orig. pub. 1514), liv. 5, tit. 108 (ed. 1514) (same as tit. 112, ed. 1521), contains the penalties for those who travel to Mina or any part of Guinea without the license of the king to "tratar, regatar, nem guerrear sem nossa licença e autoridade." The penalty was death and forfeiture of all goods. One interpretation of this holds that the purpose was to facilitate collecting taxes on commerce. Baião et al., *Expansão portuguesa*, 2: 365.
53   De Laet, *Nieuwe Wereldt*, 109; *Beschrijvinge van Virginia*, 15. The West India Company repeatedly insisted that Dutch title to New Netherland rested upon discoveries and

Dutchmen therefore expected trading vessels of other powers to be similarly certified.[54] Instructions to the first director of the West India Company in 1625 insisted that ships from "foreign nations be required to show their commission."[55] Dutch officials often demanded that Swedish and English vessels coming to exchange with natives produce official authorizations for trade – requests that Swedish vessels complied with more readily than English ones.[56]

Despite the many features of the Dutch commercial empire derived from a Portuguese model, the Dutch did not mimic it precisely. Every copy inevitably incorporates a slight alteration of the original. Not having pioneered the scientific discoveries that made high-seas navigation possible, the Dutch could not claim a critical aspect of Portuguese title – technological innovation. Nor did they employ stone pillars to mark the outer edges of their knowledge. But the Dutch did indeed seek to establish their discovery in several unique ways. The first such method used verbal corroboration by native peoples. Several such accounts circulated, some relying upon a unique Dutch understanding of the verb *to sail.*

To sail or navigate in Dutch is *varen.* But *varen* can also be used as a metaphor for ordinary existence. An old-fashioned expression, "Hoe vaart u?" means "How are you?" but literally asks, "How are you sailing?" Life may be sailing along well or badly, but moves like a ship across water. In the sixteenth century, it became customary to describe departing for the afterlife using *varen.* The saying became "to sail to heaven or hell (*ten hemmel/helle varen*)."[57] In a story told by Indians, the saying recalled the Dutch arrival.

> Those natives of the country who are so old as to recollect when the Dutch ships first came here, declare that when they saw them they did not know what to make of them, and could not comprehend whether they came down from Heaven, or were of the Devil.

commerce carried out under orders "dispatched by ministers of the chartered East India Company." Assembly of the XIX to the States General, Oct. 25, 1634, in *New York Colonial Documents,* 1: 94; Huygens, "Report . . . in 1638," in ibid., 106–107; "Report and Advice on the Condition of New Netherland . . . by the commission of the Assembly of the XIX," Dec. 15, 1644, in ibid., 149.

54 De Vries, *Korte historiael,* 175–176.

55 Van Laer, *Documents,* 55–56. Van Laer translates this as he should take away their commission, but the sentence reads that they have to be required to show it (*vorderen*) before they can be relieved of it (*lichten*) or have it copied.

56 *New York Colonial Documents,* 1: 116–117. Only Sweden's Thomas Yong's 1634 voyage up the Delaware appeared to lack such authorization. When asked for a copy of the commission to take back, Yong refused. "Relation of Thomas Yong, 1634," in Albert Cook Myers, ed., *Narratives of Early Pennsylvania, West New Jersey, and Delaware, 1630–1707* (New York, 1912), 44–46.

57 *Woordenboek de nederlandsche taal,* 26 vols. (The Hague, 1882–1993), lists no examples of this use before the sixteenth century. "Varen" (IV), A 1: 1, a, col. 516.

Instead of the Dutch having sailed to (reached) heaven or hell in the New World – in this inversion of the story – it is the natives who cannot tell whether the Dutch themselves are sailors from hell or from heaven.[58] A slightly less Dutch-inflected version of this story has natives imagining a Dutch ship as either a fish or a sea monster – also presumably depending upon where it originated.[59]

The story of the sailors from heaven or hell was used as evidence that natives verified Dutch claims to be the first Europeans in the New Netherlands region. "We have also heard the savages frequently say," wrote Adriaen Van Der Donck, "that they knew nothing of any other part of the world or any other people than their own, before the arrival of the Netherlanders."[60] "The natives noticed that the Netherlanders who first arrived at that land in 1609 were the first Christians and wind sailors/traders (*winderswaren*)."[61] Unlike the French, the Dutch did not argue that the Manhattes (tribe) or Mohicans had consented to their presence, merely that the latters' previous unfamiliarity with Europeans confirmed Dutch entitlement through "discovery."

Besides quoting indigenous peoples, the Dutch claimed discovery of the New World in another distinctive way. Sharing the Portuguese concern with nautical precision, Dutch navigators did not, however, use stone pillars to record the extent of their voyages. Instead they preferred to describe their findings using charts and highly detailed writings.

Providing descriptions rather than stone monuments to note the scope of new lands they claimed, Dutch writers characteristically amassed extensive details. This painstakingly collected information was linked to both unique Dutch meanings of the word *discovery* and the importance attached in the seventeenth-century Netherlands to describing. While in other sixteenth-century European languages, notably French, *to discover* meant simply to view from afar,[62] in Dutch *discovery* implied far greater meticulousness.

DISCOVERY AND DESCRIPTION

The principal Dutch word for discovery is *ontdekking*, which connotes uncovering, finding out the truth, but can also mean detecting a mistake. In Dutch, therefore, the word may signify not an original invention, but correcting a mistake that someone else has made. Hudson "judged that the Cape (Cod) was 75 leagues further to the west of the regions of Europe than ordinarily appears on marine charts."[63] The

---

58 Van Der Donck et al., *Vertoogh*, in Jameson, ed., *Narratives*, 293.
59 Ibid.   60 Ibid.
61 Adriaen Van Der Donck, *Beschrijvinge van Nieuw Nederlandt* (Amsterdam, 1656), 3.
62 "Descouvrir," in Edmond Huguet, *Dictionnaire de la langue française du seizième siècle*, 7 vols. (Paris, 1925–1972) 3: 56.
63 De Laet, *Noveau Monde*, 75.

corrections that Dutch voyages made on existing nautical charts of the New World could be considered *ontdekking,* discovering, rectifying mistakes.

De Laet and other Dutch writers often used the phrase *nadere ontdekking* (precisely or fully discovered) to describe Hudson's voyage to the New World. The phrase implied an understanding of discovery as a fine-grained scrutiny of coastlines, latitudes, and harbors.

A second common Dutch verb for discovery is *openbaren,* meaning broadly to reveal or disclose, but also having the distinctive Dutch meaning of "showing excellent qualities."[64] In Dutch "discovery" could therefore also entail disclosing the qualities of something already known to exist.

A third, less common synonym in Dutch for discovery is *onderscheiden* (distinguishing, discriminating, or telling one thing from another).[65] Discerning again suggests an actively produced, finely detailed kind of scrutiny. Discovery meant not distant viewing, as in sixteenth-century French, but closely monitoring all visible and measurable dimensions of regions newly encountered.

To prove discovery Dutchmen meticulously described the regions they uncovered. The verb *to describe* in Dutch, as in English, is related to the word *scribe* or writing. To describe was to de-scribe, that is, to write down or to in-scribe. Indeed, most Dutch writing on the New World was labeled "description." While the first edition of De Laet's work was called *The New World,* subsequent editions were titled the *Description of the New World.* Where Gonzalo Fernández de Oviedo called his depiction of flora and fauna of the New World a "natural *history,*" De Laet, Van Der Donck, and other Dutchmen called their accounts "descriptions."[66]

Dutch travel writings often provide superb verbal and visual images of their discoveries, particularly coastlines throughout the world.[67] The New World was no exception. Extraordinary details of coastlines appear in De Laet's account of the New World:

> The coast extends from this cape, in the first place, northwest and southeast for five leagues and then north by east and south by west for six leagues to another sandy point. . . . According to some accounts there are sandbanks or a reef extending out to sea in a southerly direction for the distance of thirty leagues. Not that it is

64 The meaning of making public exists in English ("discover," *OED,* § 4); the sense of revealing the excellent qualities of something does not.

65 While at one time English shared this meaning with Dutch, it is now obsolete. "Discover," *OED,* § 9, 11.

66 E.g., Van Der Donck, *Beschrijvinge van Nieuw Nederlandt, Beschrijvinge van Virginia;* De Laet, *Beschrijvinge.*

67 Isaäk Commelin, *Begin ende Voortang van de Vereenighde Nederlandtsche geoctroyeerde Oost-Indische Compagnie,* 8 vols. (Amsterdam, 1646).

very shallow for so great a distance, but only that the bottom can be reached with the lead; and there is the least depth of water eight or nine leagues off from the shore.[68]

De Laet's description of the New World reads like a coastal sailing log – the famous Dutch rutters – describing where the sandy bottoms were, the exact directions "north by east" "south by west," and distances to sail.

But describing did not simply provide useful information to sailors or visually pleasing images. Describing formed part of the process of laying claim to new regions. "In New Netherland . . . these rivers [were] described by ours." The North and South rivers "and all the other rivers and bays *here claimed were described by ours.*"[69] Describing demonstrated knowledge of a region, knowledge which could have been obtained only by extensive exploration. But there were other forms of description besides words.

In the seventeenth-century Netherlands according to Svetlana Alpers, description was also becoming a pictorial form.[70] While Portuguese pilot Master John wrote that he was "only sending a drawing" of the stars rather than a set of numbers, the Dutch over a century later did not say they were "only" describing when drafting a map.

Official reports of discovery to the States General included maps. When informing the States General of having found the Delaware River and Bay in 1616, Cornelius Henricxson enclosed a latitude-scaled map to "more fully" describe the region.[71] In later years Dutch commanders were explicitly ordered to make "perfect maps and descriptions" of their findings.[72] Dutch discovery therefore culminated in what Raleigh Skelton called "geographical discovery,"[73] fixing a place upon a map. To the Dutch, putting a place upon the map ren-

68 The translation is in De Laet in Jameson, ed., *Narratives,* 39–48. chaps. 9 and 10. For similar descriptions see also De Vries, *Korte historiael.*

69 De Laet, *Nieuwe Wereldt,* 109 (emphasis added). These are the Hudson and Delaware rivers, respectively.

70 Svetlana Alpers, *The Art of Describing* (Chicago, 1983), 136, 147, 158.

71 Resolution of the States General on a Report of Further Discoveries in New Netherland," Aug. 18, 1616, in *New York Colonial Documents,* 1: 12.

72 "Intructie voor den schipper commandeur Abel Jansen Tasman, Aug. 13, 1642, in R. Posthumus Meyjes, *De reizen van Abel Janszoon Tasman en Franchoys Jacobszoon Visscher ter nadere ontdekking van het zuidland in 1642/3 en 1644* (The Hague, 1919), 147.

73 Skelton claims that "the first phase in discovery of an island (let us say) is closed . . . only when the island is correctly located on the world map." Portuguese navigational instructions did rely upon charts and compasses, but the accuracy of their locations derived initially from their ability to measure latitudes. Thus, geographic discovery – the proper notation upon a map – was the *second* not the first stage in discovery. Raleigh A. Skelton, "Map Compilation, Production, and Research in Relation to Geographical Exploration," in Herman R. Friis, ed., *The Pacific Basin: A History of Its Geographical Exploration* (New York, 1967), 40–56, exp. 40. The question of the relation of geography to discovery was initially raised by Wilcomb Washburn, "The Meaning of Discovery," *American Historical Review,* 68 (1962): 14.

dered it more than a record of "discovery (*ontdekking*)"; it transformed the map into a critical sign of possession (see Figure 4).

Naming was also critical to proving discovery. "Our Dutch ship-masters and traders were the first to discover and to trade to them, *even before they had names*, as the English themselves well know," wrote a group of dissident Dutchmen.[74] That a region "lacked names" apparently meant that it lacked names on nautical charts. While sailing around the northeast coast of Canada, Hudson and others carefully noted which features *had* names, meaning those already labeled on maps. When places did not have names on maritime charts, Hudson labeled them.

Dutch writers recognized other states's claims to territory based upon map names. De Laet acknowledged French discovery of an area north of Dutch settlement by citing its name. One such place was called "Cape Malbarre or Port Fortuné according to the discovery by the French."[75] De Laet even registered disputes over territory by a conflict over its name. One such island "by ours was named Hendrick Christianson Island, and by the English Martha's Vineyard."[76]

But where only Dutch names prevailed, the Dutch claimed to have been there first. A group of Dutchmen led by Adriaen Van Der Donck declared that "all the islands, bays, havens, rivers, kills [channels] even to a great distance on the other side of New Holland or Cape Cod have Dutch names, which we gave to them. These [Dutchmen] were the first to discover and to trade to them."[77] De Laet wrote of "that quarter of the West Indies, (I say) *named* by ours 'New Netherland' [because] our Netherlanders first discovered it."[78]

Linking discovery to naming involved a precise description and ubication. "From 38°30′ to 44° named Pyebaye by one of our ship masters; lying at the height of 42°30′ from here to a point (which Adriaen Block named) . . . [followed by] Wyckbay, another bay so named by ours . . . [a] cape was also named Blackhoek by ours. . . . . There lies yet another island on the coast, which was also named by our Netherland mariners."[79] Dutchmen largely noted names for landmarks visible from the sea-islands, bays, havens, rivers, and channels.

74 Van Der Donck et al., *Vertoogh* (1650), in Jameson, ed., *Narratives*, 306.
75 De Laet, *Nieuwe Wereldt*, 109.   76 Ibid., 102.
77 Van Der Donck et al., *Vertoogh*, in Jameson, ed., *Narratives*, 306. Giovanni Verrazzano had earlier given names to areas along the coast, but the names were not given with any precision, and hence were extremely difficult to replicate. Wroth, *Verrazzano*, 70–91. By contrast the Dutch (and Portuguese) names were given to precise latitudes. Here too, there is no evidence of trade by Verrazzano either in these regions.
78 De Laet, *Nieuwe Wereldt*, 109 (emphasis added); *Beschrijvinge van Virginia*, 14; De Laet, *Noveau Monde*, 75. A similar statement appeared in the dissident report of Van Der Donck et al., *Vertoogh*, in Jameson, ed., *Narratives*, 293.
79 De Laet, *Nieuwe Wereldt*, 101–102. Part of the description is repeated on page 109.

Figure 4. The map completed by Cornelius Henricxson's expedition. From Alegemeen Rijksarchief.

Appealing to their own leaders to act against Swedish encroachments in the Delaware Valley, Dutch citizens cited geographic names. "There are in the river [Schuylkil] several beautiful large islands, and other places which were formerly possessed by the Netherlanders, and which *still bear the names given by them.* Various other facts also constitute sufficient and abundant proof that the river belongs to the Netherlanders, and not to the Swedes."[80]

Dutch names on the landscape (and thus the record of Dutch claims) became well known in the Netherlands through the widespread popularity of printed maps. By the 1570s most European maps were printed in Antwerp, and shortly thereafter in Amsterdam.[81] These newly printed maps registered the growing transformation of far-flung reaches of the world into Dutch possessions by showing them bearing Dutch names, thus spreading news of the extent of Dutch discoveries broadly among Netherlanders.

Two other slightly different Dutch explanations of how parts of the New World received their name (other than discovery) appeared on separate occasions. Both invoked an analogy with nature. "On account of the similarity of climate, situation, and fertility, this place is rightly called New Netherlands," wrote dissident Adriaen Van Der Donck in 1650.[82]

While similarity in terrain and temperature might reasonably account for the name, another analogy was playful. Since Europeans rarely joked about their rights to possess the New World, Dutch humor about these rights stands out. Near the end of the account of his adventures throughout the world, David de Vries observed of New Netherland, "On summer days beautiful crabs that are very good to eat come up on the flat beaches. Their claws are the colors of our Prince's flag; they are orange, white, and blue. So that the crabs suffice to show that we are fit (*behoren*) to people that land, and [we] have a right to it."[83] If the French could dramatize their right to the New World by dressing natives in royal colors, de Vries could point to crab claws – already in nature – as proof of Dutch entitlement to the New World.

While the principal mode of manifesting possession was describing, the Dutch occasionally planted physical objects as signs of possession. But these objects rarely established colonial authority. Rather, they were primarily warnings posted for the benefit of other European powers cautioning them to keep out.

80 Jameson, ed., *Narratives of New Netherland*, 314–315 (emphasis added).
81 Most scientific and printing activities were transferred to the north to escape the Spanish military presence in the southern Netherlands. Skelton, "Map Compilation," 49; for the subsequent history, see Van Berkel, *Het voorspoor van Stevin.*
82 Van Der Donck et al., *Vertoogh* (1650), in Jameson, ed., *Narratives*, 293.
83 De Vries, *Korte historiael*, 260. These were the colors of the flag at the time of De Vries's writing. Shortly thereafter the colors became blue, white and red.

A Dutch expedition to the East Indies in 1598 landed on the uninhabited island of Mauritius, where the vice-admiral nailed a wooden board bearing the arms of Holland, Amsterdam, and Zeeland to a tree.[84] Lying near the conventional passage through the Mozambique Channel to Southeast Asia, the island was a likely spot for Portuguese and Spanish soldiers to contest Dutch dominion. Hence, Dutch sailors carved the name of their religion *in Spanish* on the board, thus clearly warning Spaniards to stay away.[85] To discourage other Europeans – principally the English and Swedish – from claiming a region, Dutchmen planted their arms near Philadelphia (where the threat was Swedish) and on Cape Cod and at the mouth of the Connecticut River (where the menace was English).

"From the beginning, our people had carefully explored and discovered the most northerly parts of New Netherlands, and some distance on the other side of Cape Cod . . . before the English were known here, and had set up our arms upon Cape Cod as an act of possession."[86] "Kievets-hoeck (now Saybrook Point at the mouth of the Connecticut River) was also purchased at the same time [1632] by one Hans den Sluys. On this cape the States' arms had been affixed to a tree in token of possession."[87]

Placing physical objects rarely claimed a region according to Dutch law. As jurist Hugo Grotius wrote, "Property passes into ownership by men's actions or by real effect." Grotius's English translator added by way of explanation that this meant that "right of property is acquired without visible signs."[88] Since tangible objects were not necessary to indicate possession, placing such markers could only be "signs" or "tokens" of possession rather than creating such rights.

But even on those rare occasions when the Dutch used objects to signal rights of possession, the English were unwilling to recognize them as such. "The English . . . have torn them [the arms] down and carved a ridiculous face in their place. Whether this was done by authority or not, cannot be positively asserted; it is however supposed that it was. . . . It has been so charged upon them in several letters, and no denial has been made."[89]

---

84 Isaäk Commelin, *Begin ende Voortang,* 1: voyage no. 3, folio 4. The previous Dutch voyage (under Cornelius Houtman) followed well-known routes and landed only in places well populated with other Europeans.

85 For a similar use by the Spanish, see real cédula, Queen Isabel to Alonso de Hojeda, June, 8, 1501, in Martín Fernández de Navarrete, *Colección de los viajes y descubrimentos que hicieron por mar los españoles desde los fines del siglo XV,* 5 vols. (Buenos Aires, 1945–1946; orig. pub. 1825–1837), 3: 100.

86 Van Der Donck et al., *Vertoogh,* trans. in Jameson, ed., *Narratives,* 309.

87 Ibid. The name is transliterated as Hans Eencluys in *New York Colonial Documents,* 1: 287.

88 Hugo Grotius, *Inleidinge,* bk. 2, deel 8, § 1; *The Introduction to Dutch Jurisprudence of Hugo Grotius,* trans. Charles Herbert (London, 1845), 97.

89 Van Der Donck et al., *Vertoogh,* trans. in Jameson, ed., *Narratives,* 309; *New York Colonial Documents,* 1: 287.

Nor did the Swedes find the plaques any more convincing. In 1646, Andries Hudde under orders from Kieft purchased land from the Indians and set up the arms of the States General in present-day Philadelphia:

> The arms of Their High Mightinesses were erected by order of Director Kieft, as a symbol that the river, with all the country and the lands around there, were held and owned under their High Mightinesses. . . . The Swedes, with intolerable insolence, have thrown down the arms. . . . True, we have made several protests as well against this . . . but they have had as much effect as the flying of a crow overhead.[90]

The idea that "there is such a thing as a 'clear act,' unequivocally proclaiming to the universe one's appropriation . . . that the relevant audience will naturally and easily interpret as property claims,"[91] certainly did not hold true for Dutch actions in North America.

Yet Dutchmen "naturally and easily" regarded the placing of the coat of arms (by any nation) as conveying claims. They "caused a yacht of two guns to be manned and convoyed the Frenchman out of the river,"[92] for attempting to place the Bourbon king's symbols on the lower Hudson. When Indians on the Delaware Bay (Swanendael) tore down a copper plate with the arms of the States General in 1631, the head of the settlement demanded that the Indians kill the man responsible and bring them his head. The Indians brought the Dutch a head, but even the Dutch were not sure that it was the culprit's.[93] What the arms meant – clearly to Dutchmen – originated from a long history in the Low Countries.

Posting municipal arms as equivalent to modern "No Trespassing" signs was a custom which began early in the twelfth century as merchant-dominated towns began to obtain collective rights to use surrounding lands, wood, or waters and to exercise some autonomy over justice, military service, and taxes.[94] Posting its arms on a tree on its

90 Van Der Donck et al., *Vertoogh*, trans. in Jameson, ed., *Narratives*, 315. The Swedish side of this event is presented in Israel Acrelius, "The Account of the Swedish Churches in New Sweden," in Myers, ed., *Narratives of Early Pennsylvania*, 75. Ironically, the Swedes, whose settlement was initially funded with Dutch capital, were the only ones to also place coats of arms. "Affidavit of Four Men from the *Key of Calamar*, 1638," in Myers, ed. *Narratives of Early Pennsylvania*, 87–88; "Acrelius's New Sweden" (for the year 1646), in ibid., 66.

91 Carol M. Rose, "Possession as the Origin of Property," *University of Chicago Law Review*, 52 (1985): 73–88, esp. 76, 84.

92 Wassenaer, *Historisch verhael* (April 1624), trans. in Jameson, ed., *Narratives*, 73. For an enormously detailed effort to ascertain the date of this encounter, see Van Laer, ed., *Documents*, xv–xxiv.

93 Van Der Donck, *Vertoogh*, in Jameson, ed., *Narratives*, 313–314. De Vries tells a nearly identical version in *Korte historiael*, 155–156.

94 Petrus Johannes Blok, *History of the Peoples of the Netherlands*, trans. Oscar A. Bierstadt and Ruth Putnam, Part 1, *From the Earliest Times to the Beginning of the Fifteenth Century* (New York, 1970; orig. pub. 1898–1912), 221. A general English-language introduction to medieval towns is Audrey M. Lambert, *The Making of the Dutch Landscape*, 2d ed. (New York, 1985), 127–173.

outskirts, the city proclaimed its freedom from the local lord, warning revenue, judicial, and military officers to "keep out" for the town administered these functions.[95] While posting arms signaled a town's independence, the plaque was less important than a written form called a charter.[96]

A city was not considered a city in the twelfth and thirteenth centuries until it had received its charter or statutes. "These charters are the criterion of a city in the Netherlands," wrote historian Pieter Blok.[97] Charters were additionally central to the emergence of the Dutch state. The revolt against Spain which led to Dutch independence was "largely built on an appeal to . . . indigenous Dutch constitutional charters . . . exemplified by the great [urban] charters of the late medieval period," wrote historian Martin van Gelderen.[98]

It was this powerful symbol of Dutch political rights, the written charter, that authorized all of the Dutch expeditions to and settlement in the New World. "That first discovery *of consequence in the year* 1609," De Laet wrote, "[was] dispatched by the ministers of the chartered East India Company."[99] All trading voyages were carried out "under special charter and other authority . . . of the United Provinces."[100] More importantly, as the Assembly of XIX, the directorate of the West India Company, declared, "In the years 1622 and 1623, the West India Company took possession, by virtue of their charter, of the said country."[101] The company (not the colonists) took possession. Adriaen Van Der Donck described colonization as "under the supervision of the chartered West India Company."[102] While resembling other states' formal authorizations, the charter contained features rendering it distinctive not only from Portuguese but also from all other European measures.

Other Europeans usually accepted a king's rights to create political authority on his own initiative, of his "own motion, certain science, and special grace or authority,"[103] a custom rejected in sixteenth-

95 Blok, *History*, 1: 222–226.   96 Ibid., 1: 113–114

97 Ibid., 1: 217. Lambert claims that towns in the medieval Netherlands were neither distinguished by possession of a wall, market, *or* urban privileges, but a permanent trading quarter connected to an administrative center. Lambert, *Dutch Landscape*, 137. However, since the urban charters registered rights of the merchants from the trading quarter, the distinction is a matter of emphasis.

98 Martin Van Gelderen, *The Political Thought of the Dutch Revolt, 1555–1590* (Cambridge, 1992), 273–274. His conclusions are an excellent summary of the distinctive features of sixteenth-century Dutch political thought. For the revolt itself see Geoffrey Parker, *The Dutch Revolt*, 2d ed. (London, 1985); idem, *The Army of Flanders and the Spanish Road, 1567–1659* (Cambridge, 1972).

99 *Beschrijvinge van Virginia*, 14.

100 De Laet, *Nieuwe Wereldt*, 109; *Beschrijvinge van Virginia*, 15.

101 *New York Colonial Documents*, 1: 149 (1644).

102 Van Der Donck, *Beschrijvinge van Nieu-Nederlandt*, 3.

103 This monarchical form derived from the medieval papal chancery. Seed, "Taking Possession and Reading Texts," 200–201.

century Dutch political practice. The provinces of the Netherlands historically lacked a monarchical tradition, having been ruled principally by dukes and counts. Furthermore, as the author of a sixteenth-century Dutch political pamphlet observes, laws "made up at the mere command, will and pleasure of the Lord . . . [and hence] from the beginning always [have] been . . . wholly powerless and void."[104]

The political form taken by the Netherlands further contributed to their omitting the monarchical formula from authorizations for overseas ventures. The United Provinces themselves were constituted as a political union at Utrecht in 1579 in revolt against Spanish domination. This association of Dutch provinces created a governing council, the States General – "those who sit together and assemble on behalf of the nobility and the towns of the country . . . [to] represent the whole people and all inhabitants of the country."[105] Therefore, instead of attributing their political authority to a monarch's special powers the Dutch East India Company claimed they were "carrying on the welfare of the united lands [Netherlands]."[106]

Among European powers in the New World, only the Dutch sustained this distinctive communal formulation of aims-seeking the good of the whole country. Yet despite the language of common good, one part of the group in fact stood for the whole. Historian Geoffrey Parker observed that "The town councils stated repeatedly that they 'represented the whole body of the town' . . . [but] the Dutch state was run by a tightly knit oligarchy . . . made up of the 2,000 or so men who governed the provincial towns."[107] Within towns as well as within the Dutch republic, merchants were often the most powerful force. Overseas charters stated this directly. The Dutch East India Company's charter declared that they were "carrying on the welfare of the united lands [Netherlands], [which] principally consists in the shipping, trade, and commerce."[108]

Given its collectively phrased ambitions, it is not surprising that Dutchmen fixed communal emblems in the New World: the coat of arms of the principal cities or the States General – representations of

104 The Placard of 1521 issued in Worms (regarding the proceedings of judicial trials) is such an example. The quotation is from *Address and Opening* (1576), in Martin Van Gelderen, ed. and trans, *The Dutch Revolt*, (Cambridge, 1993), 99.
105 *Brief Discourse on the Peace Negotiations now Taking Place at Cologne between the King of Spain and the States of the Netherlands (1579)*, in ibid., 133, 135.
106 "Octrooi der vereenigde O.I. compagnie, March 20, 1602," in J. A. Van Der Chys, *Geschiedenis der Stichting van de V.O.C.* (Leiden, 1857), 118–135, esp. 118.
107 Parker, *Dutch Revolt*, 244–245. In the north (Holland and Zeeland), the town *vroedschap* (practical wisdom) was usually a closed group of wealthy citizens guiding municipal affairs. In the south, there were more elected officials. In both cases, these were collective organizations. Gelderen, *Political Thought*, 24–26; Blok, *History*, 1: 328–329; 2: 17–18, 34–35.
108 "Octrooi der vereenigde O.I. compagnie", in Van Der Chys, *Geschiedenis van de V.O.C.*, 118.

the merchant-dominated urban regions and Dutch Republic. (The Portuguese equivalent of planting the arms of the three cities would have been planting the flags of Coimbra, Oporto, and Lisbon – an English equivalent, planting those of London, Plymouth, and Bristol.) Occasionally the plaques showed the Dutch lion brandishing weapons in each paw but referring to the confederative nature of Dutch politics by the motto "Unity Makes Strength."[109]

Authorized by one written form – the charter – and laying claim to possession by another – maps and descriptions – the Dutch enacted colonial power in writing: tracing coastlines, noting their exact latitudes, drawing locations, describing places, and inscribing names. Yet these predominantly written forms of claiming conflicted most sharply with those of the English. Convinced that only clear acts (which they recognized) or physical objects created possession, Englishmen minimized or dismissed the role of written documents legitimating possession. "The many nations of Dutch, Zewes [Swedes], and French," wrote Edward Johnson," were to lay claim to lands they never had any right unto, but only a paper possession of their own framing."[110] The list of written documents disparaged as "only a paper possession" included charters, descriptions, names, and trading licenses.

While Dutchmen revered charters, English settlers respected but did not revere them. The first Pilgrim settlement occurred in a region outside the bounds within which it had been chartered to settle.[111]

Such actions were virtually unthinkable under Dutch law. Under Dutch law (since medieval times in most areas of the Netherlands), houses and land had to be conveyed before the district judge.[112] Even when land was acquired by prescription, the title had to be established before the sworn officers of the community, a custom in many parts of the Netherlands since the thirteenth century.[113] Such protocols were observed in the New World. The Reverend Jonas Michaëlis wrote in

---

109 De Vries, *Korte historiael*, 156. The arrow-brandishing lion (*hollandtsche-thyn*) along with the red St. Andrew's cross were originally emblems of the duke of Burgundy. Parker, *Dutch Revolt*, 35.

110 *Johnson's Wonder-Working Providence, 1628–1651*, ed. J. Franklin Jameson (New York, 1937; orig. pub. 1654), 219.

111 Karen Ordahl Kupperman, *Settling with the Indians: The Meeting of English and Indian Cultures in America, 1580–1640* (Totowa, N.J., 1980), 20, 30; idem, *Providence Island, 1630–1641* (Cambridge, 1993). See also Samuel E. Morison, "The Plymouth Colony and Virginia," *Virginia Magazine of History and Biography*, 62 (1954): 147–165.

112 Grotius, *Inleidinge*, bk. 2, deel 5, sec. 8, 40.

113 Ibid., sec. 7, 42–43. Before the advent of writing, a stick (*festuca*) thrown into the lap of the recipient, was used to transfer property. Within twelve months a "handing over" occurred in the presence of the king. Witnesses to the ceremony of throwing the stick could be called to provide evidence that ownership of the property had been transferred. According to W. H. D'Arnis Maigne, *Lexicon manuale ad scriptoes mediae et infimae Latinitatis* (Paris, 1890), the tossing of the stick conveys possession. Katherine Drew, *The Law of the Salic Franks* (Philadelphia, 1991), 110–111.

1628 that a war between the Mohawks and Mohicans had resulted in the latter's flight from the area near Manhattan. "The lands left unoccupied . . . are very fertile and pleasant. It grieves us," he wrote, "that . . . there is no order from the Honorable Directors [of the West India Company] to occupy the same."[114] In other words, Dutchmen would not move to occupy even territory abandoned by the natives as a result of war without a legal order from the West India Company.[115]

When running into conflict with the English, the Dutch always first demanded to see the patent or formal legal authorization by which Englishmen had come to settle in a place. When the English colonists were unable to produce such documents, outraged Dutchmen complained indignantly. Adriaen Van Der Donck compared talking to the English about the legality of their settlement to "knocking at a deaf man's door" (as in the Dutch proverb).[116] "They did not regard . . . or even take any notice. . . . On the contrary they have sought many subterfuges, circumstances, false pretenses, and sophistical arguments to give color to their doings, to throw a cloud upon *our lawful title* and valid rights."[117]

In 1659 Peter Stuyvesant complained about English threats of force against a Dutch settlement in Delaware Bay. He pointed out that the Dutch charter long antedated the English charter to the region. Furthermore, he complained that Nathaniel Utye from the Maryland colony was acting "without lawful order, act, or qualification from any State, Prince, Parliament or Government, shewing only an authorized Instruction or Cartabel without tyme or place or when written nor by order of any State, Province, or Parliament, or Government." The Dutch possessed "Pattent of the High and Mighty Lords States General," making the English actions "contrary to the Law of Nations."[118] Adriaen Van Der Donck and his associates delivered themselves of a similar message regarding Puritan encroachments from New England. "The English have, *contrary to the law of nations, regardless of right or wrong*, invaded the whole [Connecticut] river, for the reason, as they say, that the land was lying idle and waste, which was no business of theirs and not true."[119]

This the English demanded in addition, just as if it were their right . . . to establish laws for our nation in its own purchased

114 Reverend Jonas Michaëlis to Adrianus Smotius, Aug. 11, 1628, in Jameson, ed., *Narratives*, 131.
115 See *Ecclesiastical Records, State of New York*, 7 vols. (Albany, 1901–1916), 1: 49–68, for a transcription of the Dutch original.
116 Van Der Donk et al., *Vertoogh*, trans. in Jameson, ed., *Narratives*, 311.
117 Ibid. (emphasis added).
118 Letter, Peter Stuyvesant, Sept. 23, 1659, in *Collections of the New York Historical Society*, 3: 371–373.
119 Van Der Donck et al., *Vertoogh*, trans. in Jameson, ed., *Narratives*, 310.

lands and limits, and direct how and in what manner it should introduce people into the country, and if it did not turn out exactly according to *their* desire and pleasure, that they have the right to invade and appropriate these waters, lands, and jurisdiction to themselves.[120]

The perceived haughtiness of the English comes through in Van Der Donck's interpretation. What De Vries had attacked, Van Der Donck and his associates conceived as arrogant as well as entirely arbitrary. Arguments advanced by Anglican preacher Richard Eburne seem to bear this out:

> They that shall at first come there may account it a benefit to find the places unbuilt, in that they may thereby choose them seats and divide the country *at their own will*; that they may enter large territories and *take* to themselves ample possessions *at pleasure for them and theirs* for many generations.[121]

Nor did the English admit any other European state's right to claim on the basis of a written document. The French were the first Europeans specifically to claim northeastern North America by means of a legal document (1530) – as well as the first to settle the region. While the Dutch West India Company director, De Laet, acknowledged the prior claim of the French, the English never did.[122] Seventeenth-century French writers such as Marc Lescarbot mocked the English for having both asserted a title to and occupied a region previously claimed by Christian princes and their subjects despite their claims to the contrary.[123] But such protests, as in Van Der Donck's Dutch proverbs, were as persuasive "as a crow flying overhead" or "knocking at a deaf man's door."

Dutch insistence upon formal written authorizations for trade were likewise summarily dismissed by Englishmen. Securing official permission mattered only if trade with natives was viewed as having an official or semi-official function, as it was in both Portuguese and Dutch empires. When trading with the Indians was politically peripheral, as in the English New World, commercial relations were haphazard, irregular, and only intermittently sanctioned. English traders with Indians in northeastern America usually had no formal commission from the king, and often lacked any authorization from leaders of their settlements.

In responding to Dutch demands to show an official permit, English merchants and officials repeatedly failed to understand that au-

---

120 Ibid.
121 Eburne, *A Plaine Pathway to Plantations*, 45 (emphasis added).
122 De Laet, *Noveau Monde*, 71.
123 Even judged by the standard of patent plus occupation, the French had prior (legal) claim. De Mont's first charter (Nov. 8, 1603) from the king of France (Henry IV) is in Lescarbot, *Histoire de la Nouvelle France*, 1: (1609), bk. 4, chap. 1.

thorized trade was at the heart of the Dutch conception of empire. Nor did they comprehend that their own indifference to formal approval stemmed from a different cultural vision of the object of empire. Hence, repeated refusals by Englishmen to produce official commissions irritated Dutch officials and sometimes outraged even ordinary Dutch settlers.[124]

On April 16, 1633, an English ship, the *William,* arrived to trade on the Hudson River. After a token effort to review the *William*'s documents, the newly arrived governor of New Amsterdam let the ship sail up the river. A Dutch merchant, David de Vries, described his response. "I said to him [the new governor] . . . that the Englishman had no commission to sail there only a customs receipt [brief] from a tollhouse." Rather than letting the vessel continue, De Vries added, "I . . . would have helped him from the fort [New Amsterdam] with bullets from eight pound irons [cannon],"[125] and he started up river after the Englishman. De Vries's attitude was apparently widely shared, for when the governor, accompanied by musketeers, attempted to stop him from chasing the *William,* "all the bystanders with a [great] outcry, heaping ridicule upon the musketeers, shouted publicly that he [the governor] should have prevented *the Englishman* from sailing up the river beyond the fort with guns and muskets"(emphasis added). Governor Wouter van Twiller then sent an armed force up the river, and after two weeks of unsuccessful efforts at dissuasion, confiscated the furs the English had bought and escorted the *William* out to sea.[126] When the English government demanded compensation for the seized furs, the Dutch West India Company responded that the English skipper had openly defied friendly warnings not to trade, and the Dutch had been obliged to resort to force. Both De Vries and the West India Company irately noted that the English ship did not have any official commission to trade in the region.[127] Furthermore, the Dutch

124 Cautioned against using unnecessary force against intruding traders (and urged to take economic action against them instead), Dutch officials were sometimes forced to respond differently by an outraged local public. Instructions to Willem Verhulst (Jan. 1625), Further Instructions to Verhulst (Apr. 1625), in Van Laer, *Documents,* 55–56, 109–110; Assembly of XIX to States General, Oct. 25, 1634, in *New York Colonial Documents,* 1: 94.

125 De Vries, *Korte historiael,* 175.

126 *New York Colonial Documents,* 1: 72–81. A slightly different account of this incident is in Oliver A. Rink, *Holland on the Hudson: An Economic and Social History of Dutch New York* (Ithaca, N.Y., 1986), 118–121. Similar kinds of interdiction of English trade in East Asia appears in John Saris, *Voyage of Captain John Saris to Japan, 1613* (London, 1900), 35.

127 The West India Company in its response of Oct. 25, 1634, observes that the skipper of the *William* was unable or unwilling "to exhibit, when demanded by our agents, *his Majesty's* Instruction or Commission, which he might have for the purpose." Since the Netherlands was a republic, the only reference for this was his Britannic Majesty, whose commission the skipper lacked. *New York Colonial Documents,* 1: 94. De Vries, *Korte historiael,* 175.

accused the English of attacking their sovereignty by sowing "injurious seeds of division sown between the Indians and our people, who had previously lived together in good union."[128] Unauthorized English trading was responsible for disrupting Dutch "long and peaceful" possession of New Netherland.

The final part of Dutch description, inscribing new names, was understood by some English colonists.[129] John Smith, most likely seeking to counter Dutch claims in New England, sought to eliminate names imposed by other Europeans. Asking Prince Charles to authorize English names, he said, would create a fictive kinship with the New World, making the prince the "godfather" of New England.[130] But the official sanctioning Smith envisioned was not forthcoming; his strategy for countering other claims failed to materialize as imperial policy. Other English monarchs had, in fact, publicly maintained that naming had no formal connection to claims of sovereignty. In a 1580 dispute with the Spanish ambassador, Charles's predecessor, Queen Elizabeth countered such assertions by remarking that having "given Names to a River or Cape . . . does not entitle them [Spaniards] to ownership."[131] To a land-based or land-focused power (such as the English), Dutch names of marine landmarks were unrelated to rights of possession. Yet the Dutch thought differently. They insisted that when Englishmen and other Europeans used Dutch names, they were proving Dutch discovery and hence entitlement to New Netherland.

Debating with an English sailor who claimed in April 1633 that the large river in New York (now the Hudson River) belonged to the English (because of Hudson's nationality), David de Vries responded that Hudson was employed by the Dutch. Furthermore, he argued, among both English- and Dutchmen, the river was still known by its Dutch name: "now it was named the Mauritius river, for our Prince of Orange."[132] Twenty-two years later Adriaen Van Der Donck confidently asserted that the English would not change the name of the river. "It is not that some of the English will name it Hudson river but [instead] they will call it Maurits river for Prince Maurits who was then Governor of Netherlands."[133] Ironically, Van Der Donck was wrong in the long run. The Hudson River was one of the few Dutch-named land-

---

128 Assembly of the XIX to the States General, Oct. 25, 1634, in *New York Colonial Documents*, 1: 94–95.

129 "We set up a cross at the head of this river, naming it King's River, where we proclaimed James, King of England, to have the most right unto it." "Observations . . . George Percy," ed. Quinn, 20.

130 John Smith, *Generall Historie*, in *Works*, ed. Barbour, 2: 401–402. I owe this reference to Karen Kupperman.

131 "Sslumen [*sic*] aut Promontorium denominaverint quae proprietatem acquirere non possunt." William Camden, *Rerum Anglicarvm et hibernicarvm Annales regnante Elisabetha* (London, 1639), 328.

132 De Vries, *Korte historiael*, 175.   133 Van Der Donck, *Nieu-Nederlandt*, 3.

scape features that the English would change when they defeated the Dutch in 1663.

Claiming possession on the basis of a name closely resembled practices of the Netherlands' arch-enemy, Spain. Beginning with a small strip of land renamed San Salvador, Columbus claimed to have named six hundred islands on his first voyage, leaving three thousand islands unnamed and thus unpossessed, "scattered on the waves."[134] On some days he plunged into what one commentator has called "a veritable naming frenzy."[135] Columbus's practice of naming – or more accurately, renaming – rivers, capes, and islands as part of the ceremony of taking possession was repeated throughout the Spanish conquest of the New World.[136] Gonzalo Fernández de Oviedo wrote that "looking at one of these [Spanish] navigational charts, it appears as though one is going along reading a calendar or catalog of the saints, [but one] that is not very well ordered."[137]

While similar to the Dutch practices, Spanish renaming was not identical. Naming geographical features did not mean describing them for the Spaniards, much less putting their position on a map. Naming in Spanish practices was a ritual speech, like the Requirement, the ritual declaration of war announced in a speech. Dutch discovery occurred by describing the features and fixing their names in writing, specifically in a description or on a map.

Invoking the claim of possession based upon naming put the Dutch at odds with the Portuguese. The Portuguese in the New World (and elsewhere) rarely renamed places. For the Portuguese discovery meant finding a place in relation to latitude – a set of imaginary mathematical lines which traversed the globe. But for the Dutch over a century later, determining latitude (numbers) was on a par with the name placed upon a map: discovery by description.

The Portuguese did not rename their discoveries with names redolent of their homeland out of simple neglect or lack of interest; there

---

134 Martyr, *De orbe novo*, ed. Gaffarel, Dec. 1, chap. 3, 45. Martyr interviewed members of Columbus's expedition, including Columbus himself.

135 Tzvetan Todorov, *The Conquest of America*, trans. Richard Howard (New York, 1984), 27.

136 "Llegados alla con la buenaventura, lo primero que se ha de fazer es poner nombre general a toda la tierra general, a las ciudades e villas e logares," Ynstrucción para el Gobernador de Tierra Firme (Pedrarias Dávila), Aug. 4, 1513, in Manuel Serrano y Sanz, *Orígenes de la Dominación española en América* (Madrid, 1916) 1: 279–280, esp. 280. Bernal Díaz cites literally hundreds of instances of renaming in his *Historia verdadera*, a point which Ranajit Guha noted in writing *An Indian Historiography of India* (Calcutta, 1988).

137 Gonzalo Fernández de Oviedo, *Historia general y natural de las Indias* (1535–1549), ed. Juan Pérez Tudela, 5 vols. (Madrid, 1959), 2: 334. By contrast Giovanni da Verrazzano's evanescent names along the coast of North America resemble a poorly ordered catalog of influential members of the French court. Wroth, *Verrazzano*, 158–160.

was an ideological motive as well. João Pinto Ribeiro claimed that the Portuguese showed "their free and disinterested spirit" since "never did they change their ancient [place]name, never did they give it the name of a city or province of Portugal."[138] This naming after a European city or province was exactly what the Dutch did in the New World, designating their possessions New Amsterdam, Orange, and Staten Island. When Portuguese writers renamed, they did not pick Portuguese places, but rather the principal economic trade good of an area: Gold Coast, Ivory Coast, Malagueta Coast (after a West African spice).[139] Even Brazil itself was named for the most initially valuable commercial good – brazilwood. Portuguese writers affirmed the superiority of their variant of colonialism because they did not customarily impose foreign place names; Dutch writers considered such naming to be a procedure by which claims were "rightfully vested."[140]

Finally, it is important to note that the Dutch accounts, by contrast with the English, make nothing of the first landing, or even the first construction of a house. De Laet simply said "our people wintered there."[141] Another writer passed over it as well. "Our saints [i.e., our Dutch] yearly continued . . . this shipping and [with] our people usually remaining in place in order to carry out the trade with the wild men [Indians]."[142] Under English conventions "people remaining in place" or "wintering" in the New World would have originated Dutch colonial rule over the New World. But the Dutch themselves made no claim to colonial possession based upon habitation. Dutchmen even took to spending the winter there – not in the interests of permanent settlement but for their commercial ties – because such ties created empire. For Englishmen in the New World, either the silent pantomime of agricultural labor or physical objects – houses, fences, and gardens – created rights. While the act of writing an authorization down on paper was indeed an action, it was not one required under seventeenth-century English law. Dutch clear actions were not English ones, nor vice versa.

138 "Mostraram os nossos Capitaes o animo livre e desinteressado com que procediam nas terras descobertas o vencidas. A nenhuma mudaram seu antigo nome, a nenhuma o deram de uma cidade ou provincia de Portugal. Se a alguma deram nove nome, foi porque não ilhe sabendo o proprio ilho davam do Santo em cuja dia a descobriram, ou do sucesso que ali tinham. Nunca os Serenissimos Reis de Portugal se intitularam de alguma provincia sujeita senão foi de Guiné e do senhorio do comercio. . . . Pelo contrario, os Castelhanos tomaram as terras e ilhes e mudaram os nomes." Francisco Jose Velozo, "A teoria da expansão portuguesa e o principio das nacionalidades no pensamento de João Pinto Ribeiro (Século XVII)," *Congreso Internacional de Historia dos Descobrimentos, Actas* (Lisbon, 1961), 5: pt. 2, 407–408.
139 Gonçalves Pereira, "As consequencias económicas dos descobrimentos e das conquistas," in Baião et al., *Historia da expansão portuguesa no mundo,* 3: 65–82, esp. 68.
140 *Beschrijvinge van Virginia,* 15; Van Der Donck, *Nieu-Nederlandt,* 3.
141 See note 36.   142 *Beschrijvinge van Virginia,* 15.

Settlement, the dominant English image of entitlement and right to rule, occupied a distinctly minor place in Dutch efforts in the New World. Like the Portuguese, the Dutch also found profits from trade in the New World to yield only limited financial rewards.[143] Yet neither power was willing to renounce their hold when faced with attempted inroads by other European powers. Thus both Portugal and the Netherlands attempted large-scale, privately funded colonization efforts largely for strategic reasons. In Brazil these efforts were called donatory captaincies; in New Netherlands they were called patroons for the patron in charge of the settlement. Organized on similar principles, only one of these efforts met with success in each colony. Duarte Coelho's settlement was the only thriving Brazilian venture; Kiliaen Van Rensselaer's the only successful Dutch one.[144] But such settlements were not regarded by either power as the root of legal rights over the region.[145] In 1621 the West India Company was instructed "to promote populating the uninhabited and fertile areas and whatever else . . . was required for the profit and increase of trade."[146] Director De Laet observed that "the Chartered West India company brought colonists . . . to continue the possession of these regions and to sustain the trade in peltries."[147] The purpose of populating uninhabited regions was not to claim the region, but to further trade. Such efforts were strategic necessities in the face of competition from other Europeans rather than a source of rights.[148]

Nor was the New World a garden for the Dutch. The first English explorers had noted the fragrant aroma coming from the land and immediately inferred that the New World was a garden, ready for English planting (possession). David de Vries, approaching virtually the same region as Amadas and Barlow nearly fifty years later, smelled the same

143 The New York region had even less valuable export goods than did Brazil, whose dyewood and sugar provided a razor-thin edge of profits.

144 Rensselaerswyck was located on the Hudson River near present-day Albany. Peter Nelson, "Government and Land System," *History of the State of New York*, 1: 264–266. The Portuguese assured their control over Brazil by assuming direct political control of the colony and expending vast amounts of cash for military equipment. The Dutch were uninterested in direct political control, particularly given the New World's lack of profitable exports, and were unwilling to spend the additional funds. Hence, the patroon system influenced the Dutch West India Company to withdraw from the region, while it persuaded the Portuguese to invest in long-term military expenditures to keep the region.

145 "La rentabilité commerciale n'est par nécessairement liée à une colonies de peuplement européen." Meyer et al., *France coloniale*, 28.

146 "Dat hy den handel van de vellen ende andersints dat daer uyt 't lant valt sa sa sa sal souken te vermeerderen." Instructions to Verhulst, Jan. 1625, Van Laer, *Documents*, 64; *Van Rensselaer Bowier Manuscripts*, trans. A. J. F. Van Laer (Albany, 1908), 90–91.

147 De Laet, *Nieuwe Wereldt*, 109.

148 Unlike the Portuguese and Dutch efforts, French colonization of Canada was state run, although the seigneurial system has several significant similarities with the patroon and donatary systems. Meyer et al., *France coloniale*, 1: 33–34, 81–82.

fragrant scent. But his response was to explain and describe the source of the odor. "This sweet smell was caused by the Indians (*wilden*) who set fire to the trees and tangled weeds around this time of year in order to hunt, and the land is full of the sweet smell of sassafras which has a sweet fragrance."[149]

Sailing in the Portuguese wake, the Dutch adopted the Portuguese concept of an overseas commercial empire founded by a process called "discovery," creating knowledge by exploring the seas. But the two powers represented their nautically acquired knowledge differently. While numbers and stone pillars pinpointed Portuguese discoveries, descriptions and maps fixed the contours of Dutch findings.

---

149 De Vries, *Korte historiael,* 154. Giovanni da Verrazzano also noted the smell. "These trees emit a sweet fragrandce over a large aueam the nature of which we could not examne for the reason state above" (density of the forests). Wroth, *Verrazzano,* 134.

CONCLUSION

THE HABITS OF HISTORY

―――――――

At the heart of European colonialisms were distinctive sets of expressive acts – planting hedges, marching in ceremonial processions, measuring the stars – using cultural signs to establish what European societies considered to be legitimate dominion over the New World. Englishmen held that they acquired rights to the New World by physical objects, Frenchmen by gestures, Spaniards by speech, Portuguese by numbers, Dutch by description.

French and Spanish ceremonies self-consciously enacted colonial power. Spanish authorities composed a ritual script, the Requirement, which was to be read to the natives as a declaration of war. Frenchmen enacted colonial power most often by staging a procession, an ordered march with accompanying music and occasionally costumes. Both actions were rituals and readily understandable as such, but not all other colonial enactments can easily be classified as rituals.

Portuguese kings did not demand what are conventionally understood as rituals – a series of gestures or speeches. Rather they initially required a set of numbers, the height of the sun and position of the stars, information which was used to claim the region by virtue of its discovery. Yet the process of obtaining those numbers could only occur by a scientific technique, an activity whose gestures and timing – only at midday – were as tightly controlled as any ritual. Dutch explorers were ordered to produce detailed descriptions (including maps) of the exact latitudes discovered, not a ritual, conventionally understood. English enactments of colonialism usually lacked the self-conscious dimension that characterizes most actions we understand as rituals. Englishmen usually established colonialism through ordinary movements rather than consciously staged ones – digging a piece of turf, planting a garden, or building a fence or hedge. Taking possession did not require a dramatic ceremonial moment, but it did require an action or set of actions understood by the English as signifying possession.

Spanish, Portuguese, and Dutch forms of enacting colonial authority required literacy. Spanish rituals of possession were speeches, read aloud from a text. The reading of the text was supposed to be recorded, implying that at least one member of an expedition should be able to

179

write as well. Portuguese astronomical rituals also required the ability to read and write, as well as to measure and calculate. Dutch commissions granting the right to trade or settle required a capacity to read; written descriptions and maps required an ability to use pencil or pen. By contrast, none of the actions of English or French settlers required literacy. The French ceremonies were ritualized movements, the English everyday movements and physical objects. Both English- and Frenchmen authenticated their rule through a set of actions; speaking, writing, or calculating numerically were not keys to possession.

French, English, and Dutch enactments of possession were relatively persuasive across a broad spectrum of their respective societies. Portuguese astronomical rituals were designed for the king and a small group of his advisors who understood the significance of the mathematical rules and scientific measurements. While created only to influence a small group, these actions soon became broadly compelling. Mariners, pilots, and ordinary seamen were soon convinced of the validity of astronomical measurements, as were the large number of merchants who invested in shipping on vessels relying upon these new instruments and measurements. Only the Spanish Requirement failed to persuade significant numbers of those who used it. Conquistadores were required to summon natives to submission to a new religion, because the relevant Spanish political and religious elites, including the crown, believed this summons legitimated their power. While degrees of consensus over the enactments of colonialism differed, so too did the significance of physical objects.

Both the Dutch and Portuguese regarded the presence of objects in the New World as secondary to other ways of expressing claims – principally numbers and descriptions. English- and Frenchmen, on the other hand, both considered such objects central but in different ways. For the French it was usually the method of placement rather than the object itself which created colonial authority, whereas for the English it was the other way around. The object itself manifested authority.

Even identical physical markers were variously understood in the different traditions. Crosses were planted by Frenchmen as signs of possession, but were supposedly guaranteed by indigenous consent. Portuguese explorers used crosses and pillars, but to mark the limits of their navigational discoveries. For the English crosses were most often "signs" of having been through a region. Dutchmen did not plant crosses at all, Spaniards did so only intermittently.

Despite manifold dissimilarities on multiple grounds, Portugal, England, France, and Spain all proclaimed Roman expansion as their central political metaphor. Yet each of the four powers invoking Rome constructed entirely different ideas about what the "Roman empire" had been.

The Portuguese viewed themselves as heirs to the Roman empire because of the size of their empire and means of having established authority. The breadth of the territory they discovered paralleled that of the Roman empire; hence, they claimed to rule over an empire that was far-flung like Rome's. They explicitly attributed Roman origins to their occasional use of stone pillars. The right of a commercial return for discovery was also Roman in origin according to the eminent seventeenth-century legal scholar Serafim de Freitas. While appealing to Roman precedent for legitimacy, Portuguese writers also frequently viewed their accomplishments as superior to those of the Romans. Their empire was even farther-flung; their scientific achievements (in nautical astronomy and cartography) were superior to those of both the Greeks and the Romans. Rome was not only the political model of legitimacy; it set a standard of achievement the Portuguese had surpassed.

For the French as well, the Roman empire was both a model and a standard they felt they had exceeded.[1] Sixteenth-century political displays self-consciously located a new historic source of legitimacy in Rome. Since political ideas were frequently communicated through visual display, elements of Roman art became increasingly incorporated into sixteenth-century French royal accession ceremonies – Apollo, Hercules, the Golden Fleece, Roman triumphal arches, even Latin inscriptions began to appear.[2] Jurists and historians translated Roman legal codes and reworked a legend that the French empire was as old as the Romans', suggesting that the same forces gave birth to Rome and France.[3] Even overseas ceremonies were sometimes given Roman precedents. Claude d'Abbeville in 1614 claimed that ritual entrances and practices of planting a standard in a central location on the isle of Maranhão derived from Roman practice.[4] Yet the history of the

---

1 For the ambivalence regarding Rome, see Michel de Montaigne, "Des coches," in *Essais*, ed. Pierre Villey, (Paris, 1922), 3: 168.

2 While the Parisian journal of 1424 claims the entry of the regent as a Roman triumph, the implementation of this idea in pageantry did not begin until after 1491. At the entry of Henry II in 1549 there were statues of Hercules, Jove, Pandora, Tiphys, the pilot of the *Argo*, and the goddess Minerva. Lawrence W. Bryant, *Parisian Royal Entry Ceremonies: Politics, Ritual, and Art in the Renaissance*, (Geneva, 1986) 59–60, 65, 83, 149. The arch was first built to resemble a Roman arch in Lyons in 1515. On the Roman origins, see Sabine MacCormack, *Art and Ceremony in Late Antiquity* (Berkeley, 1981).

3 Jacques Godefroy (1587–1652), trans., *Codex Thedosianus* (Mantua, 1740–1750) 5 vols. For the histories, see Richard A. Jackson, *Vive le roi!: A History of the French Coronation from Charles V to Charles X,* (Chapel Hill, N.C., 1984), 179–181.

4 "The first thing that the ancient Romans customarily did in making their conquest was when they entered into a newly conquered land or a town, they planted their standards as soon as possible in the center of the place, and in the most prominent location, in order for all to know that they had become and would continue to be their sovereign masters, and possessors of the place." Claude D'Abbeville, *Histoire de*

Roman empire in France was (and often still is) also remembered as founded upon violence.[5] Even today France's most popular cartoon character is Asterix, the Gaul who heroically resists "Roman" brutality.[6] By contrast with the "Roman and tyrannical ambition to try to win over foreign peoples,"[7] Frenchmen considered themselves to implant a less brutal form of colonialism, creating "alliances" with the natives and receiving consent to place their signs of possession in the New World. Both French and Portuguese actions claimed to imitate Roman *practices*, but English and Spanish traditions did not.

Planting gardens, building fences, and releasing domestic animals neither imitated Roman acts of possession nor recalled Roman laws and codes. Nonetheless, English authors also justified their actions overseas by reference to Rome, but they did so differently. Englishmen drew upon writings customarily understood in other traditions as aesthetic – literature, histories, poetry. Englishmen quoted Virgil's *Georgics* to justify gardens as a form of possession and cited Herodian's *Histories* to justify occupation of land.[8] Leading sixteenth- and seventeenth-century political writers quoted artistic works as if they contained the authority to legalize English political actions overseas. "Rome" meant not a political or religious unit for the English, but a language. If a phrase could be quoted in Latin, English colonial political authority could be linked to Rome. Ironically, Latin was introduced into England as a *language* of authority by the Norman invasion.

Following their eleventh-century conquest, Normans began to reverse the traditional use of English in legal decisions and laws by introduing the Latin customary in their native Normandy. Thus, legal

---

la Mission des Pères capuchins en l'isle de Maragnan et terres circonvoisins (Graz, Australia, 1963; orig. pub. 1614), 163v. Such references to Rome were not restricted to Catholics. Villegagnon wrote in a letter to Cardinal de Granvelle that "I will never make peace with the enemies of our holy faith, and he may hold me to formally consecrated to doing them as much harm . . . as was Hannibal in going against the Romans." May 27, 1564, in Paul Gaffarel, *Histoire du Brésil français au XVIe siècle,* (Paris, 1878), 417.

5   Montesquieu describes Rome as "always at war" in *Considérations sur les causes de la Grandeur des Romains et de leur décadence,* ed. Gonzague Truc (Paris, 1954; orig. pub. 1734), 5. These are the characteristic perceptions of subjects of a country historically engaged in continual border skirmishes with Romans. The view from the metropolis (Rome) was quite different.

6   Historian Edward James points out that a Gaul was likely to have been a Gallo-Roman and that the people he was fighting were likely to have been Franks. Asterix's costume follows Frankish not Gallic dress. James, *The Franks* (New York, 1989). I am indebted to my colleague Hugh Elton for this reference.

7   René Laudonnière, *L'histoire notable de la Froride située es Indes Occindentales,* in *Les Française en Amérique pendant la deuxième moitié dy XVIe siècle* (Paris, 1958; orig. pub. 1536), 35.

8   "From . . . (1670) onwards the text of the *Georgics* came to be foregrounded in the debate about agriculture, horticulture, and *patria*." Douglas Chambers, *The Planters of the English Landscape Garden: Botany, Trees and the Georgics* (New Haven, 1993), 7, 186. The Royal Society instituted a "Georgical" or agricultural committee in 1664. Neal Wood, *John Locke and Agrarian Capitalism* (Berkeley, 1984), 26.

decisions which had been composed in English since the eighth century began to be composed in Latin. Using Latin to express culturally specific English legal practices, however, produced confusion in English legal writings. The eminent historian of the common law, S. F. C. Milsom, wrote that by the thirteenth century English law books written in Latin were providing "clear headed English answers" that to Latin scholars were "muddled Romanist answers."[9] Latin had become the *language* of legal authority, even as the meanings often remained English. (The use of Latin continues in both English *and* American law courts even to this day.)[10]

Spanish officials also believed themselves to be heirs to the Roman tradition, but they understood it neither as a language nor a set of practices, but as a religious tradition. Since submission to the superiority of Christianity functioned as the source of Spanish legitimacy, Spanish authorities created connections between themselves as heirs to the Roman empire, but only during its Catholic era. When Charles V of Spain inherited the dynastic mantle of the Holy Roman Emperor, this conviction of the continuity of Spain with Catholic Rome was even more powerfully reinforced. While their practices of establishing authority owed as much to their Islamic as to their Christian past, the Spanish viewed themselves as sole legitimate heirs to the *Catholic* Roman empire and to its vision of universal Christendom.

Only Dutch authorities failed to invoke Rome as a source of legitimacy. Resisting Spanish military forces that once represented "the Holy Roman Empire," sixteenth-century Netherlanders associated Rome with an oppressive imperial power. According to the 1576 political pamphlet *Address and Opening*, Romans "handed all force and power over to their dictator Julius Cesar . . . to govern everything at their [dictator's] own will and pleasure . . . [and] fell into gruesome slavery of their emperors."[11] To designate the Dutch enterprise in the New World – or even elsewhere – as a continuation of the Roman policies that legitimated the king of Spain's power was unthinkable. In later years, however, Dutch scholars would reinvent their overseas legal code as "Roman–Dutch" law.[12]

The novelty of creating empires far from Europe was partially smoothed over by naming the process as a Roman one. Naming Rome signified "imagining" Rome, remembering a set of practices of puta-

---

9 Stroud Francis Milsom, *Historical Foundations of the Common Law* (London, 1969), 43.
10 Phrases such as *res adjudicata* (something already litigated); *terra nullius* (land of no one) continue to be used by English-speaking lawyers. French (introduced by the Normans) also appears in the category *tort*, the French word for wrong.
11 *Address and Opening* (1576), in Morten Van Gelderen, ed. and trans., *The Dutch Revolt*, (Cambridge, 1993), 106.
12 D. P. Visser, *Essays on the History of Law* (Cape Town, 1989); J. W. Wessels, *History of the Roman Dutch Law* (Cape Town, 1908); Hugo Grotius, *The Introduction to Dutch Jurisprudence*, trans. Charles Herbert (London, 1845; orig. pub. 1631).

tively Roman origin. Planting stone pillars or planting crosses in the center of native villages were highly specific national practices, but Portuguese and Frenchmen remembered them as having been Roman, thus imagining themselves continuing a centuries-old political tradition. By contrast, Spaniards imagined themselves extending the traditions of Catholic Rome; Englishmen imagined that their legal system perpetuated Rome's through their use of Latin. Despite being rhetorically justified in terms of Rome, each country's practices – English gardens, French ceremonial processions, Spanish warfare policies, Arabic and Hebrew science – were largely rooted in specific cultural histories. Invoking Rome also served to foster the sense that Europe was indeed engaged upon a single legitimate project – domination of the peoples/lands/commerce of the New World in the name of recreating the imagined ideal of the Middle Ages – the medieval dream of a single unified Rome.

Another origin which sometimes encouraged the sense of an identical project among European powers was the invocation of universal Christianity: the hope in some quarters that the diversity of religions would come to an end, and Christianity be reunified. But as religious diversity became well entrenched – and no single religion emerged victorious – the dream of universal Christendom faded, and the origin of the authority of empires shifted decisively to secular concepts of the nation and its rhetorical allegiances.[13]

The unrealized aim of universal Christianity has created confusion in our understanding of the role of religion in the conquest of the New World. Because the differences among forms of colonialism in the New World have long been recognized, these differences have been mistakenly grouped under religious divisions rather than the emergent political ones actually operating.

The most traditional explanation of difference among forms of colonization is the distinction between Catholic and Protestant expansion. Usually the religious labels are metonyms for Spanish (Catholic) and English (Protestant) settlement in the New World. But what this distinction fails to indicate is the multiple forms of Protestant domination over the New World, not all or even a majority of them English.

The label Protestant covered a diverse group of people from a variety of different national groups. Protestants were Dutch (Calvinists and Anabaptists), French (Huguenots), and English (Puritans, Anglicans, and Quakers). Among these groups there was no common pattern of overseas settlement. Dutch Protestant communities in New York organized around riverine forts and differed substantially from the open-field English Protestant settlements less than a hundred

13 Parker, *Dutch Revolt*, 33.

miles to the east. Both differed substantially from French Protestant colonies in Florida and Brazil in the 1560s. Nor did Protestants share similar methods of taking possession. French Protestants enacted authority in ways more like those of French Catholics than those of other Protestants. To argue for a Protestant model for colonization it would be necessary to show that distinctive features of a Protestant relationship to the New World and its peoples superseded the national differences between England, the Netherlands, and France.

The same holds true for the label Catholic. There were French Catholic, Spanish Catholic, and Portuguese Catholic colonies, all of which had fundamentally different positions regarding their right to the New World, the texts and sources of their legitimacy in establishing colonial empires.

The first Protestant settlements in the New World were Huguenot – the French branch of Calvinism – under Ribault and Laudonnière in Florida in the 1560s and under Villegagnon in Brazil in the 1550s and 1560s. If there were differences between Catholic and Protestant forms of expansion in the New World, an ideal comparison would be of French styles of these. Thus, the Catholic colonies established by Champlain and D'Esnambuc should have differed significantly from Protestant ones by Laudonnière and Villegagnon because the former were Catholic and the later Protestant.[14] While they did indeed differ, the central dissimilarity rested with the reluctance of French kings to grant official letters patent to Protestant colonists or to provide state funds for Protestant evangelization. These differences altered neither French political rationales, sources of legitimacy, ceremonies, nor relationships to indigenous peoples. Thus, within a single nation, differences between Catholic and Protestant overseas ventures were restricted to the extent of official authorization and state funding of religious missions. In legitimating and enacting colonial power overseas, national differences were far more powerful than religious ones.

Economic practices also contradicted the rhetorical allegiance to universal Roman or Christian rule. State bureaucracies were established to regularize and govern economic relations with overseas possessions. Records were kept and income received neither for a pan-European organization nor an imagined universal Rome or Christendom, but by separate nations.

Yet the myth of a common Europe, a common colonial project, the common view of themselves as the heirs to Christian or Roman universalism remained unchallenged and unexamined by all participants

14 Nor is there anything distinctive in the ways in which the Protestant commander the Lord de La Ravadière enacted French colonial rule in Brazil, from the way that the Catholic relative of Richelieu's (Razilly) acted in the same set of ceremonies.

in the New World enterprise.[15] In the sixteenth century, the nation as the symbolic object to which people owed their allegiance, and by which they legitimated their political empires overseas had simply not yet come into being. European colonialists imagined the object of their ambitions as the re-creation of a Roman or a Christian empire, an empire of broad political power extended over multiple linguistic and cultural groups. The imagined universal Christianity or Roman rule rather than that of a particular nation guided the symbolic allegiances of colonialism.

The politics of legitimation of overseas empires – the elaborate revivals of Roman and canon law – were created to justify conquest of peoples who had never been conquered by the Romans and who did not regard Greek or Roman law as their own, much less a legitimate framework for conquest. For New World peoples who enjoyed wholly different religious and cultural heritages the Greco-Roman and Christian heritages of Western Europe were unpersuasive. Such rationales could only convince European audiences, for it was to their various constituencies that these rationales were ultimately addressed.

Furthermore, many ceremonies and practices used to institute colonial authority were neither Roman nor Christian. Islamic and Jewish science lay behind the Portuguese pioneering efforts in nautical astronomy and eventually became the basis of all of Europe's technical and scientific approach to high-seas navigation and domination of the seas. Islamic warfare practices shaped Spanish ones in the New World, as Bartolomé de Las Casas had noted. Beneath the symbolic allegiances to Christianity and Rome were far more complex, heteroglot cultural constructions.

Cultural practices appearing in the enactments of colonial power in the New World did more than diverge sharply along the lines of emerging cultural differences of nations. They also originated at times as disparate as the cultures themselves. The Spanish Requirement – a sixteenth-century hybrid – traced its roots to classic Iberian Islamic jurisprudence of the eighth and subsequent centuries. French ceremonies in the Amazon were inspired by increasingly elaborate coronation rituals in thirteenth- and fourteenth-century France. Dutch charters emerged in the twelfth and thirteenth centuries. All were unmistakably products of a period beginning in the eighth century and extending over a broad sweep of what is usually called the medieval era.

The developing cultural and political patterns of this "middle" period were also related to the emergence of new vocabularies and linguistic forms. The distinctive English definition of *wild* as uncultivated

---

15 The word *Europe* was in fact little used before the fifteenth century, thus suggesting that in fact the idea of a common "Europe" either emerged, or was fundamentally strengthened by, overseas colonization. Jean-Baptiste Duroselle, *L'idée de L'Europe dans l'histoire* (Paris, 1964).

emerged in the eighth century and was elaborated by the eleventh. The French meaning of *ceremonial* as having rules emerged in the fourteenth century. Yet in Portugal the concept of discovery emerged during the fifteenth century. Print capitalism was able to expand swiftly because it used vernacular vocabularies already created and in widespread use during the Middle Ages. These vernaculars also became the principal medium for describing gestures, actions, movements, and objects used in asserting political control over the New World.

The languages and practices that coalesced into accepted ceremonies of possession thus emerged from nearly invisible quotidian cultural processes within separate European communities. From roughly the eighth century onward, languages and actions became continually re-presented and reenacted, reinforced by ordinary symbolic objects such as fences and hedges, as well as sustained by the shared meanings of everyday language in vocabulary and expressions such as "possession."

Seen retrospectively from the conquest of America, this period constituted perhaps less a Middle Ages than an emergent modernity, evolving linguistic, political forms that would be carried forward into the sixteenth century, when they would travel beyond the bounds of Europe and leave their legacies upon the formerly colonial world well into the twentieth century.

The same emerging cultural differences among Europeans also shaped the distinctive economic ambitions and interests in the New World. English colonists' principal economic interest lay in acquiring indigenous land. Where land could not be readily obtained (subsequently in Africa and South Asia) British colonial officials either taxed natives on the basis of their houses or their land.[16] By contrast Spanish settlers and monarchs both sought the economic benefits of indigenous labor. The Spanish state taxed indigenous peoples on their persons, a tax called tribute; Spanish settlers also sought to appropriate native labor. The Portuguese crown and the Dutch East and West India Companies taxed the goods that indigenous peoples traded. Taxing commerce, people, and land are fundamentally different ways to collect revenue. All created substantively different European economic interests in overseas empire. Spanish interests in preserving indigenous peoples so as to tax them were matched to a lesser extent by the original interest of French, Portuguese, and Dutch settlers in having trading partners to provide them with a source of goods. Only the English had comparatively little interest in preserving indigenous peoples; their presence constituted a barrier to English occupation. To tax native land, peoples, or goods were fundamentally different economic

16 It was not until the census of 1871–1872 that the British began to show interest in direct counts of people. Bernard S. Cohen, *An Anthropologist Among the Historians and Other Essays* (Delhi, 1987), 224–254, esp. 233.

ambitions in the New World, each consistent with the cultural definitions of basic economic interests.

To track the economic benefits of each type of rule over indigenous
peoples, countries sent different human agents. English colonialists
sent a surveyor with his instruments to register the boundaries of land
carefully. The initial representative of Portuguese colonialism was the
astronomer taking measurements of the sky, his successor the treasury
agent collecting taxes, just as Dutch colonial officials did. The emissary of French colonial authority operated as a theatrical director,
choreographing and staging the ceremonial alliance of French and indigenous peoples. Spanish colonialism's initial envoy proclaimed the
superiority of Christianity; his successor was the census taker listing the
names of tributary subjects of Spanish rule.

To attain these economic ends, the agents of colonial authority created diverse kinds of state bureaucratic records. Spaniards created demographic lists of indigenous people in order to tax on an individual
basis (tribute). The Portuguese developed public accounting, creating
a massive fiscal bureaucracy to register and tax the flow of commercial
goods as a foundation of empire.[17] The Dutch did likewise, only placing
it in the hands of a quasi-governmental body rather than under direct
political control. Each established a different form of economic record
keeping: The English kept survey maps, the Spanish censuses, the Dutch
and Portuguese commercial data.[18] (Both the latter also kept naval
records, as well as nautical charts and data in official hands.) The vast
bureaucratic enterprises of modern states owe part of their origin to
tracking the culturally specific sources of colonial economic profits.[19]

Just as certain features of state power – record keeping and fiscal
domination – had their origins in colonialism, so too did related forms
of scientific and technological knowledge. The modern techniques of
land surveying were invented by the English in India in order to tax on
the basis of landownership. Unable to understand property configura-
tions based on local knowledge, they created a scientific procedure to
obtain an independent, supposedly neutral source of information on
landholding. Similarly, the Portuguese created the mathematics and
technology of high-seas navigation in order to reach the sources of

17 From the early sixteenth century Vitorino Magalhães Godinho wrote, "State and sta-
   tistics are henceforth interlinked . . . [and] lead to the development of public accounting." "Estadistica," Joel Serrão, ed., Dicionario de História de Portugal, 3 vols.
   (Lisbon, 1963–1971), 2: 256.
18 The English created their famous revenue surveys in India in order to tax indigenous peoples according to a map.
19 State bureaucratic apparatuses were commonly created within Europe to track
   people (in order to mobilize them for war). Jean Meyer, Jean Terrade, Annie
   Rey-Godlzeiguer, and Jacques Thobie, Histoire de la France coloniale des origenes à 1914,
   2 vols. (Paris, 1990), 24.

trade goods. Global latitude markings were invented by Portuguese chart makers in the first decade of the sixteenth century. Also, the mathematical insights (the relationship of rhumb lines) that made possible Mercator's projection and modern globes were discovered by Portuguese cosmographer Pedro Nunes in 1537. When we look at a globe or map, travel by ship or plane, we are using technological advances initially created by colonial expansion. Modern maps, nautical charts, land surveys, and even the Mercator projection we owe to one form or another of European colonialism.

Because the practices and vocabularies that legitimated colonial authority were cultural, they instituted power over the New World in familiar language, gestures, and objects. Hence, historical traces of colonialism remain in precisely those objects and language used to establish rule over the New World. Portuguese and Dutch colonists carried nautical and commercial guides – the latitude of each place they traded with, the anchorages and harbors, hidden reefs or sandbars, and the goods to be bartered or purchased there. Along with descriptions and guides, English colonists carried books on surveying and gardening – how to establish physical boundaries, and how to plant gardens in the New World – far more than did other European colonists.[20] English surveying and gardening books, Portuguese and Dutch nautical itineraries remain as traces to be found in libraries and private collections around the world. But their legacies remain in contemporary practices as well.

Even the relatively simple question of establishing property boundaries remains within the cultural framework of the original colonizing powers. Picket fences and hedges define the boundaries of private property in the contemporary United States. Yet the picket fences beloved in American folklore originated with the sharp pointed sticks used in the thirteenth century to enclose deer in a private hunting area. English colonists brought them to the New World to signify the boundaries of individual private property. On the other hand, geometrical figures and mathematical lines are the common understandings of how demarcation is established in contemporary Brazil. While the English (and later the U.S.) descriptions of the boundaries of ownership stem from physical objects placed on the landscape, Brazilian images derive from an equally colonial origin in geometrical figures and mathematical lines.

The cultural traces of colonialism often remain in names as well. The Southern Cross remains the name of the most famous constellation of the southern hemisphere. The Spanish practices of taking pos-

20 The most popular was W. Folkingham, *Feudigraphia: The Synopsis or Epitome of Surveying methodized* (London, 1610), noted in Alexander Brown, *Genesis of the United States*, (New York, 1964), 359.

session often involved renaming places with appelations derived from the realm of the sacred – saints (Los Angeles; Nuestra Señora de la Reina de Los Angeles), and sacraments (Sacramento) – and that of nature – good airs (Buenos Aires).[21] The Portuguese preoccupation with economic benefits led to designating places by the name of the first important economic product – Brazil for the initially valuable dyewood called brazilwood.

The Tappan Zee Bridge in New York uses the Dutch name for the native people who inhabited the Hudson River – the Tappans. *Zee* is the Dutch word for sea, so the Tappan Zee Bridge is the bridge over the sea of the Tappan peoples. Staten Island is Dutch for State's Island, but *states* is a reference to the States General of the United Provinces (the Netherlands), not the United States.

French, Spanish, and Dutch settlers both named and claimed to possess through naming. Portuguese settlers recognized naming as a means of establishing power, but viewed it as an oppressive form of colonialism. English rulers disparaged naming as a legitimate claim, with the ironic result of retaining a considerable number of indigenous names simply because naming was not pivotal to establishing colonial authority.

The ceremonies and means of creating different European colonialisms were described with distinct vocabularies, employed different objects, and relied upon separate conceptual means. English fences, Portuguese astronomical measurements, Spanish speeches, French ceremonies, and Dutch descriptions all had different cultural origins, bore different cultural meanings.

Yet surprisingly, Europeans failed to demonstrate any curiosity about dissimilarities with each other's methods. Discrepancies in defining Roman antecedents or fixing legal authority, let alone simply undertaking apparently odd or unusual ritual actions, never led citizens and subjects of other powers to any interest in the nature of these differences.

Instead, divergences in speech, language, and actions were dismissed as irrelevant, erroneous, or morally wrong. Representatives of France, Spain, Portugal, the Netherlands, and England each shared the unmistakable conviction that their and only their position was right and that all others were bull-headedly wrong. Summary derogatory dismissal is the customary way to reject cultural variations because such differences are rarely obvious, articulated, or understood as such. But one's own cultural position is seen as natural, clear, or obvious. Others simply "do not *really* understand," "are wrong and don't recognize it," or are "naive." Dutch settlers in New York accused the Eng-

---

21 The two Spanish exceptions were Golden Castile (Castilla de Oro) and the Gulf of Pearls (Golfo de Perlas). Jaime Cortesão, *A política de sigilo nos descobrimentos* (Lisbon, 1960), 11.

lish of acting arbitrarily and without the force of law for disregarding written authorizations. Englishmen accused the Dutch of neglecting to create property rights through farming with boundaries and hedges – the essential means to ownership rights in the English system. In each case, one side defined the other's legal practices and customs as inadequate because they neglected to perform a pivotal practice from one's own familiar legal and political context.

In expressing their rights to the New World, individuals and officials from each European state failed to articulate a positive statement of what they stood for or considered legal means of enacting authority – "We English do it this way." Such a statement would have been possible only if they were conscious of cultural differences. Unaware of such differences or unwilling to recognize them, Europeans simply relied upon the assumption that the familiar was right, the unfamiliar wrong.

These mutual accusations of illegality were never convincing beyond a particular European group, serving instead to reinforce each community's sense of entitlement – because only they were creating colonial rule in ways they found acceptable. Shared hostilities concerning cultural styles of colonializing contributed to an emerging consciousness of shared political identity within European societies that eventually would become identified as nationalism.

National customs appear obvious and familiar; they primarily belong to the sphere of culture (language, law, and action). As cultural conventions, they strengthen convictions that the known and the correct are linked. Contemporary nationalism combines cultural hostility to unfamiliar practices with a heightened and widespread consciousness of common political identity. It was this awareness of political fellowship that had yet to be fully realized during the sixteenth and early seventeenth centuries. However, when the nation came to be "imagined" as a self-conscious political community in the eighteenth and nineteenth centuries, there already existed a basis for it in language, political experience, and cultural practice.

Overseas enactments of colonial authority thus formed part of these emerging national traditions. The citizens, subjects, and leaders of each European power enacted domestically familiar means of political authority overseas. In so doing they simultaneously defined what was imperative and indispensable to their own legal system, as well as strengthened their convictions that *international* legality was rooted in the culturally familiar.

Each national tradition considers "its own language as the verbal and semantic center of the ideological world," wrote Mikhail Bakhtin. "Verbal-ideological *de*centering will occur only when a national culture loses its sealed-off and self-sufficient character, when it becomes conscious of itself as only one among *other* cultures and languages. . . .

[Upon such realization] there will arise an acute feeling for language *boundaries* [social, national, and semantic]."[22] This awareness of difference, a consciousness of language boundaries, was not apparent in the sixteenth century and is often still missing in national accounts of overseas expansion. Only after decentering "will language reveal its essential *human* character. From behind its words, forms, styles, nationally characteristic and socially typical faces begin to emerge; the images of speaking human beings."[23]

Because there was in practice no common political or legal heritage, conflicts occurred often among Europeans seeking to control colonial possessions. While such clashes were inevitable, given the competitive character of imperial drives in the sixteenth and seventeenth centuries, the form these disputes took owed much to the cultural traditions of politics. The incomprehension, criticism, and misunderstandings by subjects and rulers from one colonial power of another were far from "merely" ideological. They were cultural disagreements rooted in basic differences about the very foundations upon which all claims to political power rested: sovereignty, dominion, possession, and the nature of empire. Each misunderstanding reflected profound embedded differences in the cultural and linguistic premises operating within different legal systems.

International understanding is not simply a question of finding underlying interests. For one of the societies in question – sixteenth-century Spain (and often many of its contemporary former colonies) – to raise the question of their own interests is in fact a morally prejudicial question. Anybody responding to the question of interests was in fact betraying him- or herself as morally corrupt or bankrupt and therefore disqualified from the task of discussion.[24] *Interests* cannot serve as a neutral ground for discussion because the term itself is not, and historically has never been, neutral. These nationally (culturally and linguistically) specific legal cultures continue to ground the ways in which judgments about other cultures are expressed and articulated.

Historians have always thought in terms of ruptures undergirded by fundamental continuities. But it has been harder to sustain this position with the extraordinary ruptures of the sixteenth century – the end to a single Christendom and the intense discovery and exploration of the Americas. What historians have usually understood as

22 Mikhail Bakhtin, "Discourse in the Novel," in Michael Holquist, and Cary Emerson, eds., *The Dialogic Imagination* (Austin, 1981), 366, 370 (emphasis added).
23 Ibid., 370. To increase the clarity of the quote, the punctuation of the original translation has been changed.
24 *Interesado* in contemporary Latin American Spanish most often means having an (often unsavory) ulterior motive. For a historical example, see Patricia Seed, *To Love, Honor, and Obey in Colonial Mexico* (Stanford, Calif., 1988), chaps. 2 and 8.

underlying continuities have usually been social and domestic issues – private spaces and lives whose changes have been glacially slow
compared with the rapid shifts of political and economic change. But
perhaps it is time to consider that there are culturally defined political and economic structures underneath the ruptures of the sixteenth
century, structures that were not static, but were evolving at a relatively
slow speed in the direction of a form that is recognizable even today.

The first phase of European expansion came to a halt in a number
of ways by the end of the seventeenth century. The beginnings of capitalism as a global phenomena, the search for raw materials to feed the
machines of an industrializing world, and the search for markets for
those manufactured goods created colonial economic relationships
substantially more intense than those of the early modern era. Having
established a common politically self-consciousness of community in
the nation, Europeans in the second wave of colonialism readily accepted the idea that colonial expansion could be legitimated by a
purely national project rather than a Roman one. Developing different rationales and more intense economic rhythms, nineteenth-century colonialists clearly differed from their predecessors, but they
considered themselves no less entitled to rule the rest of the world.

This second wave of colonialism also instituted rule through political and bureaucratic organizations under national supervision. Revenues were collected and spent by national bureaucratic organizations;
political officials imposed national laws and customs on peoples overseas. Yet these patterns and practices of the colonial project had been
laid down in the sixteenth and early seventeenth century before the nation existed. Political control of colonialism has receded, in the
process leaving cultural legacies and traces in political and everyday
life, as well as in the names of familiar objects in our universe. Perhaps
it is because colonialism is and was so closely linked to state control that
it has reached this end. The late twentieth century has witnessed the
singular unraveling of large-scale political empires and with it the dis-
solution of state-directed, politically motivated forms of colonialism. As
a consequence the rationales for overseas expansion – the politics of
legitimation – are undergoing a very dramatic historical reevaluation.

That author of colonial empire – the nation – is starting to fray
around the edges. Once the sovereign organizing principle of expansion, the nation is now beginning to contend with other powerful
transnational organizations for the dominance of international exchange. Facing challenges from transnational corporations, Internet
communication highways, and regional trade alliances, the nation is
having to reshape its definition, reconfigure its boundaries. Yet we are
creatures of habit, the habits of our history and our culture. How we
refashion those is the next question.

INDEX

═══════════

agricultural practices: as English symbol of possession, 31–9; Spanish system of protection for indigenous peoples, 86–7

aljama status: conditions in Spain for granting, 8; of Indians conquered by Spanish, 85; of Jews and Muslims in Spain, 85

Alpers, Svetlana, 162

astrolabe (nautical): adoption by mariners of other countries, 136–7; development and description, 120–1; invented by Jewish astronomers, 117–18; Portuguese design change, 122; universal, 121

astronomical observation: as alternative to compass directions, 113–14; astrolabe as instrument of, 120–8; importance to Portuguese, 106

astronomy: Islamic, 107, 114, 116, 120–5; Jewish, 107, 117, 120, 125; Portuguese creation of nautical, 102

Averroes. *See* Ibn Rushd (Averroes)

Baigent, Elizabeth, 146

Bakhtin, Mikhail, 94, 98, 191–2

ballet, French court, 66

Barré, Nicolas, 59, 60

Blackstone, William, 35

Blok, Pieter, 168

Bodin, Jean, 51, 62, 65

body language (*see also* ballet): in French ceremonies, 55; French understanding of, 66

boundaries (*see also* enclosure movement, England; property boundaries; surveys): descriptions of English colonial, 144–7; English rights linked to, 19–23; Portuguese numerical and mathematical descriptions, 140–4; setting by perambulation, 143; used by English for gardens, 28

boundary stones, 146–7

Bradford, William, 16

Brown, Alexander, 23

Bryant, Lawrence, 53

Cabral, Pedro Álvarez, 103, 104

Cape Bojador, 109 13, 131

caravel, 110

Cartier, Jacques, 56–7

Catholicism: in different national groups, 185; French introduction in colonies, 42–3; Spanish as heirs to Roman, 183–4; Spanish requirement as submission to, 70

ceremonies (*see also* claiming possession; coronation ceremonies; processions): French, 54–5, 67–8; (word) different meanings in different countries, 48

Charles I (king of England), 23

charters, Dutch, 153, 156–7, 168–71

choreography, French ceremonies, 55

Christianity (*see also* Catholicism; Protestants): acceptance of French introduction of, 43–4; religion as basis for using force, 89–92; as source of Spanish legitimacy, 183; unrealized goal of universal, 184, 186

claiming possession: "clear act" concept, 38–9; Dutch practices related to, 150–2, 167–8; English conventions related to, 16–18, 176; French rituals and symbols, 42, 44, 56–7, 66–7; interpretation of differences in, 11–13; Portuguese acts of, 15, 129–33, 153–4; Portuguese determination of latitudes as, 101–3

Coelho, Nicolaú, 1, 103, 133

Cohen, Jeremy, 33–4

colonial authority. *See* political authority

colonialism: English establishment of, 179; French procession to enact, 179; Portuguese affirmation of, 176; Roman empire as model for European, 180–2; Spanish ritual of the Requirement, 179

colonial power. *See* political power